The EZ Model of Learning Language

A Multi-Modal Approach

A Musical-Audio-Visual-Lingual album

A Curriculum for English Second Language Learners

Elham Zandvakili

First Edition

ISBN: 979-8-218-11562-3

Registration Number: TXu002216109

In each story, any references to historical events, real people, or real places are used fictitiously. Names, characters, and places are products of the author's imagination.

Printed in the United States of America.

First printing edition 2022.

[1]**"Ezekiel saw the wheel, Way up in the middle of the air**

The big wheel runs by faith, And the little wheel runs by the grace of God

There is a wheel in a wheel."

"William L. Dawson"

چو شادی بکاهد بکاهد روان   خرد گردد اندر میان ناتوان

" فردوسی "

Translation:

When happiness is gone, the psyche is incapable, Then wisdom becomes weak and feeble

When the fountains of happiness begin to flow, Then the psyche and the wisdom begin to grow

[2] *"Ferdowsi"*

"Hold fast to dreams. For when dreams die, life is a broken wing bird that cannot fly."

"Langston Hughes"

---

[1] "Ezekiel Saw the Wheel" is a folk song written by William L. Dawson.
[2] The Shahnameh ("The Book of Kings", 2021) is a long epic poem written by the Persian poet Ferdowsi between c. 977 and 1010 CE and is the national epic of Iran. Consisting of some 50,000 "distiches".

Acknowledgment

Thank you to my family who supported me all my life and contributed to the cultivation of my growth and development. A special thanks to my brother who is an inspirational guru and instrumental in the creation of the photographs, the audio files, and the whole package. With you everything is possible and without you, life is a "broken wing bird that cannot fly."

Contents

Preface

This book facilitates the learning of language as a therapeutic process in which the second language learner acquires skills to solve problems. Through yoga, the learner is engaged in the processes of understanding the affective domain and emotional development to remove the affective barriers and in preparation for success in the cognitive realm. Yoga opens the doors for the activation of meta-affection (thinking about feelings) and its relationality to the other domains such as meta- cognition (thinking about thoughts). Through music, stories and narratives of wise people, the social domain is activated, and it leads to the development of "meta-mention"[3]/cybernetics of the self that helps the learners in the journey of self-development.

In the process of learning English, you will be engaging in the American cultural experience. You will be joining the hundreds of millions of others who have come to these shores willingly and unwillingly to engage in the great American dream. In the process, you will transform the American dream and be transformed by that cultural experience. To quote Dr. Martin Luther King Jr, "I Have a Dream Speech, I have a dream that is rooted in the American dream, that all men are created equal." There are obstacles, there are barriers, but there are no limits. Understanding yourself is the first step. Remember the longest journey begins with the first step, and that first step determines the direction your journey will take.

The EZ model of second language learning was born out of my passion for integrating language, yoga, music, storytelling, thinking, and the wisdom of famous people. Seventeen years of experience in coaching, teaching, researching and coaxing students to learn the English language has inspired me to share my experiences and engage students in feeling the joy and

---

[3] Meta-mentation: Gordon (2022), Personal Communication

excitement of learning a language and a new culture. Teaching is my passion, and I am always excited when I see students learning. I, too, am one of those restless students who find it difficult to sit still, listen to boring lectures and practice the endless drills of a traditional language class. The EZ method is an easy way to learn a language. Gone is the total reliance upon drill, drill, and the killing of interest. Learning begins with yoga and music. Each chapter in this book begins with a yoga posture. Practicing these yoga postures is necessary to give the students a sense of peace, relaxation, attention, purpose, and grounding. Songs are the EZ way to begin learning English, and music is an effortless and natural way for students to begin immersing themselves in English.

The EZ model of second language learning taps into the power and lifestyles of adolescents and young adults. This musical model releases the agency, creativity, emotions, and the craving for novelty and excitement integral to growing into adulthood. As students learn this new language, they are also empowering and changing themselves. The yoga, music, storytelling, and thinking connect them with others who are present or only imagined in the virtual museum where learners meet famous women and men in history. Learning vocabulary and the meaning of words come alive in conversations with great and wise leaders. In the museum of reincarnation, the portraits are alive, and Martin Luther King Jr., Ludwig van Beethoven, Marie Curie, Hatshepsut, George Washington, Florence Nightingale, and Albert Einstein share the wisdom and knowledge of their lives. Students are reincarnated as they absorb the spirit, wisdom, and knowledge of these great leaders. Reincarnation occurs when the spirits from the past enter the minds and bodies of those from the present. Spiritual messages are reincarnated time and time again as learners meet with great leaders from the past.

The curriculum is authentic because it represents real life, it is learner-centered, and it is task-based. Music and yoga are part of everyday real-life activities. In the past, yoga, music, and critical thinking have been exiled from language learning. In the EZ method, these elements merge in a seamless and fun way. Students will sing songs and read stories of adventure, love, passion, loneliness, disappointment, risk-taking, and justice as they learn a new language. Music is a universal language of human beings. It is a world without any borders. Music has a communicative power that brings members of communities together and conjures up the deepest of human emotions.

A student clicks on an audio file, and the learning begins. Each song is presented with lyrics to draw students into the bodily feeling of enjoying music, language, and culture. Magic happens when music, storytelling, and language learning join. Time stops, time speeds up, memories pop up, images appear, feelings take over, and you come alive. The melody is in your head, on your mind, and you pat your feet. The words find their place in the melody and rhythms of the song.

The lyrics and the music are in the language of popular music to capture and appeal to young second language learners. The learning activities that follow are built upon pop lyrics and music. The lyrics of each song are used as a base for a short story. These lyrics and short stories tell the story of the challenges and dreams of a young woman from her teenage years into adulthood. Each of the six short stories is a separate and different challenge on the way to adulthood. The Aristotelian critical thinking questions: "what, when, where, how, why, and who" are threaded throughout the activities that follow as a way of comprehending and understanding life's challenges. These questions originated over two thousand years ago as a scheme to determine if an action was right or wrong. "Over the centuries, these questions have been adopted by the courts to determine the truthfulness of witnesses and by journalists to tell a complete story. When used by students today, these questions are a framework for organizing their thinking and writing" (Zandvakili et al., 2018).

The EZ approach breaks the cycle of negativity surrounding learning a second language in school settings. Through yoga, the negative emotions of anxiety, fear, and loneliness disappear from the school settings in which students learn English. The EZ method is designed to teach students that language learning can be fun, pleasant, and even a reflective and joyful experience. Imagine what it would be like for a second language learner to look forward to going to class! The creation of that experience is my passion.

The audiences for this approach are second language teachers, teenagers, young adults, and all the English language around the world. The distance between junior high school and college is large, but music has the power to engage students across a decade of developmental differences and SPARK/C feelings, imagination, and learning. The great human potential of students is waiting to be released and to contribute to the larger society. The overall aim of this book is to improve the learning and achievement of English language students and help them realize the potential that is the legacy of every human being. It is necessary to mention that this book is a prototype for this new model. All the lyrics, audios, videos, and the website are original and created out of my passion for integrating education with yoga and music. It is recommended that teachers guide students through the first chapter of this book. After learning the procedures, students can proceed on their own.

Teachers and Students Need This Book

This supplementary book is constructed to provide teachers with a text to accompany instruction in second language learning. To fulfill this supplementary function this text has identified a series of activities that can be applied and used to teach all languages.

Students will find this text to be self-instructional such that a student will be able to acquire a set of skills that can be applied to a wide range of subject matters in addition to language learning. In this book, you are learning a new language and culture, the skills of breathing (relaxation of mind), yoga (relaxation of the body), storytelling and music (joyful feelings), wisdom of famous people from history (Museum of Reincarnation), the mechanics of language (vocabulary, syntax, pragmatics, conversation, and writing) and critical thinking (linguistic thinking) as a set of cognitive skills and a framework for thinking and writing. Teachers will find the activities in this volume are a check list of skills essential to creating a productive framework for effective instruction. Teachers can select the activities that are appropriate for the contexts of their classes. Chapter 1, an introductory chapter, is a guideline of how to use this book and each section is elaborated completely.

Elham Zandvakili

Overview: Chapters and Sections in the Book

There are seven chapters in this book. This introductory chapter (Chapter 1) is constructed to give you a general picture of the structure of all the chapters that are to follow. In chapter 2 and in the chapters that follow, it will not be necessary to repeat the lengthy explanation of each section in this chapter. So, whenever there is any question about the rationale of each section, you can always refer to this introductory chapter.

Chapters 2 to 7 tell the story of Natalia and her growth and development. Chapter 2 is about Natalia's first teenage party. Chapter 3 is about Natalia as an eighteen-year-old girl pretending she and her friend are superstars going to a party. In Chapter 4, Natalia falls in love with a young man she meets in the park. Chapter 5 is about Natalia waiting for her boyfriend to come home from a business trip. Chapter 6 is entitled, Liar, and Natalia discovers that her love has been deceiving her. Chapter 7 is about Natalia becoming a warrior and finding justice after having her heart broken and her money taken.

Sections in Each Chapter

Magic happens when yoga, music, video, lyrics, storytelling, thinking, culture, and the wisdom of famous people merge while learning English. Learning, the EZ way, is fun. Together these different ways of understanding the world flow together in a waterfall of meanings, knowledge, and languages. The EZ way is a holistic and humanistic approach that blends mental and physical activities, visual imagery, music, storytelling, and thinking. There are educators who advocate visual thinking, some advocate musical thinking, and others language thinking. Each of these is a piece of the puzzle of teaching and learning a second language and culture. You are a natural-born learner of languages. This is your evolutionary heritage from the beginning of human time. Language is as natural as breathing and necessary for becoming fully human. Imagine a vehicle from the future in which there are seven wheels giving the vehicle great stability, and as the vehicle gathers speed, the wheels come together, with one-wheel fitting in the other wheel in infinite variety. Language learning the easy way is a wheel in a wheel way up in the middle of the air.

The EZ way releases the unlimited powers of your human potential as you learn English. These powers are the sources of inspiration that, upon your reflections, will offer you tools for learning, problem-solving, and understanding from this day forward. This method is a humanistic and creative way to learn because it is based on you as a natural language learner who is a thinking, affective, social, creative, and moral human being.
Each of the seven chapters in this book contains the following sections:

Section 1 is yoga, section 2 is music and lyrics, section 3 is reading a short story, section 4 is syntax notes or grammar notes (The arrangement of words and phrases to create well-formed and meaningful sentences in a language), section 5 is the Museum of Reincarnation where learners meet famous people from history, section 6 is conversation creation, section 7 is cultural notes, section 8 is creative writing, section 9 is a quick quiz, and section 10 is the end notes including transcriptions of the listening part in the museum, the models of the conversations and the vocabulary list. These sections are interconnected, and all based upon an original song written and produced for each chapter.

Yoga is the first section in the EZ method because when the mind and body are at peace, language flows as easily as a stream down a mountain. The EZ method begins with putting the mind and body at ease through the practice of yoga. The wisdom of the millennia is in the different poses that are physical archetypes of the human experience. Breathing and practicing the posture relaxes the body and relieves the mind and sets an intention for a relational being in the world.

Section 2 is music, and lyrics, in the EZ method, and students learn vocabulary and syntax as they learn the lyrics to the song. Music is a universal experience valued and practiced by all cultures. Lyrics are a natural accompaniment to music, and the two are found universally among cultures. Music blends with lyrics (spoken language) in a seamless way.

Section 3 is the application of the critical thinking questions: "what, when, why, how, who, and where" to a short story based on the lyrics in the chapter. The short story, with its categories of the past, present, and future merge and transform each other while generating an infinite set of possibilities.

Section number 4, syntax, is studying the ways in which words and/or combinations of words give meaning to sentences in a language. Syntax deepens our understanding of language through exploring and using the arrangements of words in sentences.

Section 5, a visit to the Museum of Reincarnation, is an imaginary visit to a museum that does not exist. The museum consists of a set of galleries/rooms dedicated to a famous person from the past who has an important message for the language learner. The famous person speaks through a portrait to the language learner. The famous person shares wisdom and advice with the language learner and brings the past into the present.

Section 6 is having the language learner create and engage in a casual conversation. Spoken language comes alive in conversation in the creation and changing of meanings in casual conversations.

Sections 7 and 8 are activities in which students learn thinking skills that are applicable in a wide range of settings. The next section is cultural notes that connect current and historical events analyzed using SPARC (Setting, Participants, Activities, Reasons, and Conclusion). "SPARC" is a concept developed by Zandvakili and the reason you are using it is to ignite the SPARC in the minds of the learner so they will fully understand the nature of context. This analytic tool gives students a framework to apply to storytelling in general. After they have absorbed this frame, students will have available a framework for analyzing the basic structure of stories that can be applied in a range of contexts. Section number 8 is creative writing, in which students apply the critical thinking questions: "what, when, where, why, how, and who", and create their own stories/lyrics to be shared.

Section 9 is a quick quiz related to new vocabulary, syntax, and cultural notes. The last section is ten, which is the endnotes, including transcriptions of the listening part in the museum, the models of the conversations, and the vocabulary list.

Chapter 1: Introductory Chapter

A Wheel in a Wheel

Climb into this luxury car
Relax, let's roll, it will take you far

In this car, there are seven wheels

Yoga is the first wheel
Breath, relax, and just feel

The second wheel is the English language
Dr. EZ makes it easy as she pledged

The third wheel is the wheel of lyrics and music
Which is joyful and chic

The fourth wheel is a new culture
Turns learning into rapture

The fifth wheel is the story
As fun as the lyrics, don't worry

The sixth wheel is the Museum of Reincarnation
Welcome to the world of imagination

The seventh wheel is Aristotle's questions
Will lead you in the right directions

Welcome to the Earth Angeles
Let's sing, dance, and learn we can handle this

There is a wheel in a wheel
Way up in the middle of the air!

Section 1: Yoga Posture: Mountain

A Rationale

"Yoga is one of the world's oldest traditions for seeking wisdom and truth." (Kripalu, 2019). When you practice breathing and yoga, you free yourself to feel, to know, to relax, to enjoy, and to free yourself of doubts, anxieties, and pressures from your past. Through yoga, the negative emotions of anxiety, fear, and loneliness disappear from the school settings in which students learn English. Through yoga, you can look deeper inside yourself, and "Looking deeper gives you more options" (Carroll[4], 2019). Yoga without intention and self-awareness is exercise. Always set an intention when you start your yoga practice to be able to be aware and understand your thoughts (Meta-cognition), and your emotions (Meta- affection). Understanding the self includes knowing your thoughts and your emotions. When you monitor and control your thoughts and emotions, this leads you to understand your thoughts and emotions better ("Intra-personal Intelligence", Gardner and Hatch, 1989), and consequently, you are able to fully engage and understand your relations with others ("Interpersonal Intelligence", Gardner and Hatch,1989).

Each chapter in this book begins with a picture of a yoga posture (Asana) which is followed by the story of the mythology of that posture. Then a connection is made between the posture and the short story. Next comes a yogic breathing (Pranayama) and warm-up exercise, and lastly, we have the posture steps accompanied by precautionary health notes.

All poses in this book are standing poses that can be performed in the classroom. The poses begin the lesson and bring unity and peace among all students. You will all begin the

---

[4] Y. Carroll (personal communication, 2019)

lesson at the same starting point. Avoid the postures if you have any doubts about your health, uncontrolled high or low blood pressure, or recent injuries to any affected areas.

The poem below includes the name of all the postures used in this book. The names are underlined so that you will be aware of the names.

🎧 Intro Poem to Yoga (Visit website to listen)

Be as determined and strong as a _mountain_
Listen to all the streams of your fountain

Imagine the big sky with a _half moon_
You are going to shine and complete the other half soon

Dream big, fly high like an _eagle_
Don't doubt your inner beauty, your inner regal

Sit on the glorious _chair_ of your life
Don't be afraid of challenge and strife

Be as patient and as generous as a _tree_
Don't say, me and me, turn it to we

Don't be hesitant,
you can break all the walls all the barriers
Be proud, be victorious,
you are the _warrior,_ you are the _warrior_

Yoga Posture: Mountain (Asana: Tadasana)
Tada: mountain; Asana: posture

Stay strong as a mountain, no matter if the earthquakes of life shake you and make you want to collapse. Always remember you are a mountain!

Mythology of Tadasana

Tadasana is the mountain pose and the foundation for all standing postures. According to Kaivalya (2016), this pose "promotes the stillness, strength, relaxed power, and stability we associate with mountains." When you are inclined to feel grounded and balanced, you can imagine yourself *as* the mountain- standing tall, steady, and expansive (McGinley, 2017). The mountain symbolizes the rise toward the goal one wants to gain. Mountains are the home of the Gods and "are comparable to the sources of wisdom from which knowledge radiates in all directions, like rivers that flow from the mountain to nourish the land. So, approach the mountain freely and openly" (Radha, 2006). The mountain pose also symbolizes the flow of the energy throughout the body from the heaven to the earth. Energy flows through the body down the spine and anchors itself in the earth.

The holiness of the mountain and its position as a place of the saints is also reflected in the mysterious and beautiful stories of the [5]Shahnameh and [6]Alborz Mountain range (Dadvar & Rouzbahani, 2016).

Connecting the content of the lesson and the posture

1- The student must feel the strength and the power of being a mountain.

2- Feel the flow of knowledge and energy through your body.

3- Feel the streams and fountains of language, music, critical thinking, storytelling, and yoga.

---

[5] The Shahnameh is a long epic poem written by the Persian poet Ferdowsi between c. 977 and 1010 CE and is the national epic of Iran.

[6] The Alborz Mountain range in northern Iran stretches from the border of Azerbaijan along the western and entire southern coast of the Caspian Sea.

Cautionary notes

Do not hold the posture for a long period of time if you have any heart or circulatory issues, high or low blood pressure.

Yogic Breathing: Dirgha Pranayama

Meaning: Prana: air; life force; Yama: to restrain or hold back

Potential effects

Enhancement of complete and full breathing, decreasing stress and tension while calming the mind and the body, helping the lungs remain healthy by increasing the oxygen flow to the blood, it massages the abdominal organs, facilitating digestion, preparing you for a better learning experience. Breathing is the key to learning. Through breathing you are breaking down the emotional barriers to learning. Stop for a minute and remember how important breathing is.

Breathing Steps (Visit website to listen)

1- Sit up straight with your shoulders back and down with relaxed abdominals. Relax the face, close your mouth, and place your hands on your belly. Breathe into your belly and feel it expand like a balloon. Repeat a few times.

2- Now, put your hands to the sides of your rib cage and breathe into them, feeling the rib cage expand, and repeat a few times.

3- Put your fingertips on your upper chest. Breathe into it and feel your hands lifting. Repeat a few times.

4-Now, place your hands on your thighs with your palms facing up and make a complete inhalation. As you are inhaling, feel the expansions of your belly, rib cage, and chest, and as you are exhaling, you feel the contractions of all three. Repeat this series several times. Release your breathing and feel the impact (Figure 1).

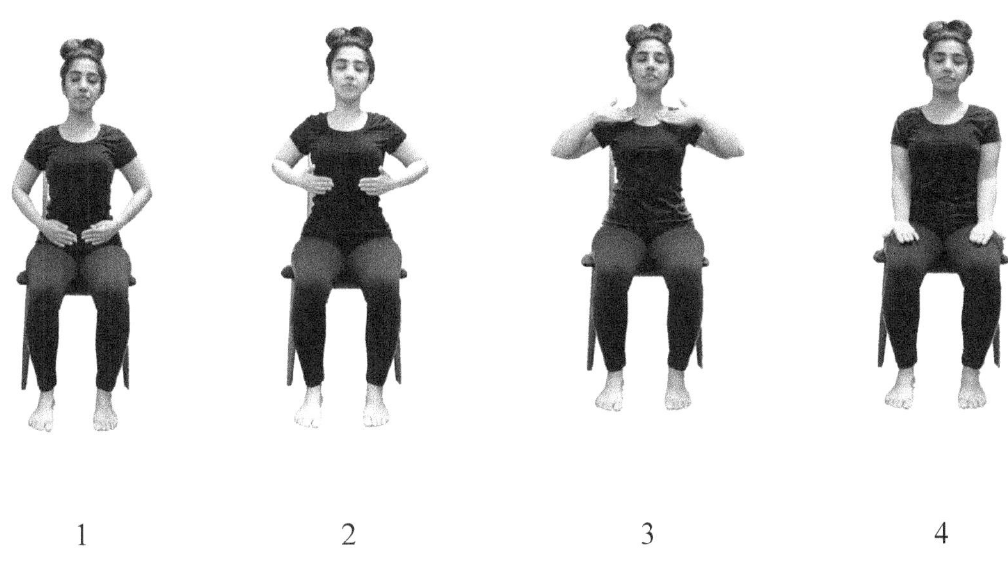

Figure 1: Dirgha Pranayama

Warm-up: Sun breaths (Visit website to listen)

- On an inhale, swing your arms toward the sky, let your fingers and palms touch centered above your head, and on an exhale, bring your hands down into the prayer position in front of the center of your chest. Inhale, raise your arms up toward the sky and exhale, bring them down in front of your chest.

- Repeat and coordinate your breath with your arm movements (Figure 2).

1   2   3

Figure 2: Sun Breaths

Posture steps for performing the Mountain Pose (Visit website to listen)

1- Stand straight with your feet parallel, rotate the sole of your right foot and place it next to the big toe of your left foot, then rotate your right foot back. This is hip-width apart. Inhale and exhale while lifting your toes up and down a few times to feel stability through the soles of your feet. Now balance your weight equally between the two feet. Straighten your knees but do not lock them. On an inhale, straighten your back. Exhale and bring your shoulders up, and then soften them back and down. Open your sternum. Feel the crown of your head reaching for the sky.

2- Inhale as you lift and extend your arms out to the sides and above your head into a V position. Relax your neck and keep your shoulders back and down. Hold this posture for a few seconds and feel grounded like a mountain.

3- To release, on an exhale, lower your arms down, relax and feel the effect of Tadasana (Figure 3).

Figure 3: Mountain Pose (Tadasana)

Section 2: Music and Lyrics: The EZ Way

In each chapter, there are audio and lyrics exercises with two parts divided into seven stages. The first part is listening (Stage 1: listening for fun, stage 2: attentive listening, and stage 3: listening and guessing). Part 2 is listening and reading lyrics. It includes (Stage 4: confirmation of guessing, stage 5: humming, stage 6: karaoke, and stage 7 is mastery). There are two audio files. One is the song with lyrics, and the other file is the song without lyrics for the karaoke part. To start, visit the www.ez-model.com website and follow the 7 stages below:

Part 1: 🎧 **Listening (Stages 1, 2 and 3), Visit website to listen**

Stage 1- (Listening for fun) Listen to the song several times, pat your feet, move your body, and enjoy the music! Do not worry about the meaning of the words yet!!!

Stage 2- (Attentive listening) Listen carefully several times to understand the lyrics.

Stage 3- (Listening and guessing) listen and read the lyrics several times to understand the lyrics. Try to guess the meaning of the words you do not know and understand. Do not look at the vocabulary list just yet. Listen to the lyrics again and guess at the meaning of the words you do not know. Write down the words you do not know.

Guess words:

....

....

....

....

....

....

Part 2: Listening & Reading Lyrics (Stages 4, 5, 6, and 7)

Stage 4- (Confirmation of guessing) Look at the vocabulary table to make sure that you know the meaning and part of speech of all the words in the lyrics.

Stage 5- (Humming) Now that you know the meaning of the whole song, listen to the music and hum along with the song several times.

Stage 6- (Karaoke), visit website to listen. See the lyrics and sing.

Stage 7- (Mastery) Listen to the music without any lyrics and sing away. Sing, Dance, and Enjoy!

Section 3: Reading a Short Story: The EZ Way

This section in all chapters includes a short story and five activities. There is continuity between the lyrics of the songs and short stories across the six songs to show the development of character. All the short stories are about a girl, Natalia, and how she becomes wiser and stronger as she grows into a warrior. Each short story is based on the lyrics you will have already learned.

In all chapters, this section starts with a warm-up activity which is listening to the short story and taking notes. The second activity is reading and guessing the missing words in the passage. In the third activity, you listen and read the short story and check to see if your guesses are correct. In the fourth activity, you scan the passage and clear up any confusion.

Reading comprehension is the fifth and last activity based on Aristotle's WH questions (what, when, where, how, who, why). These questions are individually quite simple, but they are a useful scheme for understanding the underlying structure of the story. The purpose of practicing the six "WH questions" is that you will be able to apply them in a variety of different settings. "WH questions" are especially useful in developing your writing skills. This section is a foundation and warm-up that prepares you to show creativity and meaningful learning in output activities such as writing. The questions are simple, and the answer key is provided in the footnote for your self-assessment. The footnotes include the missing word and a synonym for the word. The first word is the correct answer for the missing answer and the second word is the synonym of the answer.

a. 🎧 Listening and taking notes: (Visit the EZ website to listen)

Please listen to the story and write down what you have understood (Listen and take notes).

………

………

………

………

………

………

b. Reading and Guessing

- Please read the short story below, guess at the missing words and fill in the blanks.

"The EZ Way"

[7] Once upon a time, Dr.EZ decided to make her dream come true and (1)……………her (2)……………. for teaching language with music, yoga, and storytelling. Her (3) ……… is to encourage English language learners to feel as if they have the strength of the mountains. They are strong as mountains, and they can reach the sky. They are not like the sands in the desert moving from one place to another. To (4) …………. this, she recognized that she needed to encourage the students to build their (5) …………. ……………. So, one day she sat and wrote down some of her ideas as an introduction to her book. Here is what came to her mind:

---

[7] at some time in the past (used as a conventional opening of a story)

"Students will learn best when they feel their inner strengths and are grounded and (6) …………. .When they have (7) ……………… this, they have become ready for learning. So, clap your hands, pat your feet! Dr. EZ is in the house. It is time to learn English in an easy way. Let us get out of the old classroom, let us find (8) …………. through yoga and then go where the music is exciting. Sing, dance, and rock to the music. Feel the strength and the power of the (9) …………. of energy as you move to the music. This is a (10) ………………… model. It is time to sing, dance, and learn English together. We can learn English forever.

c. 🎧 Listening and checking your guessing (Visit website to listen)

Read and listen to the short story. While you are listening, check to see if the guesses you have made are correct. If the guesses are correct, please go on. If your guess was not correct, please make a change and fill in the blanks. Then check your [8]answers in the footnotes.

d. Clearing up all confusions

Read the short story by yourself without listening to it. Highlight or underline the parts that are unclear to you in the story above. Use your dictionary or a partner to clarify highlighted parts. Write your notes below for further review.

………………………………………………………………………………………………………..

………………………………………………………………………………………………………...

………………………………………………………………………………………………………...

e. Reading Comprehension based on "WH Questions"

Look at the figure below for the boxes and read the questions (Q) and answers (A). While you are reading the questions, answer by filling in the blank with the "WH questions" (who, when,

---

[8] 1- integrate: combine, 2- passion: love 3- goal: purpose, 4- accomplish: obtain, 5- inner strength: internal power, 6- balanced: stable, 7- achieved: attained, 8- peace: calmness, 9- flow: movement 10- distinguished: great

where, what, why, and how). Choose the answers that are the best fit. You do not have to use all the "WH questions". Notice that the title of the reading is in the middle of a circle and the questions pivot around the title of the story in the figure. Both questions and answers are provided, and you only need to put the correct "WH question" in the blank. Notice the questions are arrange in a clockwise mode.

- After you have finished filling in the blanks below, practice asking and answering the questions.
- Check your answers with the [9]answer key in the footnote.

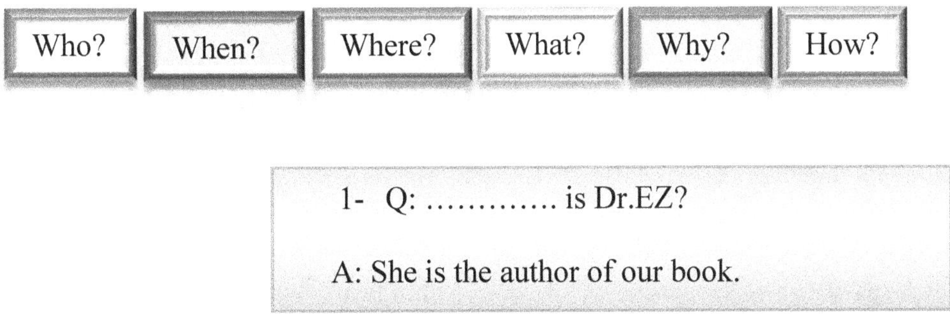

1- Q: …………… is Dr.EZ?

A: She is the author of our book.

2- Q: …………..did Dr.EZ decide to do?

A: She decided to make her dreams come true.

5- Q: ………….. does Dr.EZ ask us to go?

A: She asks us to get out of the old classroom and go where music is fun.

The EZ Way

3- Q: ………. activities do you do with Dr.EZ?

A: Singing, dancing, and learning language and yoga.

4- Q: ………... does Dr.EZ teach?

A: She combines language teaching with music.

---

[9] 1- Who, 2-What, 3- What, 4- How, 5- Where

Section 4: Syntax Notes: Infinitive, Let's, Adverbs of Time

Syntax or grammar is about how best to express and rearrange words to convey the meaning of a linguistic expression. In other words, syntactic expressions in a language are not about if a sentence is true or false. It is about how to rearrange words to clear away confusion in the communication between language users. As an English second language learner, you may have acquired the syntax points because you have been exposed to the usage of the language, but you have not recognized and learned how the words are *arranged* in English. You will be asked to generate your own examples of the syntax notes and to include them in written and spoken forms. Like vocabulary, the key to learning syntax is to use it in a real-life context to stabilize it in your mind in a meaningful way.

In each chapter, there are three syntax points, and each syntax point begins with an example from a line in the lyrics of the song, and it is followed by a quick warm-up question in which you are asked to guess what the syntax note is about based on its use in the lyrics. The purpose of this activity is to activate your previous knowledge. This is followed by a simple and limited explanation of the syntax points you may already know. This section ends by asking you to create your own real-life example of the syntax note.

Syntax Note 1: Infinitive

Example from a line in lyrics: It's Time to sing together

Warm-up question: Based on the line above, what do you think the syntax point is about? Please Explain.

………………………………………………………………………………………………

………………………………………………………………………………………………

Using an Infinitive: Showing purpose and intended action

- You know the vocabulary verbs: sing, dance, and learn. When you add a "to" to the verb, you have formed an infinitive. When using an infinitive, there is no doubt about what is on the mind of the speaker. She intends "To Sing" together.

- By using the structure It's time + an infinitive (to + base form of the verb), you are letting someone know that something needs to be done at the present time. (It's time + an infinitive) leaves no doubt about when the action is to occur.

Example: It's time to sing. It's time to learn.

Write a real-life example of the use of the syntax note above in a sentence below.

…………………………………………………………………………………………………

Syntax Note 2: Let's

Example from a line in the lyrics: Let's go dance and learn English.

Warm-up questions: Based on the line above, what do you think the syntax note is about?

…………………………………………………………………………………………………

…………………………………………………………………………………………………

Using "Let's" (short form for "let us") as a friendly way to suggest doing something so it offers a suggestion as an option rather than an order.

American use "let's" to suggest doing something in a friendly way.

For example: Let's dance together.

Write an example of the use of "Let's" in a sentence below.

…………………………………………………………………………………………………

Syntax Note 3: Adverbs of time

Example from a line in the lyrics: *Today, tomorrow, maybe forever*

Warm-up questions: Based on the line above, what do you think the syntax note is about?

……………………………………………………………………………………………………

……………………………………………………………………………………………………

Adverbs of time

They are used to let us know when an action happens. These adverbs are usually placed at the end of the sentence, which is a neutral position, but sometimes they can be placed at the beginning of a sentence for more emphasis. Look at the table below and recognize the other adverbs of time and then use them in a sentence.

List of some adverbs of time		
No.	**Adverbs**	**Example in sentences**
1	**Yesterday** /ˈjestərdeɪ/	I went to a party yesterday.
2	**Today** /təˈdeɪ/	He saw Sara today.
3	**Tomorrow** /təˈmɑːrəʊ/	She will sing tomorrow.
4	**Every day** /ˈevrideɪ/	I dance and learn English every day.
5	**Now** /naʊ/	They are singing, dancing, and learning English now.
6	**Later** /ˈleɪtər/	I will study English without music later.
7	**Tonight** /təˈnaɪt/	I will go to a party to learn English tonight.
8	**Forever** /fərˈevər/	I learn English forever.

9	**Last night** **læst naɪt**	**Last night, he sang and learned English. (More emphasis on last night)**

Write an example of the use of adverbs of time in sentences below.

....

....

....

....

....

....

....

....

....

....

Section 5: Museum of Reincarnation: Martin Luther King Jr

Leffler, W. K., (1965) *Martin Luther King*

The Museum of Reincarnation celebrates famous women and men who have changed the world. In the museum, the portraits of famous people talk to the visitors. A visitor to the museum will enter a large space where she or he will be able to chat with famous people. There are seven galleries in the museum for Martin Luther King Jr, Ludwig van Beethoven, Marie Skłodowska Curie, George Washington, Florence Nightingale, Hatshepsut, and Albert Einstein. Each famous person will be introduced, and then the famous person will come alive and talks to the visitor. When the visitor enters the gallery, the quotations from the famous person are blended into a speech. Reincarnation occurs when the visitor is learning to use the vocabulary of a famous person. The learner listens to the famous person and completes questions about vocabulary. The reincarnation of knowledge, vocabulary, and spirit leads the learner to a new way of thinking. There are three stages to stabilize the usage of the vocabulary and syntax notes in the Museum of Reincarnation.

Stage 1. Completing the vocabulary list. Before going into the museum, the learner completes the vocabulary table, including the meaning of each vocabulary word.

Stage 2. Listening to the biography. The learner is introduced to the famous person. The learner takes notes and writes down some keywords from the biography of that famous person. (The transcript of this biography is in the endnotes.)

Stage 3. Reincarnation with the famous person. The famous person comes alive and uses the vocabulary list in the table in their quotations.

    a. **Listening.** The learner listens without being concerned about filling out the table.

    b. **Listening and filling out the table**. Beginning with vocabulary word number 1, the learner listens carefully to the famous person and writes down the sentence with the vocabulary word used by the famous person in the table. She completes the table by writing down the sentences said by the famous person. The learner listens several times, plays and pauses as necessary. (The transcript of the quotations is in the endnote.)

    c. **Part of Speech and Highlighting**. After filling out the table, in each sentence, the learner highlights/underlines the vocabulary, identifies the parts of speech (noun- adjective- adverb- pronounce- idioms/expressions) of the word, and fills out part "c" of the table. The learner also identifies and highlights some of the syntax notes used by the famous person.

(Please check your answers in the vocabulary section in the endnotes)

    d. **Completing the Process of Reincarnation and Leaving the Museum**. In this part, the learner is still under the influence of the famous person. The learner writes their usage of the vocabulary words and the quotations in a sentence in part "d" in the table. The syntax notes should also be included in their sentences. When the learner creates their own example, their sentences can be a comment on the quotations, can be paraphrasing (rewriting the famous person's sentence in their own way), or it can be a quotation created by herself/himself under the influence of the famous person. Please be creative.

Stage 1. Completing the Vocabulary List

No.	Vocabulary	Meaning
1.	culture	
2.	integrate	
3.	unique	
4.	technique	
5.	make (made)	
6.	believe me	
7.	through	
8.	rhythmic	
9.	beyond	
10.	further	
11.	distinguished	
12.	extinguished	
13.	desire	

Stage 2. Listening to the biography part of the museum (Visit website to listen)

Please reply to the question below.

Who is the famous person? Why is the person famous?

……………………………………………………………………………………………

……………………………………………………………………………………………

……………………………………………………………………………………………

Stage 3. Reincarnation with the famous person (Vocabulary part)

a. Watching and Listening. (Visit website to listen)

b. Watching, listening carefully, and writing down the usage of the words by the famous person.

c. Identifying the parts of speech

d. Writing your own sentences using the vocabulary words and syntax notes.

a. Watching and Listening		
No.	**Vocabulary**	**b. Sentences with the vocabulary word used by the famous person**
		c. Part of speech
		d. Sentences with the vocabulary word used by you
1	**Culture**	b. Sentences by the famous person: ……………………………… ………………………………………………………………………………
		c. Part of speech: ……………

		d. Your sentence: ……………………………………………… ………………………………………………………………
2	**Integrate**	b. Sentences by the famous person: ……………………… ………………………………………………………………
		c. Part of speech: ……………
		d. Your sentence: ……………………………………………… ………………………………………………………………
3	**Technique**	b. Sentences by the famous person: ……………………… ………………………………………………………………
		c. Part of speech: ……………

		d. Your sentence: …………………………………………… …………………………………………………………………
4	**Made**	b. Sentences by the famous person: ……………………………… …………………………………………………………………
		c. Part of speech: ……………
		d. Your sentence: ……………………………………………… …………………………………………………………………
5	**Believe**	b. Sentences by the famous person: ……………………………… …………………………………………………………………
		c. Part of speech: ……………
		d. Your sentence: ………………………………………………

		……………………………………………………………………………
6	**Through**	b. Sentences by the famous person: ……………………………… ……………………………………………………………………………
		c. Part of speech: …………….
		d. Your sentence: ………………………………………………… ……………………………………………………………………
7	**Unique**	b. Sentences by the famous person: ……………………………… ……………………………………………………………………………
		c. Part of speech: …………….
		d. Your sentence: ……………………………………………………. ……………………………………………………………………

8	**Beyond**	b. Sentences by the famous person: …………………………………
		c. Part of speech: ……………
		d. Your sentence: ………………………………………………
9	**Extinguish**	b. Sentences by the famous person: ………………………………
		c. Part of speech: ……………
		d. Your sentence: ………………………………………
10	**Desire**	b. Sentences by the famous person: ………………………………

		c. Part of speech: …………….
		d. Your sentence: …………………………………………………… ……………………………………………………………………………
11	**Distinguished**	b. Sentences by the famous person: ……………………………… ……………………………………………………………………………
		c. Part of speech: …………….
		d. Your sentence: ………………………………………………… ……………………………………………………………………………
12	**Desire**	b. Sentences by the famous person: ……………………………… ……………………………………………………………………………

<table>
<tr><td></td><td></td><td>c. Part of speech: ……………</td></tr>
<tr><td></td><td></td><td>d. Your sentence: …………………………………………………

…………………………………………………………………</td></tr>
</table>

Section 6: Conversation Creation

Conversations have different purposes. One purpose of conversation is pedagogical, to learn new words and new syntax notes. The second purpose is rhetorical, which is the intention of the speaker to persuade and impress the listener. The aim of these conversations is to teach and practice your social skills. You will engage in role-playing, which is a highly effective strategy for pedagogical and rhetorical purposes. Learning these skills gives you the necessary confidence to accomplish your educational and rhetorical goals.

As we mentioned, a major purpose of the rhetorical part of the conversation is to convince the listener that the story of the speaker is true. The story may be true, false, or partially true. In any event, it is in the best interest of the speaker to convince the listener that the story is true. This is called "rhetoric" in classical literature. The Irish call it "blarney," Persian/ Farsi speakers use the slang "making him/her donkey", the African Americans call it "rapping it down," and Americans call it "smooth/sweet-talking". All cultures value the importance of language skills in convincing others that what they are saying is true.

In all conversation sections in this book, there is an element of convincing others. For example, in chapter 1, in the first conversation, Natalia is convincing her dad to throw a party for her. In the second conversation, Sam meets Natalia, and his intention is to convince her to dance with him.

The first activity of this section is to choose one of the topics related to the lyrics/short story of that lesson. After choosing your topic, it is time to create the actual conversation. There are different models of conversation based on the short story in the endnotes to each chapter. You can look at the models and use or modify the conversation you are creating, or you have created. The conversation you create should use the syntax notes and some of the [10]vocabulary from the museum. After creating the conversation, the last step is role-playing. In this activity, you practice and role-play the conversation with your partner, friend, brother/sister, or even with yourself in front of the mirror. The purpose of role-playing is to become comfortable using casual conversation.

a. Choosing a topic. Choose one of the following potential topics and participants related to the short story/lyrics of the lesson.

Topic 1: A teacher's dream, Participants: Dad with Son Or daughter who is a teacher

Topic 2: My dream, Participants: You with your brother/sister/Mom or dad

b. Conversation Creation. After choosing your topic, create your conversation below. Note: There are two models of conversations in the endnotes to this chapter. You can look at the models and use or modify the conversation you have created. When you are creating your conversation, you should use the syntax notes in this chapter and some of the vocabulary from the museum.

---

[10] The chosen vocabularies are recognized as intermediate and advanced words by the Cambridge Dictionary.

Topic of the conversation:

Participants:

………

………

………

………

………

………

………

………

c. Role-playing. Practice and role-play the conversation with your partner, friend, brother/sister, or even with yourself in front of the mirror. The purpose of role-playing is to become comfortable using language in a casual and conversational way.

Note: Role-play the other conversations in the endnotes for additional practice. Feel free to change the language as you see fit.

Section 7: Cultural Notes: Immigrants in the Music Industry

Cultural notes are chosen to deepen your understanding of language and culture. The purpose of including the cultural notes is to make connections between you and the characters in the cultural notes. Thus, we aim to activate the SPARK/C in your character and culture.

This section starts with a warm-up activity. This activity is based on the topic of the cultural note. You guess what the cultural notes are based on the topic. The warm-up activity is followed by reading the cultural notes. If you do not know a word or phrase, do not panic. The purpose of reading in this part is to get the gist (the general meaning) of the text. If you really need to know the meaning of a word, first apply the guessing strategy (guess the meaning of the words based on the context), and then, if necessary, use a dictionary.

The last part is "SPARCing" the cultural notes. SPARC stands for Setting, Participants, Activity, Reasons, and Conclusions. Setting is when and where the cultural points took place. Participants are the characters in the cultural notes. Activity refers to the how or the way in which the participants engage in making and changing the culture, and conclusion is the SPARC that asks, "what are the connections between you and the SPARCs of the cultural notes?"

Topic: Immigrants in the Music Industry in America

a. Warm-Up (Brainstorming)

Please look at the topic above and guess what the cultural notes are about.

....

....

....

b. Reading

Read the following cultural notes. If you do not know a word or phrase, please use the guessing strategy (guess the meaning of the words based on the context) and use a dictionary when necessary.

"Immigrants in the music industry" in the USA

With the help of immigrants, American music is loved around the world. [11]Slave songs and [12]gospels from the Caribbean, Africa, and the Bahamas changed into the blues (sad songs),

---

[11] a person who is legally owned by someone else and must work for that person
[12] A music genre that originated during African American slavery

[13]hip hop, and [14]R&B. We watch famous people on Dancing with the Stars performing salsa dance to the sound of Latino musical instruments. Country music is known as an American genre, with deep roots in the European immigrant musical traditions that were brought to the Appalachian region (Ideal Immigration, 2019).

There are many immigrants who have become famous musicians, such as Rihanna.

Pop star Rihanna was born in Saint Michael Parish, Barbados. After moving to the United States

in 2004, she signed with Def Jam Recordings, starting her music career. (Newsday.com, 2017); Not only did she bring a different taste of pop music to America but also, she recently [15]donated $5 million to help fight the [16]coronavirus. She is 32 years old, and she is the richest female singer in the world (Ellasar, 2020).

Immigrants are the source of change, inspiration, and new directions in popular music. These newcomers to America bring something new to the American musical experience. Their contributions continue to give new life, purpose, and meaning to popular music.

c. SPARCing the Cultural Notes

Using the information above, please complete the SPARC (Setting, Participant, Activities, Reasons, and Conclusion). You can write about Rihanna or anyone of your choosing.

- Setting (when and where?): ……………………………………………………………………………
- Participants (who?): ……………………………………………………………………………

---

[13] a type of popular music in which the words are spoken rather than sung and the subject of the songs is often politics or society

[14] a type of popular music, originally by African American artists, that can have features of soul, jazz, funk, and hip-hop

[15] to give money or goods to help a person or organization

[16] a type of virus that includes the SARS virus

- Activities (how did they become famous?):

  ……………………………………………………………………………………………………

- Reasons (why are they successful?):

  ……………………………………………………………………………………………………

- Conclusion (what is your SPARC?):

  ……………………………………………………………………………………………………

  ……………………………………………………………………………………………………

Section 8: Creative Story/Lyrics Writing

Creative writing is putting your ideas, emotions, thoughts, and dreams out into the world. Therefore, it is a way of organizing your writing to share with others. In this section, based on what you have learned in the chapter (Yoga, lyrics, vocabularies, syntax notes, museum of reincarnation, conversations, and cultural notes), you will follow seven stages of creative writing. You begin with stage 1, which is brainstorming. In this stage, you fill out the figure provided in the diagram that includes the categories of storytelling: participants in your story who), the settings (when and where), the activities of your story (how), the reasons for your story (why), and the conclusion of your story (what). In the second stage, you write your story/lyrics, which can be a rap, rhyming, story, etc. The third stage is sharing your story/lyrics and getting feedback. Stage 4 is applying your story/lyrics to music which can be the karaoke version of the song or your own music. In stage 5, you practice, sing, and enjoy. In stage 6, you record yourself and share your product with someone else to get feedback and revise if necessary. In stage 7, in the future, you send your creation to the EZ website (www.ez-model.com). If your creation is selected, your contribution will be featured in the next edition of this volume.

Please keep in mind that making mistakes and receiving feedback plays an important role in learning everything. So, make mistakes and learn. By getting feedback and correcting the mispronunciations and mistakes in your speaking or writing, you are creating the good habits of speaking and writing. If you keep making a mistake, it will turn into a bad habit, and it will be harder to create good habits to replace them. You want to avoid "fossilization". Fossilization is continuing to make the same mistakes. According to Selinker (1972), the most important factor related to learning a second language is avoiding the fossilization of mistakes. Monitor yourself, stop, and think if you keep making mistakes (meta-cognition).

Based on all the points you have learned in this chapter, follow the steps below:

Stage 1: Brainstorming/ SPARCing

Insert the title of your story/lyrics in the middle of the figure below and then fill in the other boxes about the participants in your story(who), the setting (when and where), the activities of your story (how), the reasons for your story (why), and the conclusion to your story (what).

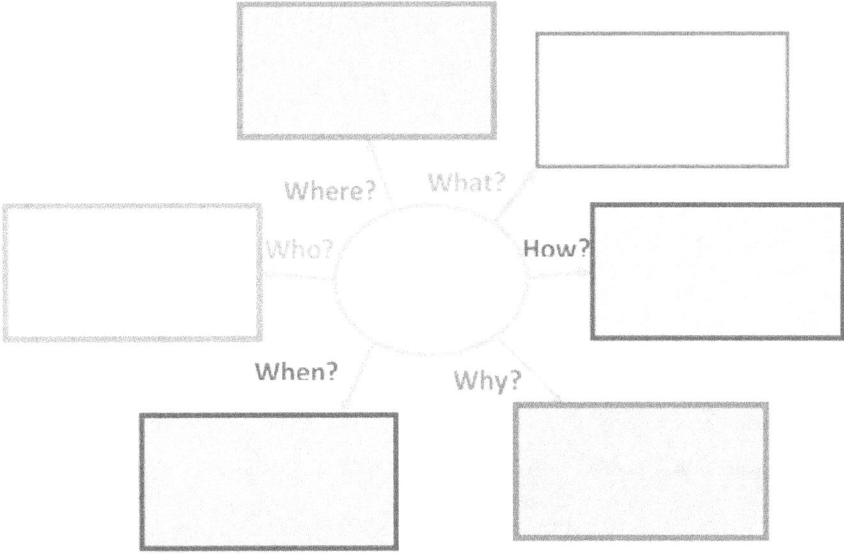

Stage 2- Writing your story/lyrics

Now, write your story/ lyrics (Your story/lyrics can be a rap, rhyming, poem, etc., Be creative and let your imagination be your limit).

The title of your story/lyrics: ……………………………………

…………………………………………………………………………………

…………………………………………………………………………………

…………………………………………………………………………………

…………………………………………………………………………………

…………………………………………………………………………………

…………………………………………………………………………………

…………………………………………………………………………………

…………………………………………………………………………………

Stage 3. Getting Feedback: Check your story/ lyrics with your teachers/parents/mentors to get feedback .

Stage 4. Applying Music: Either apply your story/lyrics on the karaoke track of the song or click on the beat's website, such as https://www.8notes.com/metronome/ , choose the right beat for your story/lyrics. Even if you play a musical instrument, apply your writing to your playing. Don't limit yourself and be creative.

Stage 5. Singing: Practice, sing and enjoy!

Stage 6. Recording: Record yourself and share your product with someone else to get feedback and revise if necessary.

Stage 7. Post your creation to the EZ website at www.ez-model.com. If you creation is selected, your contribution will be featured in the next edition of this volume.

Section 9: Quick Quiz

The quiz in this section is designed to help you review and remember the materials you have learned. The answer key is always provided in the footnotes. If you have any doubts about the correct answer, please check the footnotes.

Please answer the questions below and check your answers in the [17]answer key in the footnote.

A. **Vocabulary**: What is the synonym and part of speech of the **Bolded** vocabulary?

1- Sara had a **distinguished** career because it was her passion.

  a. Adjective: terrible   b. Noun: horrible

  c. Adjective: great   d. Noun: infamous

2- The building was on fire, but now the fire is **extinguished**.

  a. Adjective: stopped/put out   b. Adverb: very good/distinguished

  c. Adjective: orange/red   d. Adjective: very warm/ hot

3- Her technique is so **unique**. It helps the students to learn easier.

  a. Noun: handwriting   b. Noun: approach

  c. Adjective: special   d. adjective: job

4- Don't **panic**; the fire is extinguished, and everything is okay.

  a. Verb: insomniac   b. Adverb: maniac

  c. Adjective: be scared   d. Adjective: fair

5- For learning a new language, we need to learn the culture of that language because **culture** is at the heart of a language.

---

[17] Answer key: 1-C, 2- a, 3- b, 4- c, 5- a, 6- c, 7- a, 8- F, 9- T, 10- T

a. Noun: a way of life   b. Noun: grammar

c. Noun : vocabulary   d. Noun : technique

B. Syntax: Which is the best way for an English speaker to express herself/himself?

6-

a. It's time dance.

b. It's time dancing.

c. It's time to dance.

d. It's time danced.

7-

a. It's time to go.

b. It's time going.

c. It's time go.

d. It's time went.

C. Culture: Based on the Cultural Notes, decide which sentence is true (T) and which one is false (F)?

8- Without the help of immigrants, American music would be the way that it is today.

9- Country music has deeper roots in European traditions.

10- Slave songs and gospels traveled from the Caribbean, Africa, and the Bahamas and changed into the blues, hip hop, and R&B.

Section 10: Endnotes

All the endnotes in each chapter include the transcripts from the museum, including the biography, quotations from the famous people (Please use a dictionary when necessary), models of conversations related to each chapter, and the vocabulary list.

Museum Transcripts

a. Biography: Dr. Martin Luther King Jr

Martin Luther King, Jr. (1929-1968) was an African American Christian [18]civil rights [19]leader who was the face of the civil rights movement. His [20]vision and philosophy of [21]non-violence was great counterpoint to the violence and threats from those who [22]advocated [23]racial [24]segregation. His career began with his leadership of the Montgomery, bus [25]boycott to [26]protest segregated seats on buses. Under his influence, buses, restaurants, and schools were desegregated. Dr. Kings' vision of civil rights evolved beyond racial segregation to confront the evils of economic [27]inequality. He was [28]assassinated in Memphis, Tenn, while organizing a poor people's march for [29]economic opportunity and equity in 1968 ("Martin Luther King Jr.," n.d.; Carson, C. (2001); Wikipedia contributors, 2022).

b. Quotations

Schools have two goals: to teach skills and techniques and to teach values and culture. Techniques belong to the material world, and values and cultures belong to the spiritual world. What matters is the spiritual world. Culture is all the good things that people value in their daily lives. I used to worry about integrating different cultures together. Today, I am not worried anymore. Now integration is the solution and not the problem. Will you be a part of culture that

---

[18] civil rights include freedom, equality in law and in employment, and the right to vote.
[19] a person in control of a group, country, or situation
[20] idea
[21] a situation in which someone avoids fighting or using physical force, especially when trying to make political change
[22] supported
[23] connected with someone's race
[24] the policy of keeping one group of people apart from another and treating them differently, especially because of race, sex, or religion
[25] to refuse to buy a product or take part in an activity as a way of expressing strong disapproval
[26] a strong complaint
[27] unfairness
[28] was killed
[29] relating to money

has made the world a better place to live? I still believe that pure truth and love are the solutions. Through nonviolence, peace is possible in the world. Nonviolence is the unique way beyond the darkness to the light. And beyond the light is where dreams come true. According to John 1:5 NLT: "The light shines in the darkness, and the darkness can never extinguish it." I have desires for non-violence, world peace, and a lack of poverty. Ultimately a distinguished nation is a compassionate nation. No individual or nation can be great if it is not worried about others. No, no, we are not satisfied, and we will not be satisfied until justice rolls down like waters and righteousness like a mighty stream. Let the rhythmic sound of freedom rings from the mighty mountains (123 Of the Most Powerful Martin Luther King Jr. Quotes Ever, Hannah Hutyra, 2019).

"Let freedom ring from the mighty mountains."

1- Direction quotations, 2- Paraphrased Quotations

1- Culture: "education has a two-fold function to perform in the life of man and in society: the one is utility, and the other is culture." 2- Schools have two goals: to teach skills and to teach culture. Culture is all the good things that people value in their daily lives.

2- Integrate: "I fear I may have integrated my people into a burning house" 2- I used to worry about integrating different cultures together. Today, I am not worried anymore. Now integration is the solution and not the problem.

3- Technique: "Every man lives in two realms: the internal and the external. The internal is that realm of spiritual ends expressed in art, literature, morals, and religion. The external is that complex of devices, techniques, mechanisms, and instrumentalities by means of which we live." 2- Techniques belong to the material world, and values belong to the spiritual world. What matters is the spiritual world.

4- Made: "Almost always, the creative, dedicated minority has made the world better." 2- Will you be a part of the minority that has made the world a better place to live?

5- Believe: "I believe that unarmed truth and unconditional love will have the final word in reality.", 2- I believe that the pure truth and love are the solutions.

6- Through: "World peace through nonviolent means is neither absurd nor unattainable." 2- Through nonviolence, peace is possible in the world.

7- Unique and Beyond: "For we are deeply in need of a new way beyond the darkness that seems so close around us."2- Nonviolence is the way beyond the darkness to the light. And beyond the light are where dreams come true.

8- Extinguish: According to John 1:5 NLT: "The light shines in the darkness, and the darkness can never extinguish it."

9- Desire: "I have a dream" 2- I have desires for non-violence- world peace, and lack of poverty.

10- Distinguished: "Ultimately, a great nation is a compassionate nation. No individual or nation can be great if it does not have a concern for "the least of these." 2- Ultimately, a distinguished nation is a compassionate nation. No individual or nation can be great if it is not worried about others.

11- Rhythmic: "Let freedom ring from the mighty mountains." 2- Let the rhythmic sound of freedom ring from the mighty mountains.

Conversations

Model 1.

Topic: A teacher's dream, Participants: Dad with Son Or daughter who is a teacher

Son/Daughter: Hi, Dad. I am thinking of a new, chic, and unique technique for teaching and learning about culture.

Dad: Oh, really, what is it?

Son/Daughter: I want to integrate music with culture. I want to teach culture through a rhythmic and romantic music.

Dad: Wow, I think that is a breezy model. So, you want to make a fun class.

Son/Daughter: Yes, I have a desire to go beyond the class. To go further, to sing, to dance, and to learn.

Dad: My dear daughter/son. I think this is a great (distinguished) model. In this way, you can learn forever.

Son/Daughter: Oh, dad, I am really on fire with this desire because I want to use pop music as a part of the lesson. Nothing can extinguish my desire. But I am afraid because I don't know where to start.

Dad: Let's talk about your plan tonight, don't panic, darling. I will help and support you forever.

Son/Daughter: Thank you, Dad.

Model 2.

Topic: My dream; Participants: You and your brother/ sister, …

A: Hi, how are you doing? Can we talk for a few minutes?

B: Oh, yeah, what's going on?

A: I wanna talk about my dream.

B: Oh, what is your dream?

A: I would love to become a musician.

B: That is great. I will help you to find a good teacher. You can also search online and find someone yourself.

A: Do you think I can be successful?

B: I believe so. You just need to practice. Practice makes perfect.

Vocabulary list as a resource

The vocabulary in the table below is the words used in the lyrics. Please keep in mind that you do not have to study them as a list. It is a resource, a dictionary, that is available for every lesson. You can use the list in different sections when you need to check the meaning of the words you are not sure about or whenever you want to check the pronunciation, meaning/synonym, spelling, and usage of the words in a sentence.

In the vocabulary table, there are four columns. Column one is simply the number of words. In the second column, there are three parts: the vocabulary word, the phonetic/ pronunciation, and the part of speech of each word. In the second column, you will find the meaning/ synonym of the word taken from the Cambridge dictionary. If you do not fully understand it, do not worry. Refer to your bilingual dictionary. In the third column, you will find the use of the word in a sentence. Learning a word in the real-life context is so helpful in learning and remembering a word. Please create your own real-life examples.

No.	a.Vocabulary b.pronunciation c. Part of speech	Dictionary definition/ synonym	Example in sentence
1.	**Time** /taɪm/ **Noun**	the seconds, minutes, hours, days, weeks, months, years, etc., in which existence is measured, or the past, present, and future considered as a whole	It is time to learn.
2.	**To connect** /kəˈnekt/ **Verb**	to join two things	We connect language and music.

3.	**To integrate** **/ˈɪntɪgreɪt/** **Verb**	to combine two or more things to make something more effective, to combine	We integrate language and music.
4.	**Language** **/ˈlæŋgwɪdʒ/** **Noun**	a system of communication, speech	The English language is beautiful.
5.	**Culture** **/ˈkʌltʃər/** **Noun**	the way of life of a particular people, A way of life	Persian and Chinese cultures are ancient.
6.	**Music** **/ˈmjuːzɪk/** **Noun**	a pattern of sounds made by instruments or by singing or a combination of both, a song	Spanish music is rhythmic.
7.	**With** **/wɪθ/** **Preposition**	used to say that people or things are in a place together or are doing something together, along	We are learning a language with music.
8.	**Chic** **/ʃiːk/** **Adjective**	stylish and fashionable, modern	This is a chic coat.
9.	**Unique** **/juˈniːk/** **Adjective**	special in some way, different	You have a unique personality.
10.	**Technique** **/tekˈniːk/** **Noun**	a way of performing a skillful activity, an approach	We have a good teaching technique.
11.	**To make** **/meɪk/** **Verb**	to cause something (made is the past tense of make)	She made the learning easy.
12.	**Sweet** **/swiːt/** **Adjective**	if an emotion or event is sweet, it is very pleasant and satisfying, mellow and musical	Learning English through music is a sweet and fun experience.
13.	**Very** **/ˈveri/** **Adverb**	(used to add emphasis to an adjective or adverb) to a great degree, extremely	The EZ model is very easy.
14.	**easy** **/ˈiːzi/** **Adjective**	effortless, smooth, simple	Language learning through music is easy.
15.	**Believe me** **/bɪˈliːv mi/** **Believe = verb** **Me= object**	said when emphasizing that something is true, trust me	Believe me. It is so much fun.
16.	**Her** **/hər/**	to refer to a woman, girl, or female	Her teaching model is new.

		Pronoun		
17.	**Method** /ˈmeθəd/ **Noun**	a way of doing something, design	The new teaching methods encourage you to have fun.
18.	**Is** /iz/ **To be verb**	present tense of to be verb goes with he/she/it	She is funny.
19.	**Fun** /fʌn/ **Noun**	pleasure, enjoyment, amusement, joy	It is so much fun.
20.	**Breezy** /ˈbriːzi/ **Adjective**	happy, cheerful (Windy, but not in this song)	She has a breezy personality.
21.	**Learning** /ˈlɜːrnɪŋ/ **Noun**	the activity of acquiring knowledge, education	English language learning (ELL) is easy.
22.	**Through** /θru/ **Preposition**	by using, via	We are learning language through music.
23.	**Story** /ˈstɔːri/ **Noun**	a description, either true or imagined, of a series of events with a past, present, and a future, an adventure	It is a unique story.
24.	**Which** /wɪtʃ/ **Pronoun**	used to add extra information, That	We are learning a story which is unique.
25.	**So** /səʊ/ **Adverb**	extremely, very	She is singing and learning. She is so excited.
26.	**Rhythmic** /ˈrɪðmɪk/ **Adjective**	a beat that is repeated, musical	The rain has a rhythmic sound.
27.	**Hey** /heɪ/ **Exclamation**	used to get someone's attention, hello	Hey there, sweet pea.
28.	**You** /jə/ **Pronoun**	the person or people spoken to, you	Hey, you. Come here?
29.	**English** /ˈɪŋglɪʃ/ **Noun**	the language of the United Kingdom, the United States and used also in many other parts of the world, speech	We learn English and Spanish together.
30.	**Learner** /ˈlɜːrnər/	a person who receives an education, a student	I am an English language learner.

	Noun		
31.	**To let** **/let/** **Verb**	to allow something to happen, permit	Let me go.
32.	**To go** **/gəʊ/** **Verb**	to move to another place, to move, to pass	I want to go to party.
33.	**Let's go (let us go)** **/letzgəʊ/** **Idiom**	Let's move.	Let's go (let us go) to the party.
34.	**Beyond** **/bɪˈjɑːnd/** **Preposition**	outside of a limit, above	When it comes to music, dancing is beyond our control.
35.	**Further** **/ˈfɜːrðər/** **Adverb**	to a greater distance, farther	Let's go further to find the magic store.
36.	**Distinguished** **/dɪˈstɪŋgwɪʃt/** **Adjective**	respected and admired for excellence, great	She/he is a distinguished person.
37.	**Can** **/kən/** **Modal verb**	to be able to, to be capable of	We can sing and learn English.
38.	**Extinguish** **/ɪkˈstɪŋgwɪʃ/** **Verb**	to stop, to kill	Nothing can extinguish my love for learning.
39.	**to sing** **/sɪŋ/** **Verb**	to make musical sounds with the voice, to chant	She/he is singing and dancing.
40.	**To dance** **/dæns/** **Verb**	to move the body and feet in rhythm to music, to disco	I like to dance.
41.	**To learn** **/lɜːrn/** **Verb**	to get knowledge, to study	I want to learn English.
42.	**Together** **/təˈgeðər/** **Adverb**	with each other, jointly	Let's sing together.
43.	**Today** **/təˈdeɪ/** **Adverb**	on this day, current	I will learn today.
44.	**Tomorrow** **/təˈmɑːrəʊ/** **Adverb**	the day after today, a future period	I will see you tomorrow.
45.	**Maybe** **/meɪ/**	shows that something is possible, perhaps	Maybe you are the one for me.

	Word	Definition	Example
	Adverb		
46.	**Forever** /fərˈevər/ **Adverb**	for all time, without end, always	We are together forever.
47.	**To panic** /ˈpænɪk/ **Verb**	to suddenly feel very worried or frightened (To be scared)	Don't panic. Things are ok.
48.	**So** /soʊ/ **Adverb**	to such a great degree, very	I love you so much.
49.	**Romantic** /roʊˈmæntɪk/ **Adjective**	feeling of love, loving	She has a romantic relationship with him.
50.	**We are all on Fire** /wi ɑːr ɑːn ˈfaɪər/ **Idiom**	We feel unstoppable.	We are on fire. We cannot stop. Let's rock.
51.	**Full** /fʊl/ **Adjective**	having or containing a lot, whole	The glass is full of water.
52.	**Desire** /dɪˈzaɪər/ **Noun**	a strong feeling of wanting something, passion	I have a burning desire to learn English.
53.	**Determined** /dɪˈtɜːrmɪnd/ **Adjective**	showing the strong desire to follow a particular plan of action even if it is difficult, resolute	You are a determined language learner.
54.	**Strong** /strɔːŋ/ **Adjective**	firm, determined	You are a strong language learner.
55.	**Mountain** /ˈmaʊntn/ **Noun**	a large hill	Which is your favorite mountain?
56.	**Stream** /striːm/ **Noun**	a continuous flow of things or people	I like to look at a mountain stream.
57.	**Fountain** /ˈfaʊntn/ **Noun**	a stream of water forced up into the air through a small hole	Drink water from the fountain.

Chapter 2

Section 1: Yoga Posture: Half-Moon
Ardha:half; Chandra: Moon; Asana

Follow your dreams, become who you are supposed to become, and shine like a moon in the sky!

Mythology of Ardha Chandrasana

This posture considers the energy of the moon as its great symbol. The significance of

this asana is to channel the moon or lunar energy within the body. More than just the moon, the

Chandra refers to something that is glittering and shining, a brilliant object that is illuminated by light on its own. In many traditional yogic texts and stories, the moon symbolizes one-half of the two polar energies in the body (Gaia, 2019).

The feminine energy of Chandra is only half of the energy in the universe. There is a second half of the energy, and it is the masculine energy. These two forces complete each other and are always searching for their compliment for completion. The idea of the complementary forces of the masculine and the feminine is found in cultures around the world, such as Mexico and Japan. In Teotihuacan, near Mexico City, there are huge pyramids known as the Pyramid of the Sun and the Pyramid of the Moon. The Moon is the counterpart that balances the sun. She represents cooling, calming, instinct, reflection, mystery, emotion, and the dream world. In Japan, Tsukuyomi-no-Mikoto is the moon god in Japanese mythology. The name "Tsukuyomi" is a compound of the Old Japanese words tsuku ("moon, month") and yomi ("reading, counting). An alternative interpretation is that his name is a combination of "moonlit night" and "looking, watching" (Kokugo Dai Jiten,1988).

Connection to the lesson

The girl of our story, Natalia, is a teenager with a lot of energy and trying to find the right chemistry with the others at her first teenage party. The restless energy of Chandra is familiar to all young people. There is a continuing search for balance for the powerful energies of the Chandra.

Cautionary notes

- Do not hold for a long period of time if you have any heart or circulatory issues.
- Place your hands on your hips, if you have any injury to the affected area or if you have back problems.

Yogic Breathing: Dirgha Pranayama
Meaning: Prana: air; life force; Yama: to restrain or hold back

Potential effects

Enhancement of complete and full breathing, decreasing stress and tension while calming the mind and the body, helping the lungs remain healthy by increasing the oxygen flow to the blood, it massages the abdominal organs, facilitating digestion, preparing you for a better learning experience.

Three Breathing Steps: (Visit website to listen)

1- Sit up straight with your shoulders back and down with relaxed abdominals.

2- Relax the face, close your mouth, and place your hands on your belly.

3- Breathe into your belly and feel it expands like a balloon. Repeat several times.

4- Now, put your hands to the sides of your rib cage and breathe into them, feeling the rib cage expand, and repeat several times.

5- Put your fingertips on your upper chest. Breathe into it and feel your hands lifting. Repeat several times.

6- Now, make a complete inhalation. As you are inhaling, feel the expansions of your belly, rib cage, and chest, and as you are exhaling, you feel the contractions of all three. Repeat this series several times (Refer to Figure 1 in Chapter 1).

Next, move into the warmup, which is the next section.

Warm-up: Arms overhead Stretch (Visit website to listen)

Stand with your feet wider than shoulder width. On an inhale, raise your hands over your head toward the sky and hold your hands as wide as your feet. Do not bend your elbows. On an exhale, stretch your arms behind your ears as is comfortable for you. Exhale to the right and inhale back to center. Exhale to the left and inhale back to center. Repeat moving from side to side in coordination with your breathing (Figure 1).

1   2   3

Figure 1: Arms Overhead Stretch

Posture steps for performing the half-moon pose (Visit website to listen)

1- While standing tall with your feet hip-width apart,

2- On an inhale, swing your arms over your head and clasp your fingers together with your index fingers pointing toward the sky. Ground the soles of your feet into the earth. Straighten your back. Drop the tailbone. Roll your shoulders back and down, stand tall.

3- Inhale and switch the weight toward your left foot and lengthen toward your right side. Distribute your weight on both feet. Keep your shoulders and hips squared to the front.

4- To release, exhale, relax your arms down by your sides, feel the difference, and feel the effects of Ardha Chandrasana (half-moon pose). Take a few breaths and perform on the other side (Figure 2).

1   2   3

Figure 2: Half-Moon (Ardha Chandrasana)

Section 2: Music and Lyrics: Moon

Part 1: Listening (Stage 1, 2 and 3), (Visit website to listen)

Stage 1- (Listening for fun) Listen to the song several times, pat your feet, move your body, and enjoy the music! Do not worry about the meaning of the words yet!!!

Stage 2- (Attentive listening) Listen carefully several times to understand the lyrics.

Stage 3- (Listening and guessing) listen and read the lyrics several times to understand the lyrics. Try to guess the meaning of the words you do not know and understand. Do not look at the vocabulary list just yet. Listen to the lyrics again and guess at the meaning of the words you do not know. Write down the words you do not know.

Guess words:

…………………………………………………………………………………………………

…………………………………………………………………………………………………

…………………………………………………………………………………………………

…………………………………………………………………………………………………

…………………………………………………………………………………………………

…………………………………………………………………………………………………

Part 2: Listening & Reading Lyrics (Stage 4, 5, 6, and 7), (Visit website to listen)

Stage 4- (Confirmation of guessing) Look at the vocabulary table to make sure that you know the meaning and part of speech of all the words in the lyrics.

Stage 5- (Humming) Now that you know the meaning of the whole song, listen to the music and hum along with the song several times.

Stage 6- (Karaoke) See the lyrics on the monitor and sing. (Visit website to listen)

Stage 7- (Mastery) Listen to the music without any lyrics and sing away. Sing, Dance, and Enjoy!

Section 3: Reading a Short Story: Moon

a. Listen and take notes

Please listen to the story and write down what you have understood.

....

....

....

....

....

....

b. Reading and Guessing

- Please read the short story below, guess at the missing words and fill in the blanks.

"Moon"

Once upon a time, Natalia was a bored 17-year-old teenager. She asked her dad if she could have her first teenage party on the weekend. He agreed, and she invited all her friends. Her friends came from far and near. It was the night of the party, and the half moon was in the sky. The music was playing, and everybody was dancing, but Natalia was wondering who could come and dance with her to make a full moon. While she was wondering, a handsome nerdy boy (1) ………………… her and said: "Would you like to dance?", she replied: "Maybe." Sam said: "Oh, come on, let's dance!". Natalia replied "Ok." They started to dance. While they were dancing, Sam said that "you (2) …………… like the moon in the sky. Natalia felt the full energy of his eyes and replied, "Thank you!". They (3) ………….. hands and kept dancing. After a while, Natalia stopped the music and (4) …………. her hands and said: "Hey, girls! , Hey guys! Welcome to my party, time to dance to "Jennifer & Pitbull," time to make a move, let's party." Everyone was so excited, and they started (5) …………… to the "On the floor" song.

It was around 12 o'clock, and the kids were still rocking and dancing away. Their cars (6) …………. the streets, and some were double-parked. Suddenly a policewoman (7) …………. on the door. Her dad answered the door. The policewoman said, "I am sorry, sir, but it is time to end the party. The cars outside are double parked and are a fire (8) …………. because a fire engine will not be able to pass if there is a fire in the (9) ………………...". Natalia's dad replied, "Ok," and then told the young people, "The party will have to end." Quickly, all the young people got into their cars and went home. Natalia's dad (10) ………….. …. …… ….. …………. as the last car left the neighborhood.

c. Listening and checking your guessing (Visit the website to listen)

 Please read and listen to the short story. While you are listening, please check to see if the guesses you have made are correct. If your guess was not correct, please make a change and check your [30]answers in the footnotes.

d. Clearing up all confusions

Please read the short story by yourself without listening to it. Highlight or underline the parts that are unclear to you in the story above. Use your dictionary or a partner to clarify highlighted parts. Write your notes below for further review.

………………………………………………………………………………………………………..

………………………………………………………………………………………………………...

e. Reading Comprehension based on the "WH Questions."

Look below for the boxes and read the questions (Q) and answers (A). While you are reading the questions, answer by filling in the blank with the "WH questions" (who, when, where, what,

---

[30] 1- Approached: Came nearer, 2- Shine: reflect light, 3- Held: Joined hands, 4- Clapped: made a short loud noise by hitting her hands together, 5- Rocking: shaking, 6- lined: parked in a row, 7- knocked: hit repeatedly, 8 - Hazard: dangerous,9-neighborhood: the area of surrounds Natalia's home, 10- Breathed a sigh of relief: felt very happy

why, and how). Choose the answers that are the best fit. You do not have to use all the "WH questions." Notice that the title of the reading is in the middle of a circle, and the questions pivot clockwise around the title of the story in the figure. Both questions and answers are provided, and you only need to put the correct "WH questions" in the blank.

- After you have finished filling in the blanks below, practice asking and answering the questions.

- Check your answers with the [31]answer key in the footnote.

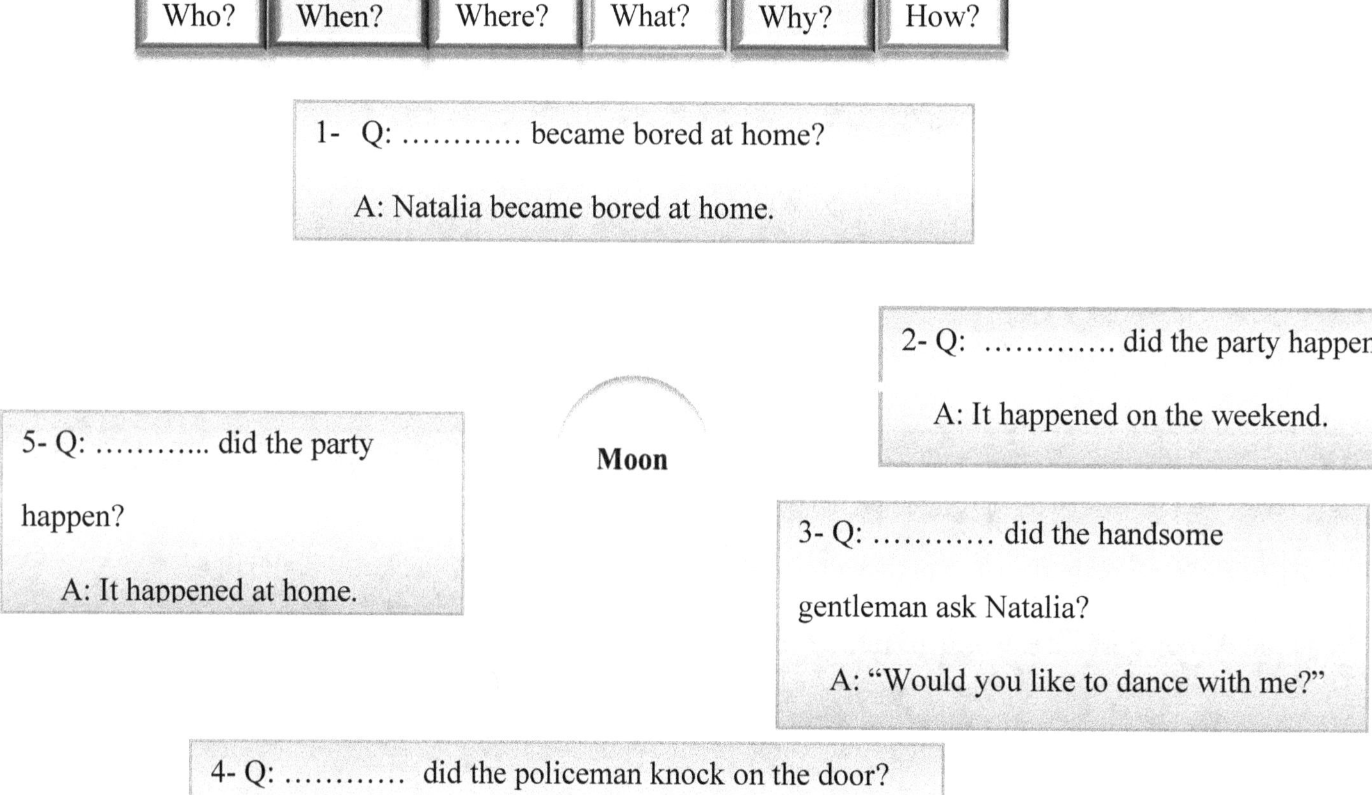

---

[31] 1- Who, 2-What, 3- What, 4- How, 5- Where

Section 4 : Syntax Notes : Impératives, Possessive Adjectives, Possessive Pronouns

Syntax Note 1 : Impératives

Example from a line in lyrics: "Put your hands in mine"

Warm-up question: what do you think the syntax note is about?

………

………

- Imperatives are used to issue a command. In fact, they tell people what to do.

How to form an imperative? The base form of the main verb, without a subject (doer).

To be polite, you may use "Please" at the beginning of the command: "Please put your hands in

mine or please come here."

Can you think of another example? Write them down.

………

Syntax Notes 2: Possessive Adjectives

Example from a line in the lyrics: "Put your hands in mine."

Warm-up question: what do you think the syntax note is about?

………

………

- Possessive Adjectives: "my, your (singular), his, her, its, our, your (plural), their"

They show possession or ownership. There is always a noun after them (hands). That's why they

are called adjectives.

Can you think of another example? Write it down.

………

Syntax Note 3: Possessive Pronouns

Example from a line in the lyrics: "Put your hands in mine."

Warm-up question: what do you think the syntax note is about?

…………………………………………………………………………………………………

…………………………………………………………………………………………………

- Possessive Pronouns: "mine, yours, his, hers, its, ours, yours, and theirs."

Possessive pronouns also show ownership. They are replacing a noun or noun phrase (your hands) that has been mentioned before in a sentence to avoid repetition. Look at the following examples:

"Put your hands in my hands (mine)". In this example, "your" is a possessive adjective and comes before a noun (hands). In parentheses, instead of my hands (a noun phrase), we can use a possessive pronoun (mine) to avoid the repetition of (my hands).

Look at the table below and notice the differences.

No.	Possessive adjectives + Noun	Possessive pronouns + ------	Examples - With possessive adjective - With possessive pronounce
1.	My	Mine	This is my car. This is mine.
2.	Your	Yours	This is your car. This is yours.
3.	His/her	His/Hers	This is her/his car. This is hers/his.
4.	Our	Ours	This is our car. This is ours.
5.	Your	Yours	This is your car. This is yours.
6.	Their	Theirs	This is their car. This is theirs.

Note: As you noticed, most of the possessive pronouns form by adding "s" at the end of possessive adjectives. The only exception is "mine," and for "his," it remains as it is.

*Please find and highlight all possessive adjectives and possessive pronouns in the lyrics. Create your own examples with them.

………

………

Section 5: Museum of Reincarnation: Ludwig van Beethoven

Wikipedia contributors, 2022, Ludwig van Beethoven

Stage 1. Completing the vocabulary list

Before going to the museum, please complete the vocabulary list below.

No.	Vocabulary	Meaning
1.	spirit	
2.	fine	
3.	forget	
4.	sadness and sorrow	

5.	The sky is the limit.	
6.	valentine	
7.	I'll tell you.	
8.	Waste no time.	
9.	dull	

Stage 2. The museum (Biography part), listening and taking notes. (Visit website to listen)

Who is the famous person? Why is the person famous?

…………………………………………………………………………………………

…………………………………………………………………………………………

…………………………………………………………………………………………

Stage 3. Reincarnation with the famous person (Vocabulary part)

a. Watching and Listening. (Visit website to listen)

b. Watching, listening carefully, and writing down the usage of the words by the famous person.

c. Identifying the parts of speech.

d. Writing your own sentences using the vocabulary words and the syntax notes.

No.	Vocabulary	a. Watching and Listening
		b. Sentences with the vocabulary word used by the famous person
		c. Part of speech
		d. Sentences with the vocabulary word used by you
1	**Spirit**	b. Sentences by the famous person: ………………………………… ……………………………………………………………………… c. Part of speech: …………… d. Your sentence: …………………………………………………….. ………………………………………………………………………
2	**Fine**	b. Sentences by the famous person: ………………………………… ……………………………………………………………………… c. Part of speech: …………… d. Your sentence: ………………………………………………….. ………………………………………………………………………
3	**Forget**	b. Sentences by the famous person: ………………………………… ……………………………………………………………………… c. Part of speech: …………… d. Your sentence: …………………………………………………... ………………………………………………………………………
4		b. Sentences by the famous person: ………………………………… ………………………………………………………………………

	Sadness and Sorrow	c. Part of speech: ....
		d. Your sentence: ....
5	**The sky is the limit**	b. Sentences by the famous person: ....
		c. Part of speech: ....
		d. Your sentence: ....
6	**Valentine**	b. Sentences by the famous person: ....
		c. Part of speech: ....
		d. Your sentence: ....
7	**I'll tell you**	b. Sentences by the famous person: ....
		c. Part of speech: ....
		d. Your sentence: ....
8	**Waste no time**	b. Sentences by the famous person: ....
		c. Part of speech: ....
		d. Your sentence: ....

9		b. Sentences by the famous person: ………………………………
		…………………………………………………………………………..
		c. Part of speech: ……………
	Dull	d. Your sentence: …………………………………………………..
		……………………………………………………………………………

Section 6: Conversation Creation

a. Choosing a topic

Choose one of the following potential topics and participants related to the short story/lyrics of the lesson.

Topic 1: "Dad, can I throw a party?", Participants: Natalia and Dad

Topic 2: Greetings, Participants: Natalia and Sam

Topic 3: Time to end the party, Participants: Dad and Policewoman

Topic 4: Saying goodbye, Participants: Natalia and her friends

b. Creating conversation

After choosing your topic, create your conversation in the space below.

Note: There are four models of a conversation in the endnotes to this chapter. You can look at the models and use or modify the conversation you have created. When you are creating your conversation, you should use the syntax notes and some of the vocabulary from the museum.

Topic of your conversation:

Participants:

………………………………………………………………………………………

………………………………………………………………………………………

………………………………………………………………………

....

....

....

....

....

c. Role-playing

Practice and role-play the conversation with your partner, friend, brother/sister, or even with yourself in front of the mirror. The purpose of role-playing is to become comfortable using the language in a casual and conversational way.

Note: Role-play the other conversations in the endnotes for additional practice. Feel free to change the language as you see fit.

Section 7: Cultural Notes: Jennifer & Pitbull singing "On the Floor"

a. Warm-Up (Brainstorming)

Please look at the topic above and guess what the cultural notes are about.

....

....

....

....

b. Reading

Read the following cultural notes. If you do not know a word or phrase, please use the guessing strategy (guess the meaning of the words based on the context) and use a dictionary when necessary.

"On the Floor Singers."

"**Jennifer Lynn Lopez** (born July 24, 1969), also known by her nickname J.Lo, is an American

actress, singer, dancer, fashion designer, producer, and businesswoman" with a Puerto Rican background. Her parents were [32]relatively poor during her childhood, but with her [33]persistence and great [34]effort, she has become one of the most successful women in the world. While she was married to Alex Rodriguez, who also came from a [35]humble beginning and became one of the richest baseball players in the world, the [36]pair [37]stepped up with a [38]generous donation after being touched by an elementary school teacher's emotional post on Facebook about having to buy a student food which went [39]viral (France, 2019). The couple also helped to ensure that families got the food they needed amid the coronavirus pandemic.

"**Armando Christian Pérez** (born January 15, 1981), known professionally as Pitbull, is an

American rapper, singer, songwriter and record producer" ("Pitbull (rapper)," n.d.). He plays hard, and he works hard. When asked for his best investment tips, Pitbull said: "Don't be afraid to lose. Listen. And always [40]invest in yourself. "According to the biography "Pitbull: Mr. Worldwide," the rapper had a reason for wanting to be known after a particular [41]breed of dog."(Pitbulls) bite to lock," the book quotes him as saying. "The dog is too stupid to lose. And

---

[32] almost
[33] Someone who is persistent continues doing something
[34] physical or mental activity needed to achieve something
[35] poor or of a low social rank
[36] two people who have a romantic relationship or are doing something together
[37] to take action when there is a need or opportunity for it
[38] willing to give money, help, kindness, etc., especially more than is usual or expected
[39] used to describe something that quickly becomes very popular
[40] to put money, effort, time, etc. into something to make a profit or get an advantage
[41] a particular type of animal

they're [42]outlawed in Dade County (Florida). They're basically everything that I am. It's been a [43]constant fight." He is also [44]inspiring the next [45]generation to be successful like him. Beyond recording music, Pitbull is using that passion for helping shape the future. He helped create the Sports Leadership and Management Academy, aka SLAM, a charter school in Miami with a sports-based curriculum (France, 2014). Miami rapper/songwriter Pitbull dropped a new single on Monday, turning the familiar sports chant "I Believe That We Will Win" into a pop anthem for the COVID-19 outbreak, with all proceeds from the song being donated to charity.

c. SPARCing the Cultural Notes

Using the information above, choose one of the two stars or combine their information and complete the SPARC (Setting, Participant, Activities, Reasons, and Conclusion).

- Setting (when and where?): …………………………………………………………………..

- Participants (who?): ………………………………………………………………………….

- Activities (how did they get there?):

  …………………………………………………………………………………………………..

- Reasons (why are they successful?):

  …………………………………………………………………………………………………..

- Conclusion (what is your SPARK?):

  ……………………………………………………………………………………………………

  …………………………………………………………………………………………………..

---

[42] to make something illegal or unacceptable
[43] all the time
[44] to make someone feel that they want to do something and can do it
[45] all the people of about the same age within a society

Section 8: Creative Story/Lyrics Writing

Based on all the points you have learned in this chapter (Yoga, vocabulary, grammar, lyrics, video, museum, and conversations), follow the steps below:

Stage 1: Brainstorming

Insert the title of your story/lyrics in the middle of the figure below and then fill in the other boxes about the participants in your story (who), the setting (when and where), the activities of your story (how), the reasons for your story (why), and the conclusion to your story (what).

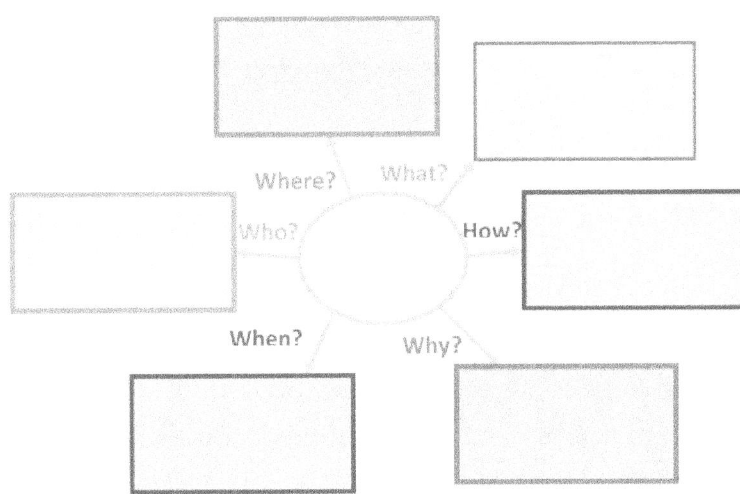

Stage 2- Writing your story/lyrics

Now in the space below, write your story/ lyrics (Your story/lyrics can be rap, rhyming, etc., Be creative and let your imagination be your limit)

The title of your story/lyrics: …………………………………….

…………………………………………………………………………………………………

…………………………………………………………………………………………………

…………………………………………………………………………………………………

....

....

....

Stage 3. Feedback

a- Self-feedback: Imagine you are a teacher, and you are correcting your creation as a teacher (You can start by analyzing the text and understanding the part of speech)

b-Peer-feedback: Check your story/ lyrics with your teacher/parents/mentors, to get feedback.

Stage 4. Applying Music: Either apply your story/lyrics on the karaoke track of the song or click on the beat's website, such as https://www.8notes.com/metronome/ , choose the right beat for your story/lyrics. Even if you play a musical instrument, apply your writing to your playing. Don't limit yourself and be creative.

Stage 5. Singing: Practice, sing and enjoy!

Stage 6. Recording. Record yourself and share your product with someone else to get feedback, and revise if necessary.

Stage 7. Posting your creation.

Section 9: Quick Quiz

The quiz in this section is designed to help you review and remember some of the materials you have learned. The answer key is always provided in the footnotes. If you have any doubts about the correct answer, please check the footnotes.

Please answer the questions below and check your answers in the [46]answer key in the footnote.

---

[46] Answer Key

    1- c, 2- d, 3- b, 4- a, 5- c, 6- c, 7- b, 8- T, 9- F, 10- F

a. **Vocabulary**: What is the part of speech and synonym of the **Bolded** vocabulary?

1- Please dance with me. You are my **valentine**.

    a. Noun: mind   b. Noun: friend

    c. Noun: love   d. Adjective: frenemy

2- Tonight, it's Sara's birthday. She is dancing and **shaking** her body.

    a. Adjective: forgetting   b.Verb: taking

    c. Noun: calling   d. Verb: rocking

3- I love you so much. **The sky is the limit.**

    a. Idiom: There is a limit   b. Idiom: There is no limit

    c. Adjective: the sky is blue   d. Adjective: They sky is big.

4- You are so fine, baby. **I have a crush on you.**

    a. Adjective: Pretty- Expression: I am attracted to you

    b. Adjective: Ugly- Phrase: I want to crush you

    c. Noun: Ugly-Expression: I want to dance with you

    d. Noun: Pretty-Phrase: I want to hold your hands

5- Oh, sweetie, **waste no time**. Let's get out of here.

    a. Adverb: Don't rush   b. Adjective: shake it

    c. Expression: hurry up   d. Expression: come here

b. **Grammar**: Which is the best way for an English speaker to express herself/himself?

6-

    a. This phone belongs to her. It is she phone.

    b. This phone belongs to her. It is his phone.

    c. This phone belongs to her. It is her phone.

d.   This phone belongs to her. It is their phone.

7-   Which of the following sentences has the same meaning as: She put her hands in his

hands?

a.   She put her hands in hers.

b.   She put her hands in his.

c.   He put his hands in his.

d.   He put his hands in shes.

A.   Culture: Based on the cultural notes, decide which sentence is true (T) and which one is

false (F)?

8-   J.Lo, is an American actress, singer, dancer, fashion designer, producer, and

businesswoman" with an American background.

9-   Jennifer's parents were relatively rich during her childhood.

10- Pitbull helped create the Music Leadership and Management Academy, aka SLAM, a

charter school in Miami with a sports-based curriculum.

Section 10: Endnotes

Museum Transcripts

a. Biography of Beethoven

Ludwig Van Beethoven (1770-1827) was born in Bonn, Germany, and is considered by many to

be the greatest composer and pianist of the 18th and 19th centuries. His [47]genius was [48]apparent at

an early age. By age 16, he traveled to Vienna to study with Mozart, the great composer, and

pianist. At the height of his musical genius, Beethoven started to become [49]deaf. Despite his

---

[47] very great and rare natural ability or skill
[48] shown
[49] unable to hear

deafness and perhaps because of it, he continued to compose at a [50]furious rate. The Moonlight Sonata was one of the most beautiful and [51]haunting of his compositions from this period of his life ("Ludwig van Beethoven.," n.d.; Thayer & Krehbiel, (2020); Wikipedia contributors (2022)).

b. Quotations

A great poet, a great music, and singing with joy and passion are the keys to the world of art. A fine poet is a gift of gold for the world. Music is the spirit of the creative life. "If you'll give happiness and joy instead of sadness and sorrows to many others, then you're a happy fellow." For the true artist, the sky is the limit. To sing a wrong note does not matter but waste no time and do not sing without passion. When there is no passion, then the day-to-day routine of life is boring and dull. So, listen to the notes of your heart and sing the melody of love with passion. Share the melody of your heart with theirs (with the hearts of other people) and make a symphony of love and peace in the world. My friend! never forget about the days we were together and always be my friend. "Love demands all and has a right to all." (Ludwig van Beethoven Quotes. (n.d.). BrainyQuote.com)

1- Direct Quotations, 2- Paraphrased Quotations

1- Spirit: "Music is a higher revelation than all wisdom and philosophy. Music is the electrical soil in which the spirit lives, thinks, and invents." 2- Music is the spirit of the creative life.

2- Fine: "A great poet is the most precious jewel of a nation."2- A fine poet is a gift of gold.

3- Forget: "Never forget the days I spent with you. Continue to be my friend, as you will always find me yours."2- My friend, never forget about the days we were together and always be my friend.

4- Sadness and Sorrow: "If you give happiness and joy to many others, you're a happy fellow."

---

[50] extremely angry
[51] beautiful, but in a sad way and often in a way that cannot be forgotten

5- The sky is the limit: "The true artist is not proud. He, unfortunately, sees that art has no limits." 2- For the true artist, the sky is the limit.

6- Valentine: "Never misjudge the most faithful heart of your beloved." 2- Always trust the heart and love of your valentine. (The one you have a crush on)

7- I'll tell you: "Music should strike fire from the heart of man and bring tears from the eyes of a woman."2- I'll tell you; music should burn the heart of a man and melts the heart of a woman."

8- Waste no time: "To sing a wrong note is insignificant but to sing without passion is unforgivable." 2- To sing a wrong note does not matter but waste no time and do not sing without passion

9- Dull: "The day-to-day exhausted me."2- The day-to-day routines of life are boring and dull.
 (Grammar)

Beethoven: Listen to the notes of your heart and sing the melody of love with passion. Share the melody of your heart with theirs (with the hearts of other people) and make a symphony of love and peace in the world.

Conversations

Model 1.

Topic: Dad, can I Throw a party? ; Participants: Natalia and her dad

Natalia: Hi Dad, I am so bored, can I have my first teenage party this weekend?

Dad: My sweet girl, why not invite all your friends over?

Natalia: Yeh, Thank you, dad.

Dad: You're very welcome. I will buy the food and drink for your party.

Natalia: Great and I am going to clean the house and invite all my friends.

Dad: Ok, we have a plan.

Model 2.

Topic: Glad to meet you; Participants: Natalia and Sam

Sam: Hey Natalia, you look so fine tonight. Can I say something?

Natalia: Sure, share with me.

Sam: I'll tell you. I have a crush on you. The sky is the limit. You are my valentine.

Natalia: Oh, thank you, I respect your feelings, but forget about it.

Sam: Oh, come on, at least, can we dance?

Natalia: Ok

Sam: Would you like a drink?

Natalia: Yes, water, please.

Sam: Here, sweetie, don't be dull. Let's rock it. Shake it. Waste no time. Cheers.

Natalia: Ok, no sorrow, no sadness. Cheers.

Model 3.

Topic: Time to end the party! Participants: Dad and Policewoman!

Police: Hello, Mr. Dad. I am sorry, but it is time to end the party.

Dad: Oh, what's wrong?!

Police: The cars outside are double parked and are a fire hazard because a fire engine will not be able to pass if there is a fire in the neighborhood.

Dad: Oh, I am sorry. I understand. I am going to ask the kids to leave immediately. To be honest with you, I am so happy you showed up.

Police: Haha! I understand. Have a good night.

Dad: Thank you, you too.

Model 4.

Topic: Saying goodbye; Participants: Natalia and her friends

Natalia: Guys, I know the policewoman was a wet blanket, but we had a great night.

Friend 1: Oh, Natali, I danced a lot... I was feeling my body begging me to stop.

Friend 2: Me too. My high heels were killing me.

Natalia: Mine too. Massage your feet and rest well because next week we will get together for

Sara's party.

Friends: Sure.

Natalia: Thanks, guys. Have a good night. See you later.

Friends: See you, bye.

Vocabulary list as a resource

	Vocabulary		
No.	Pronunciation Part of speech in the song	Meaning (synonym)	Example in sentence
1.	**To see** /siː/ **Verb**	to be *conscious* of what is around you by using your eyes, to watch	See the moon in the sky. Isn't it beautiful?
2.	**Sky** /skaɪ/ **Noun**	the area above the earth in which clouds, the sun, and the stars can be seen	The moon is in the sky.
3.	**Half** /hæf/ **Noun**	either of the two equal or almost equal parts that together make up a whole, partly	Always hear the other half of the story.
4.	**Moon** /muːn/ **Noun**	an object, like a planet, that revolves around the earth and moves through the sky and	The moon is beautiful tonight.
5.	**To Hold** /həʊld/ **Verb**	to take and keep something in your hand or arms, to keep	I like to hold your hands in mine.
6.	**Hands** /hændz/ **Noun**	the part of the body at the end of the arm, fist	Wash your hands for 20 seconds. I washed my hands to not get the coronavirus.

#	Word	Definition	Example
7.	**To Shine** /ʃaɪn/ **Verb**	to send out or reflect light	The moon is shining tonight.
8.	**Like** /laɪk/ **Proposition**	similar to; in the same way or manner as	You sing like an angel.
9.	**Full** /fʊl/ **Adjective**	Complete, whole	Tonight, the moon is full.
10.	**To Put** /pʊt/ **Verb**	to move something, to place	Put your cup on the table. I put my cup on the table.
11.	**Mine** /maɪn/ **Pronoun**	belongs to me	Put your hand in mine.
12.	**Valentine** /ˈvæləntaɪn/ **Adjective**	someone you love or admire affectionately, honey	Be my valentine!
13.	**To Have a crush on someone** /həv krʌʃ ɑːn ˈsʌmwʌn/ **Idiom**	to Like someone (To be attracted to someone) I have crush on you= I am attracted to you	I have a crush on you.
14.	**So** /səʊ/ **Adverb**	to such a great degree, very	She is so strong.
15.	**Cute** /kjuːt/ **Adjective**	charming and attractive, pretty	She is so cute.
16.	**I'll tell you** /ˌaɪlˈtel jə/ **Idiom**	used to emphasize what you are saying (I believe what I am saying to you is true)	I am telling you; You are the cutest.
17.	**Time** /taɪm/ **Noun**	the seconds, minutes, hours, days, weeks, months, years, etc., in which existence is measured, or the past, present, and future considered as a whole	It's time to sing and learn.
18.	**To dance** /dæns/ **Verb**	to move the body and feet in rhythm to music, to move the body	She can dance and sing.
19.	**To stop** /stɑːp/ **Verb**	to finish doing something or to end, to cease	Stop calling me.
20.	**Tonight** /təˈnaɪt/	(during) the night of the present day, this evening	I have a date tonight.

	Word	Definition	Example
	Adverb		
21.	**Be** /biː/ **Verb**	used to say that someone should or must do something in the lyrics: Be+ Adj	Be quick! Be strong! Be smart!
22.	**Dull** /dʌl/ **Adjective**	not interesting or exciting, boring	Don't be dull. Let's do something.
23.	**Boring** /ˈbɔːrɪŋ/ **Adjective**	not interesting or exciting	You are boring tonight.
24.	**To shake** /ʃeɪk/ **Verb**	to move something backward and forward or up and down in quick, short movements, to rock	Shake your body.
25.	**Till** /tɪl/ **Preposition**	up to, until	I can dance till tomorrow.
26.	**Tomorrow** /təˈmɑːrəʊ/ **Adverb**	the day after today	I will dance till tomorrow.
27.	**To forget about** /fərˈget əˈbaʊt / **Verb**	to stop thinking about someone or something	Let's forget about our sadness.
28.	**All** /ɔːl/ **Adjective**	everyone, entire	All my friends are beautiful.
29.	**Sadness** /ˈsædnəs/ **Noun**	the feeling of being sad or unhappy, unhappiness	She left, and I felt sadness.
30.	**Sorrow** /ˈsɑːrəʊ/ **Noun**	a feeling of great sadness, pain	Her death was a great sorrow for everyone.
31.	**To Waste no time** /weɪst nəʊ taɪm/ **Idiom**	to immediately begin an activity, to rush, to hurry up	Waste no time and come dance with me.
32.	**Fine** /faɪn/ **Adjective**	excellent or much better than average	You are so fine.
33.	**The Sky is the limit** /ðə skaɪ iz ðə ˈlɪmɪt/ **Idiom**	there is no limit. There are unlimited possibilities	The sky is the limit for our love.
34.	**To look at** /lʊk æt/ **Verb**	to direct your eyes to see	Look at the sky and see the moon.

| 35. | **To feel**
 /fiːl/
 Verb | to experience something physical or emotional | I feel joy when I am with you. |
| 36. | **Spirit**
 /ˈspɪrɪt/
 Noun | enthusiasm, energy, or courage | You sing the song with great spirit. |

Chapter 3

Section 1: Yoga Posture: Eagle

Yoga Posture: Eagle (Asana: Garudasana)
Gardua: Eagle; Asana: posture

Open the sharp vision of your heart, dream big, fly high, and do not be afraid to become what you are supposed to be, be an eagle!

Mythology of Garudasana

The Eagle is the king of birds, a symbol of power and victory. It is an emblem of victory in battle and the triumph of spirit over matter. Today the person of outstanding intelligence, who has lofty thoughts and conceives of high-flying projects, is often compared to an eagle. The eagle depicts the age-old conflict between power of the mind (soaring eagle) and matter (temptation). Ask yourself: "Can I see my struggle clearly (sharp vision)? What is my target? (Can I act at the right time and at the right place)" (Radha, 2006).

According to Paul Tillich (2008), it requires courage to be an eagle. The Eagle is a strong and regal bird and known in various myths as one of God's messengers. As you sit deeply into the eagle pose, you can imagine yourself flying between the earthly and spiritual planes, with an Eagle Eye that takes in the greater perspective of life. *Garudasana* (Eagle pose) demands great focus and patience, as does living a life in accordance with Spirit. It is easy to get bogged down with the challenges of life (or of this pose!), but a calm connection with the Divine can help you soar on to your journey.

Many cultures have associated the eagle with the most important of their gods. In Egypt, the solar symbolism was shared by the falcon and the eagle, and this heavenly principle is the divine vision. The symbol of the United States is the eagle. Many cultures have adopted the symbol of the eagle, and even in modern times, Austria has the double-headed eagle as its special emblem. The arms of Mexico show the eagle with the serpent. Aristotle tells a story of the eagle's fabulous eyesight, which allowed it to look directly at the sun. This story was later expanded to symbolize Christ as the eagle who could look directly at his father (Hatha yoga).

Connection to the lesson

In this song, the girl of the story, Natalia, is switching between different feelings and planes of imagination. Starting a relationship with the boy (temptation) and feeling the power of independence (soaring eagle).

Cautionary notes

If you have a persistent heart issue, high/low blood pressure, or weak knees, please consult your physicians and avoid holding the posture for a long period of time.

Yogic Breathing: Dirgha Pranayama (Visit website to listen)
Meaning: Prana: air; life force; Yama: to restrain or hold back

Potential effects

Enhancement of complete and full breathing, decreasing stress and tension while calming the mind and the body, helping the lungs remain healthy by increasing the oxygen flow to the blood, it massages the abdominal organs, facilitating digestion, preparing you for a better learning experience

Three Breathing Steps:

1- Sit up straight with your shoulders back and down with relaxed abdominals.

2- Relax the face, close your mouth, and place your hands on your belly.

3- Breathe into your belly and feel it expands like a balloon. Repeat several times.

4- Now, put your hands to the sides of your rib cage and breathe into them, feeling the rib cage expand and repeat several times.

5- Put your fingertips on your upper chest. Breathe into it and feel your hands lifting. Repeat several times.

6- Now, make a complete inhalation. As you are inhaling, feel the expansions of your belly, rib cage, and chest, and as you are exhaling, you feel the contractions of all three. Repeat this series several times (Refer to Figure 1 in Chapter 1).

Next, move into the warmup, which is the next section.

🎧 Warm-up: Balancing knee (Visit website to listen)

1- Stand tall in Tadasana and keep your feet parallel and close to each other. Shift your weight from your left foot to right and from your right foot to your left several times.

2- On an inhale, sweep your arms to the sides, palms facing down.

3- On an exhale, raise your left knee up in front of you until your thigh is at a 90-degree angle with the floor. On an inhale, bring your foot down. Feel the difference and repeat on the other side (Figure 1).

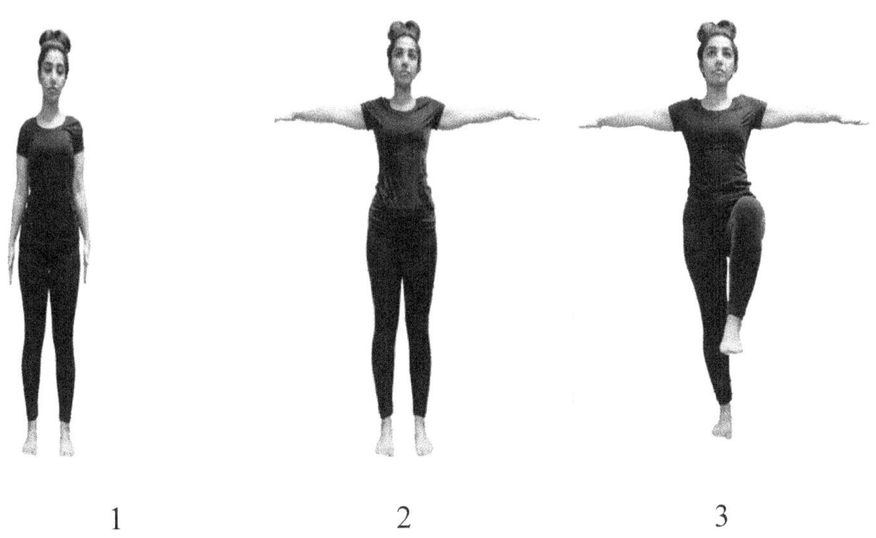

Figure 1: Balancing Knee

Posture steps of Garudasana (Eagle Pose): (Visit website to listen)

1- Stand tall with your feet hip-width apart and parallel to each other.

2- On an exhale, blend both knees, until you feel the engagement of your quad muscles.

3- Inhale and shift your weight onto your right foot and lift your left foot. On an exhale, rotate your left knee out and high and swing it over your right leg. While maintaining the balance, on an inhale, bend your left knee as comfortable. Keep your pelvis neutral, and your hips squared and parallel.

4- On an inhale, swipe your arms to the sides and then cross your right arm over your left. On an exhale, bend your elbows and lift your hands in front of your face.

5- Inhale while slowly bending your right knee and let your hips sink down a bit while pressing your legs and arms together. Keep breathing and balance your torso until your elbows are just above your knees. Hold the posture for a few seconds.

6- To release, exhale, uncross your arms and then your legs. Relax, rest, feel the effect of Garudasana (the eagle pose) and repeat on the other side (Figure 2).

Figure 2: Eagle (Garudasana)

Section 2: Music and Lyrics: We are Superstars

Part 1: Listening (Stage 1,2 and 3), (Visit website to listen)

Stage 1- (Listening for fun) Listen to the song several times, pat your feet, move your body, and enjoy the music! Do not worry about the meaning of the words yet!!!

Stage 2- (Attentive listening) Listen carefully several times to understand the lyrics.

Stage 3- (Listening and guessing) listen and read the lyrics several times to understand the lyrics. Try to guess the meaning of the words you do not know and understand. Do not look at the vocabulary list just yet. Listen to the lyrics again and guess at the meaning of the words you do not know. Write down the words you do not know.

Guess words:

....

....

....

....

....

....

....

Part 2: Listening & Reading Lyrics (Stage 4, 5, 6, and 7)

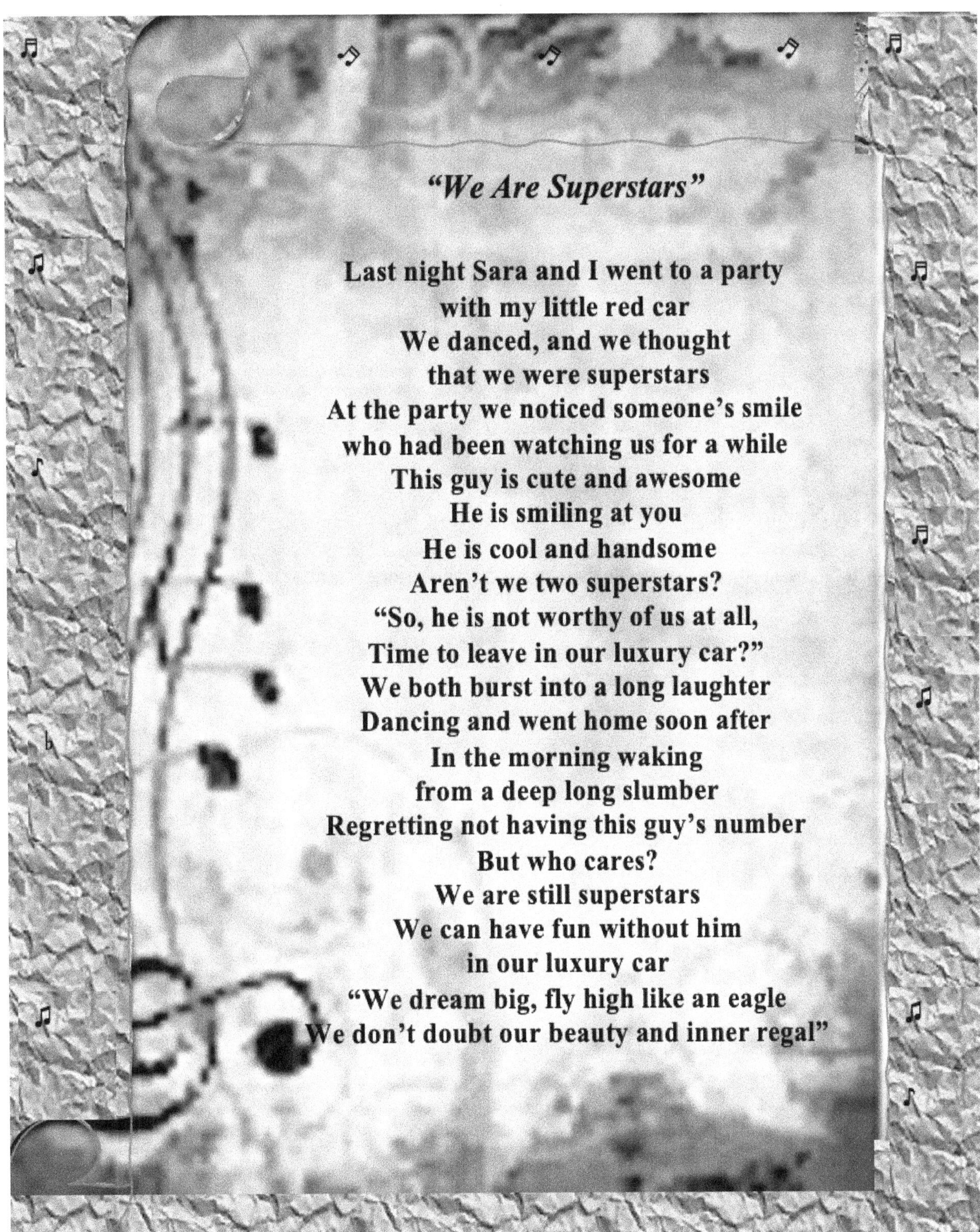

Stage 4- (Confirmation of guessing) Look at the vocabulary table to make sure that you know the meaning and part of speech of all the words in the lyrics.

Stage 5- (Humming) Now that you know the meaning of the whole song, listen to the music and hum along with the song several times.

Stage 6- (Karaoke) See the lyrics on the monitor and sing.

Stage 7- (Mastery) Listen to the music without any lyrics and sing away. Sing, Dance, and Enjoy!

Section 3: Reading a short story: We are Superstars

a. Listening and taking notes (Visit website to listen)

Please listen to the story and write down what you have understood. (Listen and take notes)

....

....

....

....

....

b. Reading

Please read and listen to the short story below, guess at the missing words, and fill in the blanks.

"We are superstars"

Natalia is now 18 years old; She recently received her driver's license. She is working afterschool and has bought her first car with the help of her dad. She is so excited about her little new red car.

One Saturday night, Natalia and her friend Sara decided to go to a party. They dressed up, and the two beautiful young girls got into Natalia's small red car and (1) …………….. toward the party. They (2) ……………….. their little red car was a (3) ……………… car. They listened to the music in the car, sang, and danced on their way to the party. They named their little red car "Luxy." They were feeling like Cinderellas going to the Ball. They arrived at the party. They had a drink and (4) …………… it all night. After a while, they started talking about their luxury car (Luxy), and they decided (5) ……………. that they were superstars the whole night. Suddenly, they noticed the prince, a young man with a smile and an attractive style. Sara said excitedly to Natalia, "The prince is smiling at you; he has a crush on you." Natalia told Sara: "Let us not (6) ……………… ourselves, we are eagles, we are superstars, he can wait." Then they burst into laughter and started dancing. The young man approached Natalia and asked her, "Shall we dance?" Natalia replied, "No, thank you. It is close to midnight, and we must go home." The young man was so polite and told Natalia, "No problem, please enjoy your night." Then Natalia and Sara got into Luxy and went home. When they got home, they were (7) …………….., and soon fell asleep. In the morning, they woke up and remembered the story of last night. Sara told Natalia, "I think we got to (8) ……………… ……… with our Superstar story girl, it's sad, you missed your chance to get his number." Natalia said to Sara, "I did. He was both polite and handsome, but don't worry, we are superstars. We can always have fun without him in our Luxy, we are eagles, and we do not doubt our (9) …………   You are a superstar. Don't wonder who you are!" While they were laughing and singing, "we are superstars," they (10) ………. …….. off their bed to have breakfast.

c. 🎧 Listening and checking your guessing. (Visit website to listen)

Please read and listen to the short story. While you are listening, please check to see if the guesses you have made are correct. If your guess was not correct, please make a change and fill in the blanks. Then check your answers in the [52]footnote.

d. Clearing up all confusions

Please read the short story by yourself without listening to it. Highlight or underline the parts that are unclear to you in the story above. Use your dictionary or a partner to clarify highlighted parts. Write your notes below for further review.

………..

………...

---

[52] 1- headed toward: went to the direction, 2- imagined: had a mental picture, 3- luxurious: very comfortable and expensive, 4- sipped: drank slowly, 5- to pretend: to behave as if, 6- doubt: be uncertain, 7- exhausted: extremely tired, 8- Got too carried away: Became so excited that we did not control what we did, 9- inner regal: inside queen, 10- got out of: left

....

....

....

....

....

e. Reading Comprehension based on WH Questions

Look below for the boxes and read the questions (Q) and answers (A). While you are reading the questions, answer by filling in the blank with the "WH questions" (who, when, where, what, why, and how). Choose the answers that are the best fit. You do not have to use all the "WH questions." Notice that the title of the reading is in the middle of a circle, and the questions pivot clockwise around the title of the story in the figure. Both questions and answers are provided, and you only need to put the correct "wh question" in the blank.

- After you have finished filling in the blanks below, practice asking and answering the questions.

- Check your answers with the[53]answer key in the footnote.

---

[53] 1. who, 2. how, 3-when 4- what 5- why

| Who? | When? | Where? | What? | Why? | How? |

1- Q: .... was smiling at Natalia?

A: A cool and handsome gentleman was smiling at her.

2- Q: .... did they get to the party?

A: They got there with Natalia's small red car.

5- Q: .... didn't Natalia dance with the handsome gentleman?

A: Because she thought she was a Cinderella superstar.

Superstars

3- Q: .... did Natalia and Sarah go to the party?

A: They went to the party on Saturday night.

4- Q: .... did Sara tell Natalia in the morning?

A: "You missed your chance to get his number."

Section 4: Syntax Notes: Past Tense, Plural Nouns, Order of Adjectives

Syntax Note 1: Past Tense

Example from a line in the lyrics: "Last night, Sara and I went to a party."

Warm-up questions: What do you think the syntax point is about? Please Explain. Please

Explain.

……………………………………………………………………………………………………

……………………………………………………………………………………………………

Past tense: An action completed at a specific time in the past.

There are three groups of verbs in the past tense:

1-The regular verbs: form the past tense by adding "ed" or "d" at the end, such as: learn: learned,

Love: loved

2- The irregular verbs: They do not follow a rule for the past tense. They need to be learned by

repetition and usage in real-life conversations such as Think: thought, go: went

3- The verbs that remain the same in the present and past tense, such as put: put, burst: burst

  a. Please find the other past tense verbs in the lyrics /conversations and highlight them. Then

   write a real-life example of the use of syntax point above in a sentence below.

………

Syntax Note 2: Plural nouns

Example from a line in the lyrics: "We are superstars."

Warm-up questions: What do you think the syntax point is about? Please Explain. Please

Explain.

....

....

Plural nouns: In English mostly, you add "s" (cars) or "es" (wishes) to make the nouns plural.

There are some plural irregular nouns (woman: women, man: men). Also, some nouns have the same form in the singular and the plural (fun: fun).

Please identify and highlight the plural nouns in lyrics and conversations. Write a real-life example of the use of the syntax point from above in a sentence below.

....

Syntax Note 3: Order of Adjectives

Example from a line in the lyrics: "I went to a party with my little red car."

Warm-up questions: What do you think the syntax point is about? Please Explain. Please Explain.

....

....

Here is the order of adjectives:

1. Determiners such as: My, a/ an, number, some, …

2. Opinion: cute, good, bad, …

3. Size/shape: little / small, big, …

4. Age: New, old, …

5. Color: Red, blue, …

6. Origin: American, Spanish, …

7. Material: metal, wood, …

8. Purpose: Sleeping, running (as in my beautiful old white running shoes)

Example 2: My cute little new red Spanish metal car.

Write a real-life example of the use of syntax point above in a sentence below.

………………………………………………………………………………………………………

Section 5: Museum of Reincarnation: Marie Curie

Bain News Services. *Marie Curie*

Stage 1. Completing the vocabulary list

Before going to the museum, please complete the vocabulary list below.

No.	Vocabulary	Meaning
1.	thought	
2.	to notice	
3.	superstar	
4.	to be worthy of	
5.	at all	

6.	Who cares	
7.	to regret	
8.	to smile	
9.	to burst into laughter	

Stage 2. 🎧 The biography part of the museum, listening and taking notes. (Visit website to listen)

Who is the famous person? Why is the person famous?

………………………………………………………………………………………………………

………………………………………………………………………………………………………

………………………………………………………………………………………………………

Stage 3. 🎧 Reincarnation with the famous person: Vocabulary part (Visit website to listen)

a. Watching and Listening.

b. Watching, listening carefully, and writing down the usage of the words by the famous person.

c. Identifying the parts of speech

d. Writing your own sentences using the vocabulary words and the syntax notes.

		a. Watching and Listening
No.	**Vocabulary**	**b. Sentences with the vocabulary word used by the famous person**
		c. Part of speech
		d. Sentences with the vocabulary word used by you

1	**Thought**	b. Sentences by the famous person: ……………………………… ……………………………………………………………………………… c. Part of speech: …………… d. Your sentence: ………………………………………………….. ………………………………………………………………………………
2	**To notice**	b. Sentences by the famous person: ………………………………… ……………………………………………………………………………… c. Part of speech: …………… d. Your sentence: ………………………………………………….. ………………………………………………………………………………
3	**Superstar**	b. Sentences by the famous person: ………………………………… ……………………………………………………………………………… c. Part of speech: …………… d. Your sentence: ………………………………………………….. ………………………………………………………………………………
4	**To be worthy of**	b. Sentences by the famous person: ………………………………… ……………………………………………………………………………… c. Part of speech: …………… d. Your sentence: ………………………………………………….. ………………………………………………………………………………
5	**At all**	b. Sentences by the famous person: ………………………………… ……………………………………………………………………………… c. Part of speech: ……………

		d. Your sentence: ………………………………………….. ……………………………………………………………………
6	**Who cares**	b. Sentences by the famous person: …………………………… ……………………………………………………………………
		c. Part of speech: ……………
		d. Your sentence: ……………………………………………….. ……………………………………………………………………
7	**To regret**	b. Sentences by the famous person: ………………………… ……………………………………………………………………
		c. Part of speech: ……………
		d. Your sentence: ……………………………………………….. ……………………………………………………………………
8	**To smile**	b. Sentences by the famous person: ………………………… ……………………………………………………………………
		c. Part of speech: ……………
		d. Your sentence: ……………………………………………….. ……………………………………………………………………
9	**To burst into laughter**	b. Sentences by the famous person: ………………………… ……………………………………………………………………
		c. Part of speech: ……………
		d. Your sentence: ……………………………………………….. ……………………………………………………………………

Section 6: Conversation Creation

a. Choose one of the following potential topics and participants related to the short story/lyrics of the lesson.

Topic 1: At home, Participants: Natalia and Sara

Topic 2: At the party, Participants: Natalia and Sara

Topic 3: At the party, participants: Natalia and the prince

Topic 4: In the morning, Participants: Natalia and Sara

b. After choosing your topic, create your conversation in the space below.

Note: There are three models of conversations in the endnotes to this chapter. You can look at the models and use or modify the conversation you have created. When you are creating your conversation, you should use the syntax notes and some of the vocabulary from the museum.

Topic of Your Conversation:

Participants:

....

....

....

....

....

....

c. Role-playing. Practice and role-play the conversation with your partner, friend, brother/sister, or even with yourself in front of the mirror. The purpose of role-playing is to become comfortable using the language in a casual and conversational way.

Note: Role-play the other conversations in the endnotes for additional practice. Feel free to change the language as you see fit.

Section 7: Cultural Notes: American Superstars: Oprah, Beyonce, Angelina Jolie

a. Warm-Up (Brainstorming)

Please look at the topic above and guess what the cultural Notes are about?

....

....

....

....

b. Reading

Read the following cultural Notes. If you do not know a word or phrase, please use the guessing strategy (guess the meaning of the words based on the context) and use a dictionary when necessary.

Oprah

Oprah, 66, is only the third woman in history to own her own television and film production studio, joining Mary Pickford and Lucille Ball. She proved that the wildest dreams could come true with hard work and determination, [54]faith, and persistence. She's journeyed from being a poor child to an international icon whose influence goes beyond the world of television into social [55]awareness, publishing, film, philanthropy[56] , and education. (Mayor, 2000), Oprah was an honors student in high school, earned a full scholarship for college, and is now a billionaire that millions look up to and admire." (Hall, 2014), Oprah Winfrey donated $10 million to coronavirus relief.

Beyoncé

"The singer, in a rare 2016 interview with Elle, explained her decision to define the word "feminist" within the lyrics of her single "Flawless." "I put the definition of feminist in my song and on my tour, not for [57]propaganda but to give [58]clarity to the true meaning. I'm not really sure people know or understand what a feminist is, but it's very simple. It's someone who believes in [59]equal [60]rights for men and women," she told Elle." (Jang, 2017). She also has donated $6m for mental health and other initiatives during the Covid-19 pandemic.

---

[54] belief
[55] information
[56] the activity of helping the poor, especially by giving them money
[57] information, ideas often only giving one part of an argument, that are published, with the intention of influencing people's opinions
[58] the quality of being clear and easy to understand
[59] the same in amount, number, or size
[60] the legal authority to publish, copy, or make available a work such as a book, movie, recording, or work of art

Angelina Jolie

Angelina, "Hollywood's most famous actresses and [61]philanthropist" (Trejo, 2019). "She gave a speech at the 2015 African Union Summit where she spoke about the importance of women's rights nationwide." (Jang, 2017). She also donated $1M to help feed hungry children during the pandemic.

"There is a [62]global [63]epidemic of [64]violence against women — both within conflict zones and within societies at peace, and it is still treated as a lesser crime and lower [65]priority," Jolie said. "We need [66]policies for long-term [67]security that are [68]designed by women, focused on women, [69]executed by women — not at the expense of men, or instead of men, but alongside and with men. "She continued, "There is no greater pillar of [70]stability than a strong, free, and [71]educated woman. And there is no more inspiring role model than a man who respects and [72]cherishes women and [73]champions their [74]leadership" (Jang, 2017).

c. SPARCing the Cultural Notes

Using the information above, please complete the SPARC (Setting, Participant, Activities, Reasons, and Conclusion).

- Setting (when and where?): ……………………………………………………………………………………

- Participants (who?): ……………………………………………………………………………………

---

[61] a person who helps the poor, especially by giving them money
[62] worldwide
[63] widespread; a particular problem that seriously affects many people at the same time
[64] actions or words that are intended to hurt people
[65] something that you do or deal with first because it is more important or urgent than other things
[66] diplomacy
[67] safety
[68] selected
[69] do, perform
[70] a situation in which something is not likely to move or change
[71] having learned a lot at school or college and having a good level of knowledge
[72] to love and protect, to care
[73] to support
[74] control and management

- Activities (how did they get there?):

  ………………………………………………………………………………………….

- Reasons (why are they successful?):

  ………………………………………………………………………………………….

- Conclusion (what is your SPARC?):

  …………………………………………………………………………………………

  …………………………………………………………………………………………

Section 8: Creative Story/Lyrics Writing

a. Based on all the points you have learned in this chapter (Yoga, vocabulary, grammar, lyrics, video, conversations), follow the steps below:

Stage 1: Brainstorming/ SPARCing

Insert the title of your story/lyrics in the middle of the figure below and then fill in the other boxes about the participants in your story(who), the setting (when and where), the activities of your story (how), the reasons for your story (why), and the conclusion to your story (what).

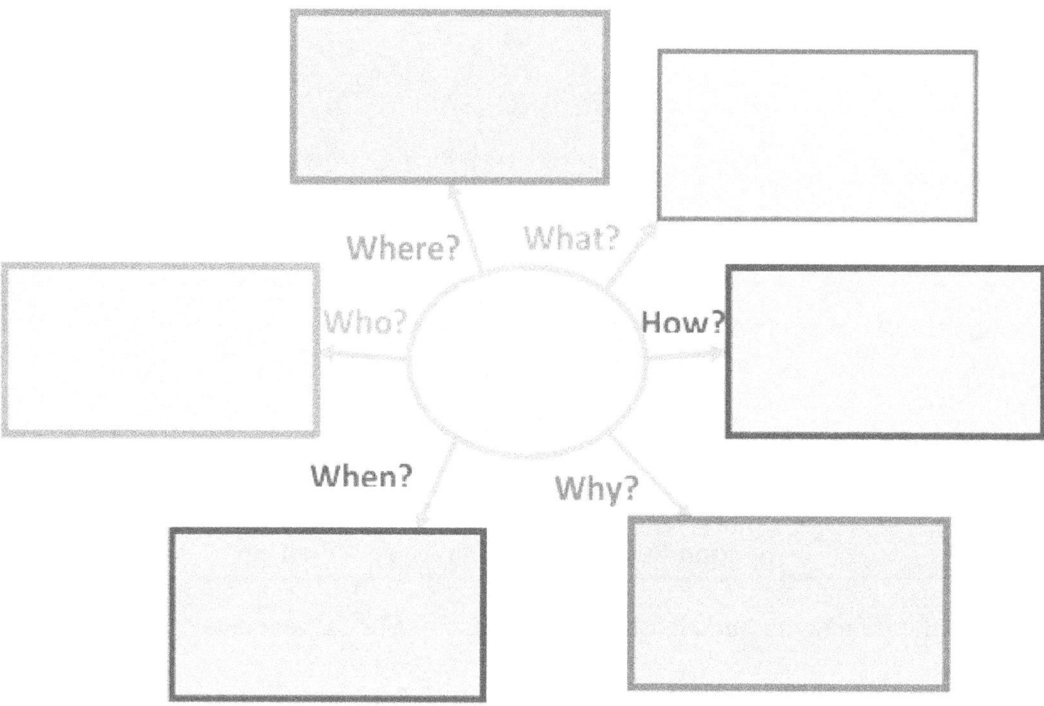

Stage 2- Writing your story/lyrics

Now in the box below, write your story/ lyrics (Your story/lyrics can be a rap, rhyming, etc., Be creative and let your imagination be your limit)

The Title of Your Story: ....

....

....

....

....

....

Stage 3. Getting Feedback: Check your story/ lyrics with your teachers/parents/mentors, to get feedback

Stage 4. Applying Music: Either apply your story/lyrics on the karaoke track of the song or click on the beat's website, such as https://www.8notes.com/metronome/. Choose the right beat for your story/lyrics. Even if you play a musical instrument, apply your writing to your playing. Don't limit yourself and be creative.

Stage 5. Singing: Practice, sing and enjoy!

Stage 6. Recording. Record yourself and share your product with someone else to get feedback, and revise if necessary.

Stage 7. Posting your creation.

Section 9: Quick Quiz

The quiz in this section is designed to help you review and remember the materials you have learned. The answer key is always provided in the footnotes. If you have any doubts about the correct answer, please check the footnotes.

Please answer the questions below and check your answers in the [75]answer key in the footnote.

a.   Vocabulary: What is the part of speech and synonym of the **Bolded** vocabulary?

1-   Do you think the handsome young man is **worthy** of dancing with Natalia?

a. is afraid of   b. is ashamed of   c. is crazy to   d. deserves

2-   I was at the party, and **suddenly** I noticed a gentleman's smile.

---

[75] Answer Key
1-   d, 2- c, 3- a, 4- c, 5- b, 6- d, 7- c, 8- F, 9- T, 10- T

a. expectedly- beam   b. slowly- laughter

c. unexpectedly- beam   d. slowly- laughter

3- I have a crush on him. He is both **handsome and awesome**.

a. good-looking-beautiful   b. good looking- dangerous

c. dangerous- beautiful   d. dangerous- beautiful

4- He told a funny joke, and everybody **burst into laughter**.

a. Suddenly began to cry   b. Expectedly began to cry

c. Suddenly began to laugh   d. Expectedly began to laugh

5- Sara **regretted** not getting his number.

a. felt crazy   b. felt unhappy   c. didn't feel sorry   d. didn't feel crazy

A. Syntax: Which is the best way for an English speaker to express herself/himself?

6-

a. Last night Sara and I goed to a party.

b. Tomorrow Sara and I goed to a party.

c. Tomorrow Sara and I went to a party.

d. Last night Sara and I went to a party.

7- Which of the following sentences is true(T), and which one is false(F)?

a. These mans and womans are attractive.

b. These men and womans are attractive.

c. These men and women are attractive.

d. These mens and womens are attractive.

B. Culture: Based on the Cultural Note, decide which sentence is true(T) and which one is false(F)?

8- According to Beyoncé "Feminist" is someone who believes in inequal rights for men and women.

9- According to Angelina Jolie, a very famous actress, and philanthropist, "there is no greater pillar of stability than a strong, free and educated woman."

10- Oprah was an honors student in high school and earned a full scholarship for college.

Section 10: Endnotes

Museum Transcripts

a. Biography of Marie Curie

Marie Skłodowska Curie (1867–1934) was a Polish and naturalized-French physicist and chemist who [76]conducted [77]pioneering research on [78]radioactivity. The [79]discovery of radioactivity by Henri Becquerel in 1896 [80]inspired Marie and her husband in their [81]brilliant research and analyses, which led to the [82]isolation of polonium, named after the country of Marie's birth, and radium. She won her first Nobel Prize in physics in [83]collaboration with her husband for the study of [84]spontaneous radiation, and she won her second Nobel prize in Chemistry for her research in radioactivity ("Marie Curie.," n.d.; Charles River Editors (2018); Wikipedia contributors (2022)).

---

[76] did, performed

[77] being the first to do or use a new idea

[78] the quality that some atoms have of producing a type of energy that can be very harmful to health

[79] finding for the first time

[80] to make someone feel that they want to do something and can do it

[81] great, extremely intelligent

[82] separation

[83] the situation of two or more people working together

[84] happening or done in a natural, often sudden way, without any planning or without being forced

b. Quotations

Who cares about the personal life of people? What matters are ideas. To be a superstar, each of us must work for our own improvement. We must have perseverance and, above all, confidence in ourselves. We must believe that we are worthy and gifted for something and that this thing must be attained. When you are working with passion, you smile, and you burst into laughter because it makes you rejoice like a child. Have passion and enjoy the present moment by focusing on your passion, or you will regret losing grace. I am one of those who thought, like Nobel, that humanity will draw more good than evil from new discoveries. One never notices what has been done; one can only see what remains to be done. Have no fear at all of perfection; you will never reach it. (Marie Curie Quotes. (n.d.). BrainyQuote.com).

1- Direct Quotations, 2- Paraphrased Quotations

Thought: "I am one of those who think (thought), like Nobel, that humanity will draw more good than evil from new discoveries."

1. To Notice: "One never notices what has been done; one can only see what remains to be done."

2. Superstar: "You cannot hope to build a better world without improving the individuals. To that end (to be a superstar), each of us must work for our own improvement."

3. To be worthy of: We must have perseverance and, above all, confidence in ourselves. We must believe (that we are worthy) and gifted for something and that this thing must be attained.

4. At all: "Have no fear (at all) of perfection; you'll never reach it."

5. Who cares: "Be less curious about people and more curious about ideas?" 2- who cares about personal life of people, what matters are ideas.

6.   To regret: "The older one gets, the more one feels that the present moment must be enjoyed, comparable to a state of grace." 2- Enjoy the present moment, or you will regret losing grace.

7.   To smile and to burst into laughter: "All my life through, the new sights of Nature made me rejoice like a child." 2- when I am working with my passion for nature, I smile. I burst into laughter because it makes "I rejoice like a child."

Conversations

Model 1.

Topic: At home, Participants: Natalia and Sara

Sara: Hey, Natalia, I have a plan for tonight's party.

Natalia: What kind of plan?

Sara: Let's pretend we are superstars.

Natalia: Ok, I am up for it, girl. Let's go get dressed.

Sara: Are we going in your car?

Natalia: It stopped in the middle of the street the other day. But that's fine. We are superstars.

We will call our bodyguards to come and fix it for us, haha. Let's go in my little red car.

Sara: Ok, since we are superstars, your car is a luxury car, so no problem. Ha,ha,ha.

Natalia: No doubt. I thought about changing its name from reddy to Luxy. Ha, ha.

Natalia: I am ready. Are you?

Sara: I am not ready at all; I don't know where I put my red high heel shoes.

Natalia: Wear your sneakers. Who cares? We are superstars.

Sara: No way, I'll borrow yours.

Model 2.

 Topic: At the party, Participants: Natalia and Sara

Sara: Hey, Natalia, A cool, handsome guy is smiling at you. Have you noticed him?

Natalia: Yes, I did, but remember, we are superstars, so no one is worthy of us at all.

Sara: Ah, right! I thought he could be a superstar too.

Natalia: Nope, he is not good enough for us.

Model 3.

Topic: At the party, participants: Natalia and the prince

Prince: Hello beautiful lady, shall we dance?

Natalia: No, thank you, it's close to midnight, and we must leave.

Prince: What's up with this midnight thing? Let's just dance.

Natalia: I am sorry, it's time to leave.

Prince: Ok, no problem, enjoy your night, and I hope to see you soon.

Natalia: Smile, Bye.

Model 4.

Topic: In the morning in bed, Participants: Natalia and Sara

Natalia: Oh, what a nice deep slumber I fell into.

Sara: Ye, we were dead tired last night. We danced a lot. Oh, God, I regret not getting the guy's number.

Natalia: Oh, don't worry. We are eagles, superstars. Ha, ha, I remember how funny it was when the prince asked you to dance, and you said, "it's close to midnight, we must go, and how we burst into laughter.

Natalia: It's time to get up and start our day. Let me go to the bathroom.

Vocabulary list as a resource

No.	Vocabulary	Meaning (synonym)	Example in sentence
	Pronunciation / **Part of speech in the song**		
1.	**Superstar** /ˈsuːpərstɑːr/ Noun	an extremely famous actress/actor, singer, musician, sports player, etc., distinguished, well-known	We thought we were superstars.
2.	**Last night** /læst naɪt/ Adverb	the night immediately before the present, evening	Last night we were at the party.
3.	**To go** **(past tense: went)** /ˈpɑːrti/ Verb	to move or travel to another place, to pass	Last night we went to the party.
4.	**Party** /bɑl/ Noun	a social event at which a group of people meet to talk, eat, drink, dance, etc.	Cinderella went to the ball.
5.	**With** /wɪð/, /wɪθ/ Preposition	using something	We got to the party with our cute car.
6.	**Little** /ˈlɪtl/ Adjective	small in size or amount	Their little red car is cute.
7.	**Red** /red/ Adjective	of the color of fresh blood	Their little red car is parked there.
8.	**Car** /kɑːr/ Noun	a road vehicle with an engine, four wheels, and seats for a small number of people	Their car is not expensive.
9.	**To dance** **(past tense: danced)** /dæns/ Verb	to move the body and feet in rhythm to music, rock	We danced, and we sang.
10.	**To think** **(past tense: thought)** /θɪŋk/	to have or to form an opinion or idea about something, realize, see	I thought for a moment about you.

	Verb		
11.	**After a while** /ˈæftər ə waɪl/ **Adverb**	following, coming	After a while, he came.
12.	**Suddenly** /ˈsʌdənli/ **Adverb**	Unexpectedly, abruptly	Suddenly I heard a sound.
13.	**To notice** (past tense: noticed) /ˈnəʊtɪs/ **Verb**	to become aware of, esp. by looking to see	We noticed a gentleman's smile.
14.	**Someone** /ˈsʌmwʌn/ **Pronoun**	a person, a character	We noticed someone's smile.
15.	**Smile** /smaɪl/ **Noun**	to have a happy expression, beam	I noticed his smile.
16.	**Who** /huː/ **subject**	used as the subject or object of a verb to show which person you are referring to, or to add information about a person just mentioned. It is used for people, not things	This is John, who I told you about.
17.	**To watch** **(had been** **watching)** /wɑːtʃ/ **Verb**	to look at something for a period of time, especially something that is changing or moving	He had been watching you for a while.
18.	**For a while** /fɔːr ə waɪl/ **Phrase**	for a long time	I haven't seen you for a while.
19.	**To say** (past tense: said) /seɪ/ **Verb**	to tell something to someone, to speak	I said: "he is so handsome."
20.	**This** /ðɪs/ **Pronoun**	used for a person, object, or thing to show which one is referred to, this person	This guy is handsome.
21.	**Guy** /gaɪ/ **Noun**	a man, boy	This guy is cute.
22.	**Is** /ɪz/ **To be verb**	be, used with he/she/it	She is smart and cute.
23.	**Cute** /kjuːt/ **Adjective**	charming and attractive, beautiful	This cute girl is a superstar.

24.	**Awesome** /ˈɔːsəm/ **Adjective**	causing feelings of great admiration, breathtaking, beautiful	You are awesome.
25.	**Cool** /kuːl/ **Adjective**	fashionable in a way that people admire, excellent, neat	She hangs out with all the cool guys at the bar.
26.	**Handsome** /ˈhænsəm/ **Adjective**	physically attractive, good-looking	He is handsome.
27.	**Just a moment** /dʒʌs ə ˈməʊmənt/ **Idiom**	wait a short period of time, wait briefly	Just a moment, please. I am thinking.
28.	**Aren't we** /ɑːrn wi/ **Contraction of are not**	contraction of are not	- "Aren't we superstars?" - "Yes, we are."
29.	**So** /səʊ/ **Conjunction**	therefore, thus	So, he doesn't deserve us.
30.	**To be worthy of** /bi ˈwɜːrði ov/ **Verb**	deserving respect, admiration, or support, to deserve	So, she is not worthy of me.
31.	**At all** /ət ɔːl/ **Adverb**	in any way	So, he doesn't deserve us at all.
32.	**Must** /məst/ **Modal verb**	used to show that it is important that something happen in the present or future, need	We must leave the party now.
33.	**To leave** /liːv/ **Verb**	to go away from someone that stays in the same place, get out	We must leave now.
34.	**Luxury** /ˈlʌkʃəri/ **Noun**	great comfort, especially as provided by expensive and beautiful things	This fur coat is a luxury.
35.	**Both** /bəʊθ/ **Pronoun**	used to refer to two people, the pair	We both burst into tears, but it was happy tears.
36.	**To burst into laughter** /bɜːrst ˈɪntə ˈlæftər/ **Idiom**	To break open into laughter, to begin suddenly to laugh	We both burst into laughter.
37.	**Dancing** /ˈdænsɪŋ/ **Verb**	Short form of We were dancing, moving our body	We were dancing and enjoying ourselves.
38.	**Home** /həʊm/ **Noun**	a house, apartment	We went home.

39.	**After** /ˈæftər/ **Preposition**	following in time, afterward	We went home after dancing.
40.	**Morning** /ˈmɔːrnɪŋ/ **Adverb**	during the early part of the day, AM	We woke up in the morning.
41.	**To wake up** (Past tense: Woke up) /weɪk ʌp/ **Phrasal Verb**	To arise, to get up	We woke up from a long sleep.
42.	**Long** /lɔːŋ/ **adjective**	continuing for an extended amount of time	I have been waiting a long time
43.	**Slumber** /ˈslʌmbər/ **Noun**	sleep	I fell into a long slumber.
44.	**To regret** /rɪˈɡret/ **Verb**	to feel sorry or unhappy about something you did	I regret not having his number.
45.	**To have** /həv/ **Verb**	to own or possess something	I don't have his phone number.
46.	**Number** /ˈnʌmbər/ **Noun**	phone number, digits	What's your phone number?
47.	**Who cares?** /huː kerz/ **Informal idiom**	used to emphasize rudely that you do not think something is important, who pays attention	- He has four college degrees - So, who cares?!
48.	**Are** /ər/ **To be verb**	be, used with you/we/they	We are superstars.
49.	**Still** /stɪl/ **Adverb**	despite that, nevertheless	We don't have luxury cars, but we are still superstars because we are smart and cute girls.
50.	**Fun** /fʌn/ **Noun**	pleasure, enjoyment, amusement, joy	Let us have fun.
51.	**Without** /wɪˈðaʊt/ **Preposition**	not having or doing (not having the help of someone)	Let's have fun without them.
52.			

Chapter 4

Section 1: Yoga Posture: Chair

Yoga Posture: Standing Squat/Chair Pose (Asana: Utkatasana)
Utakata: Powerful, exceeding the usual measure; asana: posture

Dream big, sit proud and strong on the glorious chair of your dream!

Mythology of Utkatasana

Sit inside the glorious purpose of your life and find strength with the chair pose. The name comes from the Sanskrit words *utkaṭa*, meaning "gigantic, powerful and proud" (Sjoman, 1999).ß

This pose follows the struggles of Rama, a divine prince, following his exile from the kingdom by his father. With courage and strength, he overcomes many struggles and challenges, and after fourteen years in exile, Rama returns to his birthplace to be crowned king and assume his rightful place on the throne. Of course, this myth is concerned with the theme of *utkata:* power, courage, and ferocity, all embodied in Rama. A throne is a type of chair reserved for the powerful that brings feelings of pride and the power of positive affirmations and gratitude (Kanzar, 2018). The significance of a throne chair is such that many of these thrones - such as China's Dragon Throne - survive today as historical examples of the nation's history.

Connection to the lesson

In this lesson, Natalia is proud and powerful when she is talking to Garcia. She is entering a college in Boston, and she feels so proud about it. She is so happy because she has overcome all academic challenges. And she feels she is entering a new period in her social life. (She is becoming familiar with Garcia and the positive affirmation that she is a Scorpio and independent).

Cautionary notes

Do not hold the posture for a long period of time If you have low, high blood pressure, heart issues, or weak knees.

Yogic Breathing: Dirgha Pranayama

Meaning: Prana: air; life force; Yama: to restrain or hold back

Potential effects

Enhancement of complete and full breathing, decreasing stress and tension while calming the mind and the body, helping the lungs remain healthy by increasing the oxygen flow to the blood, it massages the abdominal organs, facilitating digestion, preparing you for a better learning experience.

Three Breathing Steps: (Visit website to listen)

1- Sit up straight with your shoulders back and down with relaxed abdominals.

2- Relax the face, close your mouth, and place your hands on your belly.

3- Breathe into your belly and feel it expands like a balloon. Repeat several times.

4- Now, put your hands to the sides of your rib cage and breathe into them, feeling the rib cage expand, and repeat several times.

5- Put your fingertips on your upper chest. Breathe into it and feel your hands lifting. Repeat several times.

6- Now, make a complete inhalation. As you are inhaling, feel the expansions of your belly, rib cage, and chest, and as you are exhaling, you feel the contractions of all three. Repeat this series several times (Refer to Figure 1 in Chapter 1).

Warm-up: Torso Cat and Dog (Visit website to listen)

1- While sitting on your chair and placing the palms of your hands on your laps, on an inhale, expand your chest and arch your back. Ground your butt into the chair and feel the stretch. On an exhale, round your back while bending forward and drop your chin and feel the stretch. Inhale, expand your chest and arch your back. Exhale, round your back, bend forward and drop the chin.

2- Repeat the Torso cat and dog several times while coordinating your breath (Figure 1).

1   2

Figure 1: Torso Cat and Dog

Posture steps for Chair pose/ Standing Squat (Utkatasana), (Visit website to listen)

1- Stand tall in the Mountain pose with your feet hip-width apart.

2- On an inhale, slowly bend your knees and lower your hips. Gradually bow your back while maintaining the length in your waist. Allow your hips to sink to engage your front thighs and feel the stretch in your hamstrings, if you feel any discomfort raise your hips and take the pressure off your knees. Do not let the knees extend over your toes. Maintain the arch in your back.

3- On an inhale, sweep your arms in front of you parallel to the floor, palms facing down. Roll your shoulders back and down. Keep breathing and hold the pose for a few seconds.

4- To release, ground yourself firmly through your feet and come up and then allow your arms to sink down by your sides. Relax and feel the effect of Utkatasana, the chair pose (Figure 2).

1   2   3   4

Figure 2: Chair Pose/Standing Squat (Utkatasana)

Section 2: Music and Lyrics: 411

Part 1: **Listening (Stage 1,2 and 3), (Visit website to listen)**

Stage 1- (Listening for fun) Listen to the song several times, pat your feet, move your body, and enjoy the music! Do not worry about the meaning of the words yet!!!

Stage 2- (Attentive listening) Listen carefully several times to understand the lyrics.

Stage 3- (Listening and guessing) listen and read the lyrics several times to understand the lyrics. Try to guess the meaning of the words you do not know and understand. Do not look at the vocabulary list just yet. Listen to the lyrics again and guess at the meaning of the words you do not know. Write down the words you do not know.

Guess words:

....

....

....

....

....

....

....

Part 2: Listening & Reading Lyrics (Stage 4, 5, 6, and 7)

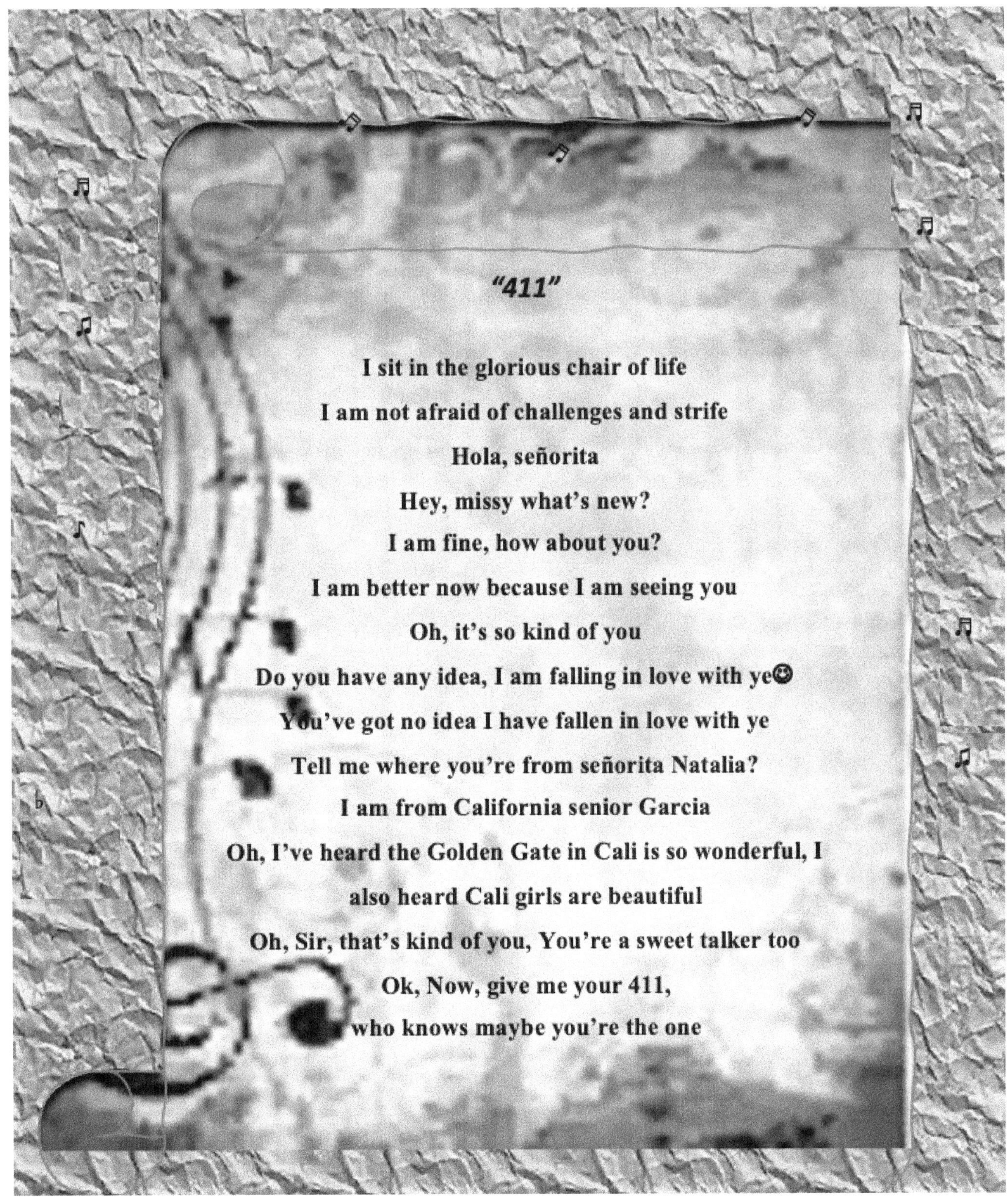

Wait, just a minute, senior,

here is my phone number

My sign is Scorpio and

I was born in November,

Never forget my mind is tough

but my heart is tender

Missy I strongly recommend that

we surely meet up this weekend

Ok, tell me what time and where?

At 6 at Copley Art Square

Ok, Bye-bye See you later

Adios, Hasta luego sweetie,

Please, please be well and take care

Section 3: Reading a Short Story: 411

Warm-up Activity

a. Listening and taking notes: (Visit website to listen)

a. Please listen to the story and write down what you have understood. (Listen and take notes)

……………………………………………………………………………………………

……………………………………………………………………………………………

……………………………………………………………………………………………

b. Reading and guessing

Please read the short story below, guess at the missing words and fill in the blanks.

"411"

Natalia and her family have (1) ………… moved from California to Boston, Massachusetts, where she is going to college.

One day while walking her dog, [85]Asal, in [86]Peter's Park near her home, she remembers her friend Sara. She misses her a lot, and she remembers them being superstars in her little red car. A smile (2) …………… on her face as she remembers the fun times with Sara. She feels so (3) …………… of herself for being a top student at Boston College. She feels great pride because she overcame all the (4) ……………. to become a (5) …………… woman and to make her dad and family proud.

____

[85] means honey in Persian (Farsi)
[86] Peter's Park is a popular dog park in Boston, MA

While in the park, she stops at a (6) …………… where a (7) …………… [87]organization is selling hand-made necklaces to help children with special needs. She buys a necklace with her name on it. A young man whose name is Garcia is standing behind her and overhears her conversation. Garcia orders a necklace for himself to (8) …………… Natalia. As she is leaving, she is listening to a song on her headphones and humming the lyrics "I sit in the glorious chair of life, I am not afraid of challenges and strife!" and she is (9) …………… the "chair pose" of yoga while she is singing along with the lyrics. Suddenly Asal begins to bark. Then Garcia (10) ……………… Natalia and asked her, "Hola, Senorita, May I talk to you?" Natalia replied, "Yes." Garcia asked curiously, "how are you? What's new with you today? Are you new to the neighborhood? Where are you from?". Natalia replied, "I am from California." Garcia said (11) ……………….., "I have heard that California is beautiful, and I have seen pictures of the Golden Gate Bridge. I have also heard that all Cali girls are (12) …………. and beautiful just like you." Natalia replied (13) ………………., "You are such a sweet talker." Garcia said (14) ………………., "Natalia, I am not trying to (14) …………. you; I am saying this from the bottom of my heart.". Then he asked, "May I call you? What is your 411?" Natalia replied, "Here is my number, but I must warn you; My zodiac sign is Scorpio, and Scorpio women are (15) …………… and (16) ……………., their minds are tough, and their hearts are so tender". Garcia said, "I admire your (17) …………… my lady,". Then he asked, "Could we meet for a cup of Chai? If you agree, we can meet this Saturday at 6:00 pm at Copley square?" Natalia replied, "Ok, Now, I must leave. See you later." Garcia replied passionately "bye, please take care."

---

[87] a group of people who work together in an organized way for

Later, they start dating, and she falls in love with Garcia. One year passes, and one day Garcia explains that he must go on a short business trip to China. He tells Natalia that he needs to borrow some money from her to make this business deal in China. He said, "Natalia, I will make a lot of money, and when I return, we can be married."

Natalia replied, "Oh, Garcia, don't worry, we are going to make a life together, and I want to help you. No problem, I will give you the money from my savings."

Garcia said, "Thank you, sweetie. When I get back, I will have a surprise for you." Natalia gives him all her savings. A few days later, Garcia leaves Logan international Airport for his trip to Wuhan, China.

c. 🎧 Listening and Checking your Guessing (Visit website to listen)

Please read and listen to the short story. While you are listening, please check to see if the guesses you have made are correct. If your guess was not correct, please make a change and fill in the blanks. Then check your [88]answers in the footnotes.

d. Clearing up confusion

Please read the short story by yourself without listening to it. Highlight or underline the parts that are unclear to you in the story above. Use your dictionary or a partner to clarify highlighted parts. Write your notes below for further review.

………..

---

a shared purpose

[88] 1- recently: not long time ago, 2- appears: starts to be seen, 3- proud: satisfied, 4- challenges: mental and physical effort, 5- educated: knowledgeable, 6- Stand: small shop, 7- Charity: a system of giving money, food, or help free to those who are in need because they are sick, poor, or have no home smart: wise, 8- impress: to cause someone to (admire) love you or respect you, 9- imagining: forming a picture in her mind, 10- approached: came nearer to 11- enthusiastically: In a way that shows you're so interested in, 12- smart: intelligent, or able to think quickly, 13- suspiciously: in a way that makes you think that something is wrong, 14- passionately: in a way that shows that you have very strong feelings or emotions -15- fool: cheat, deceive, 16 - serious: not joking , 17 - independent: not getting help from other people, 18- character: qualities that are interesting

……...

……………………………………………………………………………………………………….

……...

e. Reading Comprehension based on the "WH Questions."

Look below for the red boxes and read the questions (Q) and answers (A). While you are reading

the questions, answer by filling in the blank with the "WH questions" (who, when, where, what,

why, and how). Choose the answers that are the best fit. You do not have to use all the "WH

questions." Notice that the title of the reading is in the middle of a circle, and the questions pivot

around the title of the story in the figure. Both questions and answers are provided, and you only

need to put the correct "wh question" in the blank.

 After you have finished filling in the blanks below, practice asking and answering the questions.

Check your answers with the [89]answer key in the footnote.

---

[89] 1. why, 2. where, 3.why 4. what 5. What time - where, 6. where

Who?	When?	Where?	What?	Why?	How?

1- Q: ………… did Natalia say her sign is Scorpio?

A: She wanted to warn Garcia that she is serious, independent, and strong-willed.

2- Q: ………… Garcia and Natalia meet each other for the first time?

A: They met each other in Peter's Park in Boston.

411

3- Q: ………… Natalia tells Garcia that "you are a sweet talker?"

A: Because Garcia told her "California girls are smart and beautiful just like you."

6- Q: ………... is Natalia from?

A: She is from California.

4- Q: After Natalia mentioned she is from California ……. did Garcia say?

A: "I have heard that all California girls are smart and beautiful just like you."

5- Q: ………… time and ……… are Natalia and Garcia are going to meet each other?

A: They are going to meet each other at 6 at Copley Square in Boston.

Section 4: Syntax Notes: Direct Speech, Present Perfect, "Who Knows," Greeting Expressions

Example from a line in the lyrics: Garcia said, "Hey, missy, what's new?"

a. Warm-up questions: What do you think the syntax point is about? Please Explain. Please Explain.

....

....

Syntax Note 1: Direct speech: (Reported Speech/ inverted commas ("")/ quotation marks) and punctuation rules in writing

Direct speech repeats, or quotes, the exact words someone has said. The most common reporting verbs are "said," "asked", "replied." They are placed either in the beginning or at the end of the quotation.

Example 2: "You are handsome," Natalia said. ("said" is placed at the end of the quotation)

Natalia said, "You are handsome." ("said" is placed at the beginning of the quotation)

Note: In writing, we place the exact words spoken between quotation marks ("") to avoid [90]plagiarism.

b. Write a real-life example of the use of syntax point above in a sentence below?

....

Syntax Note 2: Present Perfect

Example from a line in the lyrics: I have heard California girls are beautiful.

---

[90] the process or practice of coping or using another person's ideas or work and pretending that it is your own

a. Warm-up questions: What do you think the syntax point is about? Please Explain. Please Explain.

……………………………………………………………………………………………………

……………………………………………………………………………………………………

Present Perfect: An action happened at some point in our life, but it is not clear exactly when

How to form the present perfect? Have/ has + past participle

I/you/they/we have seen the pictures of the Golden Gate Bridge.

He/she has seen the picture of the Golden Gate Bridge.

You cannot use the present perfect with specific adverbs of time that determine a specified time

in the past, such as: 1 hour ago, yesterday, one year ago, last week, two weeks ago, when I lived

in California, at that moment, that day, ….

We use the present perfect with unspecific expressions such as: never, ever, yet, already, several

times, ….

c.   Write a real-life example of the use of syntax point above in a sentence below.

……………………………………………………………………………………………………

Syntax Note 3: "Who Knows," Greeting Expressions

Example from a line in the lyrics: Who knows, maybe you are the one for me

a.   Warm-up questions: What do you think the syntax point is about? Please Explain. Please

Explain.

……………………………………………………………………………………………………

....

"Who knows" is used for questions, but it can also be used for statements.

English speakers often use this phrase as a statement when they are surprised or frustrated.

- Who knows why she said that?

- Who knows when the party will end?

b.   Write a real-life example of the use of syntax point above in a sentence below?

....

	d. Some English Greeting Expressions	
No.	**Possible Questions**	**Possible Answers**
1	"Hello / Hi / Hey"	"Hello/ Hi"
2	"Long time no see !"	"Yes/ye, it has been a long time."
	What have you been up to? / What are you up to? / How have you been?	"Not much," or "Nothing."
3	"What's new? / What's up? / Anything new?"	"Not much/ Nothing/ Nothing much"/ or explain what you are doing like: "I am getting ready for tonight's party."
4	"How are you? / How is everything? How are you doing? / Is everything Ok? /How are things?"	"I am fine/ good / I am ok, thanks." "Very good/ Pretty good." "Excellent, Terrific, Great"

		"Not so good, not bad, So So, not great"
		"Terrible/don't ask."
		"I am hanging in there" (means I am not giving up on something, even if it's difficult)
5	How's life?	"Not much. Same old, same old."
6	I am glad/happy to see/to meet you. It's nice to see/to meet you. Good/glad/nice/happy to see/to meet you	"You too" "I am glad/happy to see/to meet you too. It's nice to see/to meet you too. Good/glad/nice/happy to see/to meet you too. "Thank you. It's very nice to meet you as well." "Likewise,"

Choose the expressions that are less familiar to you and create a short greeting conversation with the expressions above.

……………………………………………………………………………………………

……………………………………………………………………………………………

Section 5: Museum of Reincarnation: George Washington

Weidenbach, A. & Stuart, G. (1876), George Washington

Stage 1. Completing the vocabulary list

Before going to the museum, please complete the vocabulary list below.

No.	Vocabulary	Meaning
1	Do you have an idea	
2	Strongly recommend	
3	Surely	
4	Fall in love	
5	Meet up	
6	Who knows	

Stage 2. 🎧 The biography part of the museum, listening and taking notes. (Visit website to listen)

Please reply to the questions below.

Who is the famous person? Why is the person famous?

……

……

Stage 3. Reincarnation with the famous person (vocabulary part)

a. 🎧 Watching and Listening. (Visit website to listen)

b. Watching, listening carefully, and writing down the usage of the words by the famous person.

c. Identifying the parts of speech

d. Writing your own sentences using the vocabulary words and the syntax notes.

a. Watching and Listening		
No.	**Vocabulary**	b. Sentences with the vocabulary word used by the famous person
		c. Part of speech
		d. Sentences with the vocabulary word used by you
1	**Do you have** **an idea**	b. Sentences by the famous person: …………………………………… ………………………………………………………………………… c. Part of speech: ……………. d. Your sentence: ………………………………………………….. …………………………………………………………………………
2		b. Sentences by the famous person: …………………………………… …………………………………………………………………………

	Strongly recommend	c. Part of speech: ……………
		d. Your sentence: ……………………………………………….. ……………………………………………………………………
3	Surely	b. Sentences by the famous person: …………………………… ……………………………………………………………………
		c. Part of speech: ……………
		d. Your sentence: ……………………………………………….. ……………………………………………………………………
4	Fall in love	b. Sentences by the famous person: …………………………… ……………………………………………………………………
		c. Part of speech: ……………
		d. Your sentence: ……………………………………………….. ……………………………………………………………………
5	Meet up	b. Sentences by the famous person: …………………………… ……………………………………………………………………
		c. Part of speech: ……………
		d. Your sentence: ……………………………………………….. ……………………………………………………………………
6	Who knows	b. Sentences by the famous person: …………………………… ……………………………………………………………………
		c. Part of speech: ……………
		d. Your sentence: ……………………………………………….. ……………………………………………………………………

Section 6: Conversation Creation

a. Choose one of the following potential topics and participants related to the short story/lyrics of the lesson.

Topic 1: At the park, Participants: Natalia talking to herself (Talking to yourself is a common experience to help you to understand something)

Topic 2: At the Park, Participants: Natalia and Garcia

Topic 3: A short business trip, Participants: Natalia and Garcia

b. After choosing your topic, create your conversation in the box below.

Note: There are two models of conversations in the endnotes to this chapter. You can look at the models and use or modify the conversation you have created. When you are creating your conversation, you should use the new syntax notes and some of the listed vocabularies.

Topic of the Conversation:

Participants:

………………………………………………………………………………………………

………………………………………………………………………………………………

………………………………………………………………………………………………

………………………………………………………………………………………………

………………………………………………………………………………………………

………………………………………………………………………………………………

c. Role-playing. Practice and role-play the conversation with your partner, friend, brother/sister, or even with yourself in front of the mirror. The purpose of role-playing is to become comfortable using the language in a casual and conversational way.

Note: Role-play the other conversations in the endnotes for additional practice. Feel free to change the language as you see fit.

Section 7: Cultural Notes: [91]Harassment

a. Warm-Up (Brainstorming)

Please look at the topic above and guess what the cultural Notes are about?

....

....

....

....

b. Reading

Read the following cultural points. If you do not know a word or phrase, please use the guessing strategy (guess the meaning of the words based on the context) and use a dictionary when necessary.

---

[91] behavior that annoys or upsets someone

"Harassment"

Street harassment is mainly sexual harassment that [92]consists of unwanted comments, [93]gestures, [94]honking, [95]wolf-whistling, [96]catcalling, exposure, stalking, persistent sexual advances, and touching by strangers in public areas such as streets, shopping malls, and public transportation.

[97]According to an article by the non-profit organization Stop Street, Harassment can also include [98]persistent [99]requests for someone's name, number, destination, or other personal information (411) after the victim has already denied the requests. The practice of street harassment is rooted in power and control and is often a reflection of societal discrimination.

In 2014, researchers from Cornell University and Hollaback conducted the largest international cross-cultural study of street harassment. The data suggests that the majority of females have their first street harassment experience during [100]puberty. (Whittaker & Kowalski, 2015).

Fortunately, many common street harassment behaviors are already illegal in the USA. In fact, since at least the late 1880s, some women have used these laws to report street harassers to the police.

---

[92] a movement of the hands, arms, or head, etc. to express an idea or feeling
[93] made up
[94] it makes a short, loud sound
[95] a whistle (= sound made by blowing air through the lips) sometimes made by a man when he sees a woman, he finds sexually attractive
[96] make a whistle, shout, or comment of a sexual nature to a woman passing by
[97] based on
[98] continuous
[99] asking for
[100] the period during which adolescents reach sexual maturity and become capable of reproduction

c. SPARCing the Cultural Notes

Using the information above, please complete the SPARC (Setting, Participant, Activities, Reasons, and Conclusion).

- Setting (when and where?): …………………………………………………………………….

- Participants (who?): …………………………………………………………………………

- Activities (how did they get there?):

  ………………………………………………………………………………………………

- Reasons (why are they successful?):

  …………………………………………………………………………………………………..

- Conclusion (what is your SPARC?):

  ………………………………………………………………………………………………

  ………………………………………………………………………………………………

Section 8: Creative Story/Lyrics Writing

Based on all the points you have learned in this chapter (Yoga (Mountain), vocabularies, grammar, lyrics, video, conversations), follow the steps below:

Stage 1: Brainstorming/ SPARCing

Insert the title of your story/lyrics in the middle of the figure below and then fill in the other boxes about the participants in your story(who), the setting (when and where), the activities of your story (how), the reasons for your story (why), and the conclusion to your story (what).

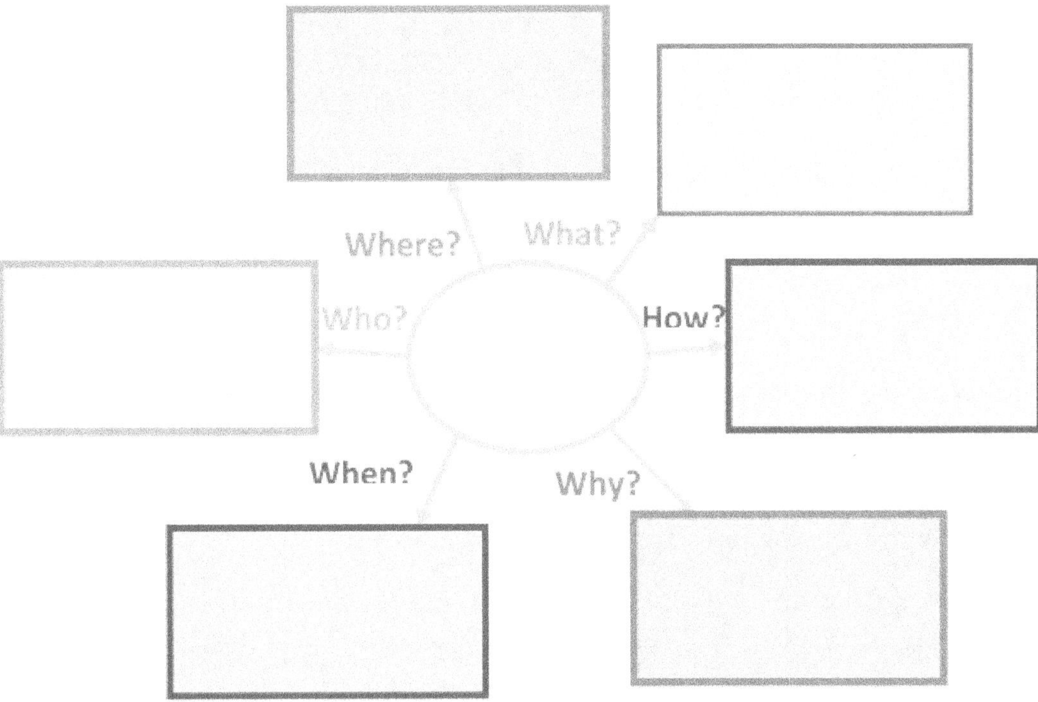

Stage 2- Writing your story/lyrics

Now in the space below, write your story/ lyrics (Your story/lyrics can be rap, rhyming, etc., Be creative and let your imagination be your limit)

The title of your story/lyrics: …………………………..

…………………………………………………………………………………………………..

…………………………………………………………………………………………………..

…………………………………………………………………………………………………..

…………………………………………………………………………………………………..

…………………………………………………………………………………………………..

…………………………………………………………………………………………………

Stage 3. Getting Feedback: Check your story/ lyrics with your teachers/parents/mentors, to get

feedback

Stage 4. Applying Music: Either apply your story/lyrics on the karaoke track of the song or click on the beat's website, such as https://www.8notes.com/metronome/. Choose the right beat for your story/lyrics. Even if you play a musical instrument, apply your writing to your playing. Don't limit yourself and be creative.

Stage 5. Singing: Practice, sing and enjoy!

Stage 6. Recording. Record yourself and share your product with someone else to get feedback, and revise if necessary.

Stage 7. Posting your creation.

Section 9: Quick Quiz

The quiz in this section is designed to help you review and remember the materials you have learned. The answer key is always provided in the footnotes. If you have any doubts about the correct answer, please check the footnotes.

Please answer the questions below and check your answers in the [101]answer key in the footnote.

a. **Vocabulary:** What is the part of speech and synonym of the **Bolded** vocabulary?

1- Hey man, **what's new**?

a. Expression: what is that?   b. Idiom: what's not old

c. Idiom: how do you do?   d. Expression: what's up?

2- Do you know **where and when** we are meeting?

a. Adverb: at what time and what location

b. b. Adverbs: at what location and what time

---

[101] Answer Key
1- d, 2- b, 3- b, 4- d, 5- c, 6- d, 7- c, 8- F, 9- F, 10- F

   c. Proposition: who and at what location

   d. Proposition: which and what time

3- My darling, **I am falling in love with you**, and I am planning to marry you.

  a. Adjective: I am falling down   b. Idiom: I am beginning to love you

  c. Idiom: I am feeling loved by you   d. Adjective: You are so lovely

4- The doctor **strongly recommends** a minimum of 30 minutes of exercise every day.

  a. Adjective: Verb nicely walks   b. Adjective, Verb: highly walks

  c. Adverb, verb: nicely suggests   d. Adverb, verb: highly suggests

5- It's my birthday. Let's have a party this **weekend.**

  a. Nouns: Sunday and Monday   b. Adjective: Thursday and Friday

  c. Nouns: Saturday and Sunday   d. Adjective: Thursday and Friday

b. Grammar: Which of the following sentences don't have the same meaning as "nice to meet you"?

6-

  a. Glad to meet you.

  b. Glad to see you.

  c. Happy to meet you.

  d. Long time no see.

7- Which of the following sentences is true (T)?

  a. I have seen the picture of the Golden Gate last year.

  b. I ever seen the picture of the Golden Gate.

  c. I have seen the picture of the Golden Gate before.

  d. I saw the picture of the Golden Gate so far.

c. **Culture**: Based on the cultural note, decide which sentence is true (T) and which one is false (F)?

8- Street harassment is mainly sexual harassment that consists of unwanted comments, gestures, honking, wolf-whistling, catcalling, exposure, following, persistent sexual advances, and touching by strangers in private areas.

9- According to the founder of the non-profit organization "Stop Street Harassment," street harassment cannot consist of physically harmless behavior, such as "kissing noises" and "non-sexually explicit comments.

10- The data suggests that the majority of females have their first street harassment experience when they are 30 years old.

Section 10: Endnotes

Museum Transcripts

a. Biography of George Washington

George Washington (1732- 1799) was a [102]military leader, [103]statesman, and the founding father of the United States. Washington was [104]elected as the first president of the U.S and served two terms from 1789 to 1797. He was first elected to the House of Burgess (representative) of the state of Virginia and was selected as a [105]delegate to the [106]constitutional [107]convention. He was the head of the constitutional convention of 1787, which established the U.S. Constitution and a

---

[102] fighting forces
[103] a politician or government official who is respected and experienced
[104] chose
[105] a person chosen or elected by a group to speak, vote, etc. for them, especially at a meeting
[106] relating to or following the rules of the US Constitution
[107] a large formal meeting of people who do a particular job or have a similar interest

[108]federal government. He was selected by the convention to lead the continental army in the war for independence from Great Britain. He led the army to [109]victory, and the Peace Treaty of Paris was signed in 1783 ("George Washington.," n.d.).

b. Quotations (Visit website to listen)

Let's start with two facts about me. Do you have an idea that I fell in love with agriculture and became an expert in it? My love for the land began with my careful planting and harvesting of the crops. I experimented with different crops and found those that were the most useful. I discovered that if you give love to the land, the land will give you love in return. My second passion was for peace among nations, and who knows what the fruits of peace and history will be? I met a French general, and we made peace. 100 years later, the French government gifted the United States the Statue of Liberty to support peace and immigration.

When you are a peace seeker, a passionate one, and you have spirit, you can do anything. When perseverance and spirit meet up with knowledge, wonders happen in all ages. Knowledge is surely, in every country, the basis of public happiness. But do not forget through your journey, you need to make mistakes to learn and to be successful. I strongly recommend not looking back at your mistakes unless you can learn a useful lesson. My last advice is "Observe good faith and justice towards all nations, cultivate peace and harmony with all."

1-Quotes taken from: (120 George Washington Quotes to Celebrate His Place in History, Hannah Hutyra, 2019), 2- Paraphrased Quotations

1- Do you have an idea: Do have an idea that (I) Washington "was quite an agricultural innovator? He supposedly experimented with the idea of crop rotation."

---

[108] relating to the central government
[109] winning

2- I strongly recommend: "We should not look back unless it is to derive useful lessons from past errors, and for the purpose of profiting by dearly bought experience." 2- I strongly recommend "not look back unless it is to derive useful lessons from past errors, and for the purpose of profiting by dearly bought experience."

3- Surely: "Knowledge is in every country the surest basis of public happiness."2- "Knowledge is (surely) in every country the basis of public happiness."

4- Fall in love: "I have always considered marriage as the most interesting event of one's life, the foundation of happiness or misery." 2- "I have always considered (falling in love) and marriage as the most interesting event of one's life, the foundation of happiness or misery."

5- Meet up: "Perseverance and spirit have done wonders in all ages." 2- When perseverance and spirit meet up, wonders happen in all ages. I met up with the French general to bring peace (Grammar point).

6- "Observe good faith and justice towards all Nations. Cultivate peace and harmony with all." Who knows how to bring peace and harmony to nations? I have always believed that good faith and justice toward all nations lead to the cultivation of peace and harmony.

Conversations

Model 1.

Topic: At the park, Participants: Natalia Talking to yourself

Natalia: Oh, I miss Sara a lot. I think I should call her.

Natalia: Yes, girl, you should get in touch with your old friend and tell her how proud you are to be in Boston and a student.

Natalia: I remember all the hard work and long nights that I spent burning the midnight oil to get into college.

Natalia: I also remember turning down all these young men so that I could spend my time studying.

Natalia: No one understood how hard it was for me to overcome the challenges I went through.

Natalia: I am so proud of myself for all the hard work and sacrifices that I made to get here.

Model 2.

Topic: At the park, Garcia making Natalia a donkey, Participants: Natalia and Garcia

Garcia: Hola, senorita, What a beautiful dog! What's your dog's name?

Natalia: Her name is Asal, and it means honey in Persian. Her breed is Lhasa Apso.

Garcia: This is Storm, and he is my dog. You know he is a Pitbull. Oh, I almost forgot, my name is Garcia, and Nice to meet you.

Natalia: My name is Natalia. Nice to meet you too.

Garcia: What's new?

Natalia: Nothing. What's up with you?

Garcia: Can I say something?

Natalia: Say!

Garcia: Do you have any idea; that I am falling in love with you?

Natalia: I have no idea. By the way, my sign is Scorpio.

Garcia: Oh, interesting. My sign is Cancer. You know Scorpio is a good match with Cancer. So maybe you are the one for me?

Natalia: Oh, Senior, you are such a sweet talker too.

Garcia: Now, may I have your 411?

Natalia: Ok, here is my number.

Garcia: Seniorita, I strongly recommend we meet up this weekend.

Natalia: Ok, when you call, we will talk about it. Have to go, bye.

Garcia: Bye, please take care.

Model 3.

Topic: Short business trip, Participants (Garcia and Natalia)

Garcia: Hi, sweetie, how are you today? What's new?

Natalia: I am good. How are you?

Garcia: Natalia, I must tell you something.

Natalia: What?! Is anything wrong.

Garcia: No, nothing is wrong, honey. I must go on a short business trip to China

Natalia: Oh really? Why? And how long?

Garcia: About two weeks. Natalia, I need to borrow some money from you to make this business deal in China. I will make a lot of money out of this deal, and when I return, we can be married.

Natalia: Oh, Garcia, don't worry, we are going to make a life together, and I want to help you, no problem. I will give you the money from my savings.

Garcia: Thank you, sweetie. When I get back, I will have a surprise for you.

Natalia: I am going to miss you, Garcia.

Garcia: Me too, darling.

Vocabulary list as a resource

	Vocabulary		
No.	**Pronunciation** **Part of speech** **in the song**	**Meaning** **(synonym)**	**Example in sentence**
1.	**To sit** /sɪt/ **Verb**	to be or stay in a position or place	I sit on this beautiful chair.

#	Word	Definition	Example
2.	**Glorious** /ˈglɔːriəs/ **Adjective**	deserving great admiration, praise, and honor	This is a glorious day.
3.	**Chair** /tʃer/ **Noun**	a seat for one person	This chair is reserved for her.
4.	**Life** /laɪf/ **Noun**	the period between birth and death, or the experience or state of being alive	I know that life is tough, but I am a fighter.
5.	**Afraid** /əˈfreɪd/ **Adjective**	feeling fear or feeling worried about the possible results of a particular situation	I know that life is tough, but I am not afraid of it.
6.	**Challenge** /ˈtʃælɪndʒ/ **Noun**	(the situation of being faced with) something that needs great mental or physical effort in order to be done successfully and therefore tests a person's ability	I know that life is tough, but I love challenges.
7.	**Strife** /straɪf/ **Noun**	violent or angry disagreement	I know that life is tough, but I am not afraid of challenges, and strife.
8.	**Hola** /Ola/ **Interjection**	Hello/ A Spanish word used to get attention or to greet someone	Hola, what's up?
9.	**Seniorita** /señorita/ **Noun**	Spanish/ Miss [noun] a polite title given to an unmarried female, either in writing or in speech	Seniorita, how are you?
10.	**411** /fɔːr wʌn wʌn/ **Slang**	Information (It is also the phone number in the US to find out a person's phone number)	- "It's has been nice meeting you. Could I have your 411." - "Let me think about it for a minute."
11.	**Hey** /heɪ/ **Noun**	used to get someone's attention, hi	"Hey, dear, how are you?" "I am good. and you?"
12.	**Missy** /ˈmɪsi/ **Noun**	Miss, girl	- "Missy, what's up?" - "not much"
13.	**what's new?** /wʌtz nuː/ **Expression Informal**	What's new? What's up? informal (also whassup, what's up)	- "what's new?" - "not much, how about you?"
14.	**I** /i/ **Subject pronoun**	used as the subject of a verb to refer to the person speaking or writing	- "What's your name?" - "I am Ellie."
15.	**Am**	"I" form of the verb be	- "How old are you?"

	/əm/ **To be verb**		- "I am twenty years old."
16.	**Fine** /faɪn/ **Adjective**	very good or very well	- "How are you, baby?" - "I am fine. How are you?"
17.	**How about you?** /haʊ əˈbaʊt jə/ **Expression** **Infor**	How about you? How are you?	- "How are you, darling?" - "I am fine. How about you?" - "I am fine."
18.	**Better** /ˈbetər/ **Adjective**	comparative of good: of a higher standard, or more suitable, pleasing, or effective than other things or people, finer	- "How are you feeling?" - "I am better now."
19.	**Now** /naʊ/ **Adverb**	at the present time rather than in the past or future, or immediately, at this moment, right now	Let us dance- now.
20.	**Because** /bɪˈkəz/ **Conjunction**	for the reason that, as, considering	- "How are you?" - "I am better now because I see you!"
21.	**I am seeing you** /aɪ əm siː ɪŋ jɑː/ **Informal Expression**	to meet or visit someone	- "How are you?" - "I am good because I am seeing you."
22.	**"It's so kind of you."** / ɪts kaɪnd əv jə/ **Expression**	generous, helpful, and thinking about other people's feelings	- "You look so beautiful." - "It's so kind of you to say that."
23.	**Do you have any idea?** / duː juː həv ˈeni aɪˈdiːə/ **Expression**	said for emphasis when you are describing how good or bad an experience is	- "Do you have any idea how cute you are?" - "Thank you."
24.	**fall in love** /fɔːl ɪn lʌv/ **noun**	if you fall in love, you begin to love someone, to love	- "I am falling in love with you." - "Me too."
25.	**Sir** /sɜːr/ **Noun**	a polite word used to address a man, Mr	- "Sir, you look so handsome." - "Thank you."
26.	**I have no idea** /aɪ həv nəʊ aɪˈdiːə/ **Informal Expression**	I don't have a belief about something. I don't have an understating about it	- "Do you have any idea how good it feels when we are together?" - "I have no idea."
27.	**To tell**	to say, to utter, to express	Tell me where you are from.

	/tel/ **Verb**		
28.	**Where are you from?** /wer ər juː frʌm/ **expression**	what city/state/country they consider "home," and that you assume it's someplace other than where you are right now, what is your nationality?	- "Where are you from?" - "I am from California."
29.	**Senior** /senior/ **Noun**	Sir/Mr. (Spanish word)	Senior, how are you?
30.	**To hear** /hɪr/ **Verb**	to be told or informed about, learned	I've heard that Californian girls are cute.
31.	**Cali** /kali/ **Noun**	nickname for the state of California.	We are going to Cali on vacation.
32.	**Is** /ɪz/ **To be verb**	he/she/it form of be	She is cute. Isn't she?
33.	**So** /səʊ/ **Adverb**	to such a great degree; truly, very	- "You are so sweet." - "Thank you, you too."
34.	**Wonderful** /ˈwʌndərfl/ **Adjective**	extremely good, great, amazing	- "She is a wonderful girl." - "I believe so."
35.	**Also** /ˈɔːlsəʊ/ **Adverb**	in addition, too	She is a fighter, and she is also very beautiful.
36.	**Girl** /gɜːrl/ **Noun**	a female child or young woman, especially one still in school	- "All the girls in the world are cute." - "True that."
37.	**Cali girls**	Californian girls, Girls from California/kali	Californian girls are smart.
38.	**Are** /ər/ **To be verb**	we/you/they form of be	We are cute and strong. We are wonder women.
39.	**Beautiful** /ˈbjuːtɪfl/ **Adjective**	very attractive, gorgeous, fascinating	- "I heard that Californian girls are beautiful!" - "All girls are cute."
40.	**Oh** /əʊ/ **Exclamation**	used to express different emotions, such as surprise, disappointment, and pleasure, often as a reaction	- "She's won the [110]Grammy awards ten times." -"Oh, really? I didn't know that!"

---

[110] A Grammy Award (stylized as GRAMMY, originally called Gramophone Award), or Grammy, is an award presented by The Recording Academy to recognize achievements in the music industry.

		to something someone has said, ah	
41.	**Sweet talker** /ˈsmuːðˌtɔːkə/ **Adjective**	a person who talks to someone in a pleasing or funny way in order to persuade them to do or believe something	- "You are a sweet talker." - "Am I?!"
42.	**Too** /tuː/ **Adverb**	in addition, also, likewise (especially at the end of a sentence)	"I love you." "I love you too."
43.	**Now** /naʊ/ **Adverb**	at the present time rather than in the past or future, or immediately, at this moment, right now	We are dancing now.
44.	**To Give** /gɪv/ **Verb**	to offer something to someone or to provide someone with something	- "Now give her your 411." - "My name is Garcia, and I am from Boston."
45.	**Me** /mi/ **Pronoun**	used, usually as the object of a verb or preposition, to refer to the person speaking or writing	- "Please give me your number(digits)." - "Excuse me!"
46.	**Your** /jər/ **Pronoun**	belonging or relating to the person or group of people being spoken or written to, belonging to you	- "I like your dress." - "Thank you!
47.	**Who** /huː/ **Subject pronoun**	which person, which people	Who knows?
48.	**To know** /nəʊ/ **Verb**	to have information in your mind, to realize	- "Do you know what her name is?" - "I don't know."
49.	**Who knows?** /huː nəʊs/ **phrase**	A rhetorical question asked to show that the person asking it neither knows the answer nor knows who might. It could be one or the other, or both	- "Do you think I'll get married to her?" - "Who knows, you might never marry."
50.	**Maybe** /ˈmeɪbi/ **Adverb**	used to show that something is possible or that something might be true, perhaps	Who knows, maybe you are my love.
51.	**You are the one** /juː ɑːr ði wʌn/ **Expression**	Used to say that someone is your true love.	You are the one.

52.	**wait, Just a minute** /weɪt, dʒʌst e ˈmɪnɪt/ **Expression**	said in order to interrupt someone, or to get their attention, or when you have suddenly thought of something important	Wait, just a minute. Let us review the situation.
53.	**Here (you are)** /hɪr/ **Expression**	used when giving something to someone	Here, try some of this. It's perfect.
54.	**My** /maɪ/ **Pronoun**	belonging to or connected with me; the possessive form of I, used before a noun	I keep thinking about my girlfriend.
55.	**Number** /ˈnʌmbər/ **Noun**	a phone number, digits	I gave him my number.
56.	**Sign** /saɪn/ **Noun**	a written or printed mark that has a standard meaning, a mark	- "What is your Zodiac sign?" - "Virgo."
57.	**Scorpio** /ˈskɔːrpiəʊ/ **Noun**	the eighth sign of the zodiac, relating to the period October 23 to November 21 and represented by a scorpion (= a small creature that has a curved tail with a poisonous sting), or a person born during this period (Zodiac sign)	- "What is her Zodiac sign?" - "Her sign is Scorpio."
58.	**Be born** /bi bɔːrn/ **Verb**	to come out of a mother's body and start to exist	I was born on the 23rd of August, and my sign is Virgo.
59.	**November** /nəʊˈvembər/ **Noun**	the eleventh month of the year, after October, and before December	I was born on the 21st of October, and my sign is Scorpio.
60.	**Never** /ˈnevər/ **Adverb**	not at any time or not on any occasion	Never forget, I am a fighter.
61.	**To forget** /fərˈget/ **Verb**	to be unable to remember a fact, something that happened, or how to do something	Never forget, you will succeed if you try.
62.	**Mind** /maɪnd/ **Noun**	the part of a person that makes it possible for him or her to think, feel emotions, and understand things	My mind is focused on my goal.

63.	**Tough** /tʌf/ **Adjective**	strong; not easily broken or made weaker or defeated	Life is not tough if you take it easy.
64.	**Heart** /hɑːrt/ **Noun**	used to refer to a person's character or the place within a person where feelings or emotions are considered to come from	My heart is tender.
65.	**Tender** /ˈtendər/ **Adjective**	gentle, loving, or kind	My heart is tender, but my mind is strong.
66.	**Strongly** /ˈstrɔːŋli/ **Adverb**	very much or in a very serious way, highly, fully	I strongly recommend that we go to this restaurant this weekend.
67.	**To Recommend** /ˌrekəˈmend/ **Verb**	to suggest that a particular action should be done, to suggest, to confirm	Coronavirus is everywhere so I strongly recommend that you stay at home.
68.	**That** /ðæt/ **Conjunction**	used to introduce a clause that reports something or gives further information, although it can often be left out	He said (that) he would love me forever.
69.	**We** /wi/ **Pronoun**	used as the subject of a verb to refer to a group including the speaker and at least one other person, you, and I	- "Can we all go to the party this evening?" - "why not."
70.	**Surely** /ˈʃʊrli/ **Adverb**	used to express that you are certain or almost certain about something. absolutely, certainly	I am slowly but surely getting my strength back.
71.	**To meet up** /miːt ʌp/ **Phrasal verb**	to meet another person in order to do something together	They suggested we meet up at Sara's.
72.	**This** /ðɪs/ **Adjective pronoun**	something that is near to the speaker in time and space	I strongly recommend that we meet up this coming weekend.
73.	**Weekend** /ˈwiːkend/ **Noun**	Saturday and Sunday, when many people do not work	We are going to the party this weekend.
74.	**Ok** /əʊˈkeɪ/ **Exclamation**	agreed or acceptable; all right, yes, okay	- "Ok, when and where?" - "At 6 o'clock at pleasant square."
75.	**When** /wen/ **Adverb**	at the time at which, at what time	- "When and where will we meet this weekend?" - "I will tell you later."

76.	**Where** /wer/ Adverb	to, at, or in what place, location	- "Where is your friend?" - "She is at home."
77.	**Lady** /ˈdɑːnə/ Noun	Lady is often used as a polite way of addressing or referring to any woman, missy	- "Sweet lady, shall we dance?" - "My pleasure."
78.	**At** /ət/ Preposition	used to show a particular place or a particular time, near to	I will see you at Assembly Square.
79.	**Copley Art Square** Noun	Name of a square in Boston	I will see you at Copley square.
80.	**Square** /skewer/ Noun	An area of approximately square-shaped land in a city or a town, often including the buildings that surround it	I will see you at Azadi square.
81.	**Bye** /baɪ/ Exclamation	Goodbye, adios, so long	Bye-bye, see you later.
82.	**To see** /siː/ Verb	to meet, visit, or spend time with someone	You can see the mountains.
83.	**Later** /ˈleɪtər/ Adverb	at a time in the future or after the time you have mentioned, again	See you later.
84.	**Adios**	A Spanish word meaning goodbye	Adios, take care.
85.	**Hasta Luego**	A Spanish phrase meaning see you later	Adios, Hasta luego.
86.	**Sweetie** /ˈswiːti/ Noun	a very pleasant or kind person	Bye, sweetie.
87.	**Please** /pliːz/ Exclamation	used to add force to a request or demand	Just a moment, please.
88.	**Be well** /bi wel/ Expression	Used to say to a person to take good care of herself/himself	Please be well until we meet again.
89.	**To take care (of yourself)** /teɪk ker/ Informal expression	used when saying goodbye to someone, goodbye, protect yourself	Please take care.

Chapter 5

Section 1: Yoga Posture: Tree

Yoga Posture: Tree (Asana: Virkshasana)
Virksha: Tree; Asana: posture

When you are overwhelmed by the difficulties in life, just be patient and strong like an oak tree and believe that the spring of your life is on its way!

Mythology of Virkshasana

"In many Indian traditions, trees are symbols of love and devotion. Many native cultures seek the knowledge of trees for healing, searching their branches, trunks, leaves, and roots for powerful medicines. Patient by nature, trees are quiet and steady, living their long lives in rhythm with the seasons and the circadian rhythm of the world. Trees often appear as sacred symbols of the universe, a bridge between the creator and the individual" (Gaia, 2018). Because of its hollow center, bamboo is resilient and less susceptible to breakage. It can bend but not break. To the Chinese, this characteristic corresponds with the ideals of a Confucian scholar - strong yet modest and flexible.

The tree pose offers a beautiful opportunity to meditate on a tree's inherent qualities. The tree is so tolerant that it even gives shade to the woodcutter, who comes to cut it down with an ax. The true yogi freely gives the fruits of spiritual wisdom and love as generously as trees. Trees tolerate all kinds of natural disturbances, torrents of rain, scorching heat, and piercing cold. The tree pose is a posture in which we give body, mind, and breath the qualities of generosity, forbearance, strength, and balance (Kaivalya, 2016).

Every part of the globe has a myth about trees. From the oak in central Europe, ash in Scandinavia, and Shorea in India, trees are revered. They cultivated and protected holy trees and would beg forgiveness from a tree if it were cut. In Korea, spirits of women who died in childbirth were thought to live in trees. Other groups of people considered trees tightly bound with their own creation. The Greeks believed the first man was made from an ash tree. In Siberia, man and woman were thought to have been created separately from a larch and a fir. Scandinavian myths state gods breathed life into two tree trunks to make the first human couple. Other northern Europeans believed man was first carved from an alder. In Indonesia, vertical slices cut into a fig tree by two gods created man, while horizontal slices created woman. In New Guinea, man was considered a tree that moved! Some trees were well known for their special attributes. In many areas, birch was the tree of health, wisdom, and safety -- used in baby cradles and cribs and used as symbols of public office. Cedars were the trees of paradise in the Mideast. They were also symbols of faithful lovers in China and were held as sacred in Nepal. Junipers were planted as protection from thieves and witches (Coder, 2011).

Connection to the lesson

In this period of her life, Natalia is so sad because Garcia, who is the love of her life, is diagnosed with a bad virus in China. She is trying to be patient, and in order to create a balance in her feelings, she writes a song and expresses her feeling to Garcia. She is trying to be strong and patient as a tree.

Cautionary notes

- Do not raise your arms, if you have heart issues.

- Keep your toes on the ground if it's difficult for you to keep your balance.

- Ensure your knees are soft if you have discomfort in your knees.

Yogic Breathing: Dirgha Pranayama

Meaning: Prana: air; life force; Yama: to restrain or hold back

Potential effects

Enhancement of complete and full breathing, decreasing stress and tension while calming the mind and the body, helping the lungs remain healthy by increasing the oxygen flow to the blood, it massages the abdominal organs, facilitating digestion, preparing you for a better learning experience.

Three Breathing Steps: (Visit website to listen)

1- Sit up straight with your shoulders back and down with relaxed abdominals.

2- Relax the face, close your mouth, and place your hands on your belly.

3- Breathe into your belly and feel it expands like a balloon. Repeat several times.

4- Now, put your hands to the sides of your rib cage and breathe into them, feeling the rib cage expand, and repeat several times.

5- Put your fingertips on your upper chest. Breathe into it and feel your hands lifting. Repeat several times.

6- Now, make a complete inhalation. As you are inhaling, feel the expansions of your belly, rib cage, and chest, and as you are exhaling, you feel the contractions of all three. Repeat this series several times (Refer to Figure 1 in Chapter 1).

Next, move into the warmup, which is the next section.

Warm up: Standing Hip Circles (visit website to listen)

Stand tall with your feet about shoulder-width apart and place your hands on your hips. Ensure that your knees are not locked, start to move your hips in a circle. Inhale and exhale, and little by little, make the circles larger and larger (Figure 1).

1   2   3   4   5

Figure 1: Standing Hip Circles

Posturer steps of Tree (Virkshasana): (Visit website to listen)

1- Stand tall with your feet hip-width apart, inhale and transfer your weight onto your left foot.

2- On an inhale, raise your right foot as high as is comfortable. While keeping your balance and breathing deeply, grasp your right foot and place it on the inside of your left thigh. (If you have difficulty putting your right foot on your left thigh, then lean your foot on the inside of your ankle).

3- On an inhale, raise your arms to the sides, palms facing forward. Keep your abs active and lengthen your back.

4- Inhale as you are rooting yourself through the standing leg, exhale and lift your arms and stretch toward the sky. Soften your shoulders, move them back and down and straighten your back. Gaze at a spot on the ground and maintain your balance. Hold the pose for a few seconds.

5- To release, on an exhale, bring your arms down by your side and then lower your raised leg down to the ground.

6- Relax and feel the difference of Virkshasana (tree pose) and repeat with the right leg (Figure 2).

Figure 2: Tree (Virkshasana)

Section 2: Music and Lyrics: Waiting for You

Part 1: **Listening (Stage 1,2 and 3) (To listen, click here)**

Stage 1- (Listening for fun) Listen to the song several times, pat your feet, move your body, and enjoy the music! Do not worry about the meaning of the words yet!!!

Stage 2- (Attentive listening) Listen carefully several times to understand the lyrics.

Stage 3- (Listening and guessing) listen and read the lyrics several times to understand the lyrics. Try to guess the meaning of the words you do not know and understand. Do not look at the vocabulary list just yet. Listen to the lyrics again and guess at the meaning of the words you do not know. Write down the words you do not know.

Guess words: ……………………………………………………………………………………

………………………………………………………………………………………………

………………………………………………………………………………………………

………………………………………………………………………………………………

………………………………………………………………………………………………

Part 2: Listening & Reading Lyrics (Stage 4, 5, 6, and 7)

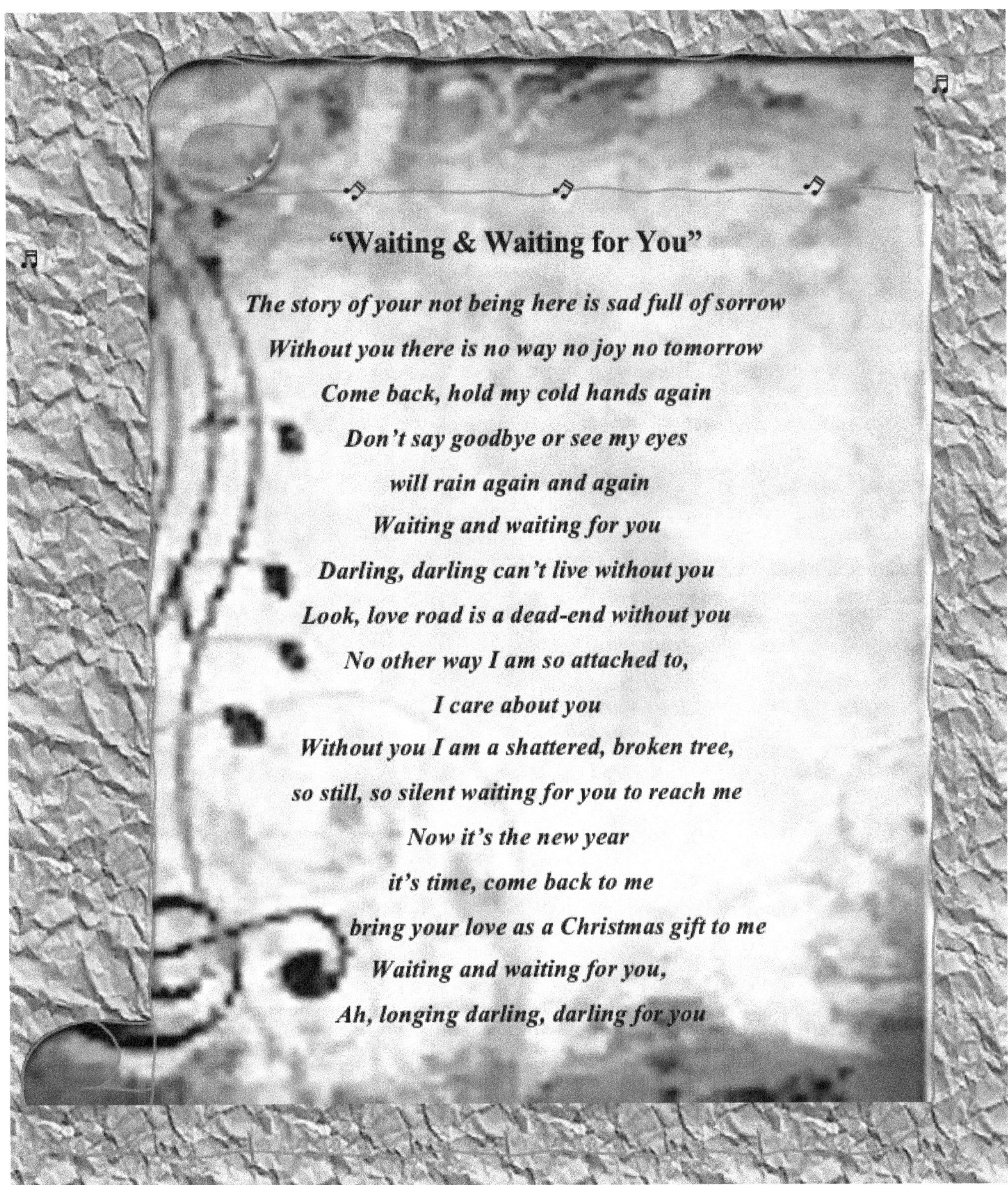

Stage 4- (Confirmation of guessing) Look at the vocabulary table to make sure that you know the meaning and part of speech of all the words in the lyrics.

Stage 5- (Humming) Now that you know the meaning of the whole song, listen to the music and hum along with the song several times.

Stage 6- 🎧 **(Karaoke)** See the lyrics on the monitor and sing. (Visit website to listen)

Stage 7- **(Mastery)** Listen to the music without any lyrics and sing away. Sing, Dance, and Enjoy!

Section 3: Reading a short story: Waiting and Waiting for You

Pre-Reading activity

a. 🎧 **Listening and taking notes**: (Visit website to listen)

Please listen to the story and write down what you have understood.

....

....

....

....

....

....

b. Reading and Guessing

-Please read the short story below, guess at the missing words and fill in the blanks.

"Waiting & Waiting for You"

It is December 2019; it is almost time for Garcia to return home. One night, Natalia receives a

call from Garcia. He tells her, "I am ill, and I am in the hospital. I will return as soon as I recover". But later, the hospital (1) ……………. Garcia is (2) ……………. with Covid-19. When Natalia learns he has the virus, and he will not be home for Christmas, she is feeling sad and remembers all the beautiful memories with him. She feels a (3) ………… in her throat and [111]drops of [112]tears (4) ……… …………. her [113]cheeks. She (5) ……… ………. her car, goes to the ocean where she used to go with Garcia, and she looks out at the waves coming into the beach. This song comes to her mind: "Come back and hold my cold hands again. don't say goodbye or see my eyes will rain again and again. Waiting and waiting for you, Darling, darling can't live without you." She remembers their sitting by the fireplace, he would hold her hands and make them warm.

(6) …… ……………….. ……. ……………. of the sadness in her heart, she returns home, and the broken-hearted Natalia picks up her guitar and starts playing this song for Garcia. She sings the song, posts it on Facebook, and tells everybody this is my Christmas gift to my dear Garcia. Because she sang it from the bottom of her heart, it touched the hearts of others who heard it on Facebook, and the song went viral.

---

[111] a small round-shaped amount of liquid
[112] a drop of salty liquid that flows from the eye, as a result of strong emotion, especially unhappiness, or pain
[113] the soft part of your face that is below your eye

c. 🎧 **Listening and Checking your Guessing (Visit website to listen)**

Please read and listen to the short story. While you are listening, please check to see if the guesses you have made are correct. If your guess was not correct, please make a change and fill in the blanks. Then check your [114]answers in the footnotes.

d. Clearing up all confusions

Please read the short story by yourself without listening to it. Highlight or underline the parts that are unclear to you in the story above. Use your dictionary or a partner to clarify highlighted parts. Write your notes below for further review.

……..

……...

e. Reading Comprehension based on the "WH Questions."

Look below for the boxes and read the questions (Q) and answers (A). While you are reading the questions, answer by filling in the blank with the "WH questions" (who, when, where, what, why, and how). Choose the answers that are the best fit. You do not have to use all the "WH questions." Notice that the title of the reading is in the middle of a circle, and the questions pivot around the title of the story in the figure. Both questions and answers are provided, and you only need to put the correct "wh question" in the blank.

- After you have finished filling in the blanks below, practice asking and answering the questions.

- Check your answers with the [115]answer key in the footnote.

---

[114] 1- discovers: to find information, 2- infected: has the virus, 3- lump: a hard swelling found in her throat, 4- slide: move easily , 5- gets into : goes inside, 6- to lighten the burden: to lift the pressure
[115] 1. why, 2. what, 3.why 4. how 5. when, 6. why

| Who? | When? | Where? | What? | Why? | How? |

1- Q: ………… was Natalia scared?

A: Because Garcia got infected by Coronavirus.

2- Q: ………… did Natalia do after writing her feelings?

A: She picked up her guitar and started playing this song for Garcia.

6- Q: ……….. was Garcia quarantined?

A: He was quarantined because he became infected with the Coronavirus.

Waiting & Waiting

3- Q: ………… did she decide to write a letter to him?

A: She thought it might help her to lighten the burden of the sadness in her heart.

4- Q: ………… did the Natalia feel on Christmas?

A: She feels sad and lonely.

5- Q: ……….. is Natalia feeling so sad and lonely?

A: She is feeling sad and lonely at Christmas time.

Section 4: Syntax Notes: Modal Verbs, Present Continuous Tense, So + Adjective

Syntax Note 1: Modal Verbs

Example from a line in the lyrics: "I can't live without you." (It is not possible to live without you)

a. Warm-up question: What do you think the syntax point is about? Please Explain. Please Explain.

……………………………………………………………………………………………

……………………………………………………………………………………………

Can (Positive)

It is used to express an ability or to express that something is possible. It is also used to show a request and permission. Can is the same for all subject pronounces (I, you, he, she, it, they).

How to form a sentence using can: subject + can + infinitive without to

Example 1: I can sing and learn. (an ability)

Example 2: You can be a good friend. (Possible)

Example 3: Can I leave the class? (Permission)

Cannot (can't): (Negative)

To form the negative: subject + cannot (can't) + infinitive without to

I cannot (can't) live without you.

Can (Questions)

To form the question: Can + subject + infinitive without to

Can I sing and learn? Yes, you can.

Can I live without you? No, you cannot(can't)

b.   Write a real-life example of the use of syntax point above in a sentence below.

……………………………………………………………………………………………………

Syntax Note 2: Present Continuous Tense

Example from a line in the lyrics: "I am waiting and waiting for you."

Warm-up questions: What do you think the syntax point is about? Please Explain. Please Explain.

……………………………………………………………………………………………

……………………………………………………………………………………………

Present Continuous tense: An action is happening right now

How to form a present continuous tense: "(am/is/ are) + verb + ing"

I am waiting for you. You are waiting for me. They are waiting for me. She/he/it is waiting for you.

Write a real-life example of the use of syntax point above in a sentence below.

……………………………………………………………………………………………………

Syntax Note 3: So + Adjective

Example from a line in the lyrics: "I am so tired without you."

Warm-up questions: What do you think the syntax point is about? Please Explain. Please Explain.

………………………………………………………………………………………………

………………………………………………………………………………………………

So + adjective (so tired)

We usually use so when we mean "to a great extent or limit." With this meaning, so is a degree adverb that modifies adjectives(tired).

Write a real-life example of the use of syntax point above in a sentence below?

………………………………………………………………………………………………………

Section 5: Museum of Reincarnation: Florence Nightingale

Wikipedia contributors. (2022). *Florence Nightingale.*

Stage 1: Completing the vocabulary list

Before going to the museum, please complete the vocabulary list below.

No.	Vocabulary	Meaning
1.	To reach	
2.	No way	

3.	Care about	
4.	Attached to	
5.	Longing	
6.	Still	
7.	Shattered	
8.	Silent	
9.	Joy	

Stage 2. The Biography part of the museum, listening and taking notes. (Visit website to listen)

Who is the famous person? Why is the person famous?

………………………………………………………………………………………………….

…………………………………………………………………………………………………..

………………………………………………………………………………………………….

Stage 3. Reincarnation with the famous person (Vocabulary part).

a. Watching and Listening. (Visit website to listen)

b. Watching, listening carefully, and writing down the usage of the words by the famous person.

c. Identifying the parts of speech

d. Writing your own sentences using the vocabulary words and the syntax notes.

No.	Vocabulary	a. Watching and Listening
		b. Sentences with the vocabulary word used by the famous person **c. Part of speech** **d. Sentences with the vocabulary word used by you**
1	**To reach**	b. Sentences by the famous person: …………………………………… ………………………………………………………………………… c. Part of speech: …………… d. Your sentence: ……………………………………………….. …………………………………………………………………………
2	**No way**	b. Sentences by the famous person: …………………………………… ………………………………………………………………………… c. Part of speech: …………… d. Your sentence: ………………………………………………….. …………………………………………………………………………
3	**To care about**	b. Sentences by the famous person: …………………………………… ………………………………………………………………………… c. Part of speech: …………… d. Your sentence: ………………………………………………….. …………………………………………………………………………
4		b. Sentences by the famous person: …………………………………… ………………………………………………………………………… c. Part of speech: ……………

	To attached to	d. Your sentence: …………………………………………………… …………………………………………………………………
5	**Longing**	b. Sentences by the famous person: …………………………… ………………………………………………………………… c. Part of speech: …………… d. Your sentence: …………………………………………………….. …………………………………………………………………
6	**Still**	b. Sentences by the famous person: …………………………… ………………………………………………………………… c. Part of speech: …………… d. Your sentence: …………………………………………………….. …………………………………………………………………
7	**Shattered**	b. Sentences by the famous person: …………………………… ………………………………………………………………… c. Part of speech: …………… d. Your sentence: …………………………………………………….. …………………………………………………………………
8	**Silent**	b. Sentences by the famous person: …………………………… ………………………………………………………………… c. Part of speech: …………… d. Your sentence: …………………………………………………….. …………………………………………………………………
9		b. Sentences by the famous person: ……………………………

	Joy	………………………………………………………………………………
		c. Part of speech: ……………
		d. Your sentence: …………………………………………………..
		………………………………………………………………………

Section 6: Conversation Creation

a. Choosing a Topic

Choose one of the following potential topics and participants related to the short story/lyrics of the lesson.

Topic 1: Topic: bad news, Participants: Natalia and Garcia

Topic 2: What's App conversation (When are you coming home?), Participants: Natalia and Garcia

Topic 3: A Chat on Facebook, Participants: Natalia and one of her Facebook followers who likes her song

b. Creating Conversation

After choosing your topic, create your conversation in the space below.

Note: There are two models of conversations in the endnotes to this chapter. You can look at the models and use or modify the conversation you have created. When you are creating your conversation, you should use the new syntax notes and some of the listed vocabulary.

Topic of Your Conversation:

Participants:

………………………………………………………………………………………………

....

....

....

....

....

....

....

c. **Role-playing.** Practice and role-play the conversation with your partner, friend,

brother/sister, or even with yourself in front of the mirror. The purpose of role-playing is to

become comfortable using the language in a casual and conversational way.

Section 7: Cultural Notes: Covid-19 and Front-line Heroes

a. **Warm-Up (Brainstorming)**

Please look at the topic above and guess what the cultural Notes are about?

....

....

....

b. **Reading**

"2019-20 Covid-19 and Front-line Heroes who have been as patient and strong as a tree"

Read the following cultural points. If you do not know a word or phrase, please use the

guessing strategy (guess the meaning of the words based on the context) and use a dictionary

when necessary.

The COVID-19 pandemic is an infectious disease resulting in acute respiratory syndrome. The outbreak was first identified in Wuhan, China, in December 2019. The World Health Organization declared the outbreak a public health emergency of international concern on 30 January and a pandemic on 11 March. As of 26 May 2020, more than 5.49 million cases of COVID-19 have been reported in more than 188 countries and territories, resulting in more than 346,000 deaths. More than 2.23 million people have recovered from the virus. ("COVID-19 pandemic," n.d.)

The 2019-20 Covid-19 is an enemy of every culture and an invisible serial killer in the world. It has torn apart countless families, shattered economies, and left people in shock and sorrow not only in the US but around the world. People around the world are waiting for the virus to go away. The coronavirus has changed every living culture. We can no longer touch those we love. We stay away from each other. We stay in the house. The virus is the cultural emergency of this century. The virus has caused time to stop as everyone is sheltered in place. The virus is not waiting for us. We are waiting for the virus to go away. Waiting and waiting at home and depending upon technology are everybody's culture these days.

The Heroes: Those Who Did Not Wait and Did Help

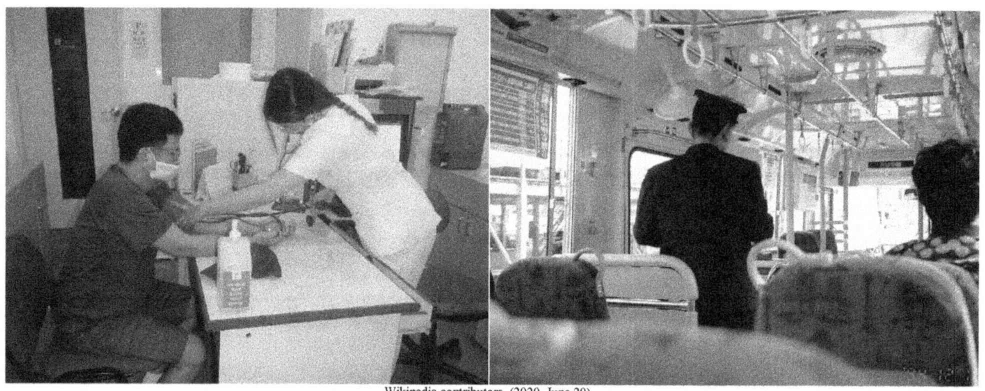

Wikipedia contributors. (2020, June 20)

The nurses in hospitals all around the country are our true heroes. They are the ones who are not waiting, and instead, they are fighting the virus. They get up each day and report to hospitals that are struggling to provide care to the victims of the covid-19 virus. These nurses are putting their health and safety on the line each day as they provide the primary care for those who are suffering. Nurses around the country report the same concerns and fears. They are working long hours and experience the fear of not knowing if they are going to be infected. They care for the dying whose families cannot be with them. Nurses have to hold the hands of the dying. Of course, they console the families and comfort them as best they can. At the end of the day, they go home and shower in the basement, and change clothes before going upstairs to be with their families. They are encouraged by the kindness shown to them by friends and neighbors who bring food and drinks and leave it at their doorsteps. The restaurants deliver meals on the weekends. The kindness of strangers is everywhere. Being kinder is everybody's culture these days.

Bus drivers, transit workers, firemen and policewomen, and men are also putting their health and lives on the line as they provide the essential services that make life in our cities and towns possible. Each day these public servants leave their families and go out to serve others. Despite the pandemic, they report to work each day to repair the buses, and trains, clean the stations and buses and report to the firehouses and police stations so that life can go on in the cities. Hundreds of these essential workers have lost their lives in cities large and small. The covid-19 virus has impacted these workers more than most, and many of these workers are people of color. The virus has had a very large impact on communities of color. This large impact on communities of color is causing a renewed conversation about the need to provide the health services necessary to keep all our citizens healthy and well. They have been strong and patient heroes and a source of strength like the trees.

Celebrities Who Celebrated First Responders and Nurses

"The stars take part in One World: Together at Home concert: Some of the biggest names in music have joined forces to celebrate healthcare workers in a globally televised concert. Lady Gaga, Paul McCartney, and Billie Eilish were among more than 100 artists who performed songs from their living rooms due to the coronavirus lockdown. The Rolling Stones even managed to play together from four separate locations. The eight-hour show also featured real-life stories from those on the front line of the fight against the Covid-19 virus. The event raised almost $128m (£102m), with proceeds going towards vaccine development and local and regional charities, Organizers Global Citizen said. Lady Gaga, who curated the line-up, called the event "a love letter to the world". Dedicating the show to first responders and medical staff, she said the participating musicians all wanted "to give back a little bit of the kindness that you've given us". (Savage, 2020).

c. SPARCing the Cultural Notes

Using the information above, please complete the SPARC (Setting, Participant, Activities, Reasons, and Conclusion).

- Setting (when and where?): …………………………………………………………………………
- Participants (who?): ……………………………………………………………………………………
- Activities (how did they get there?):

  ……
- Reasons (why are they successful?):

  ……

- Conclusion (what is your SPARC?):

………………………………………………………………………………………………

………………………………………………………………………………………………

Section 8: Creative Story/Lyrics Writing

Based on all the points you have learned in this chapter (Yoga, vocabulary, syntax, lyrics, video, conversations), follow the steps below:

Stage 1: Brainstorming

Insert the title of your story/lyrics in the middle of the figure below and then fill in the other boxes about the participants in your story(who), the setting (when and where), the activities of your story (how), the reasons for your story (why), and the conclusion to your story (what).

Stage 2- Writing Your Story/Lyrics

Now in the space below, write your story/ lyrics (Your story/lyrics can be rap, rhyming, etc., Be creative and let your imagination be your limit)

The Title of Your Story:…………………………

....

....

....

....

....

....

....

....

Stage 3. Getting Feedback: Check your story/ lyrics with your teachers/parents/mentors, to get feedback

Stage 4. Applying Music: Either apply your story/lyrics on the karaoke track of the song or click on the beat's website, such as https://www.8notes.com/metronome/. Choose the right beat for your story/lyrics. Even if you play a musical instrument, apply your writing to your playing. Don't limit yourself and be creative.

Stage 5. Singing: Practice, sing and enjoy!

Stage 6. Recording. Record yourself and share your product with someone else to get feedback, and revise if necessary.

Stage 7. Posting your creation.

Section 9: Quick Quiz

The quiz in this section is designed to help you review and remember the materials you have learned. The answer key is always provided in the footnotes. If you have any doubts about the correct answer, please check the footnotes.

Please answer the questions below and check your answers in the [116]answer key in the footnote.

c. Vocabulary: What is the part of speech and synonym of the Bolded vocabulary?

1- We must make a U-turn; this is a **dead-end street**.

   a. Adverb: this street is big   b. Adjective: this street is closed at one end

   c. Adverb: this is a small street   d. Adjective: this street is closed at two ends

2- Baby, I am **shattered** without you.

   a. Adverb: shady   b. Adverb: shabby

   c. Adjective: broken   d. Adjective: strong

3- He has missed her a lot, and he is **longing** to hear her sweet voice

   a. Adjective: Becoming longer   b. Adjective: becoming loving

   c. Verb: having a weak desire   d. Verb: having a strong desire

4- My girlfriend is a liar, but the problem is that I am very **attached to her**.

   a. Adjective: hate her very much   b. Adjective: like her very much

   c. Verb: tired of her too much   d. Verb: meet with her too much

5- She dived into the **still** water of the pool.

   a. Adverb: wild   b. Adjective: calm   c. Adverb: blue d. Adjective: clean

A. Syntax: Which is the best way for an English speaker to express herself/himself?

---

[116] Answer Key

   1- b, 2- c, 3- d, 4- b, 5- b, 6- d, 7- d, 8- F, 9- F, 10- T

6-

    a. She can meet up with her boyfriend.

    b. She can to meet up with her boyfriend.

    c. She can meeting up with her boyfriend.

    d. she can meet up with her boyfriend.

7-

    a. She is singing and learn language.

    b. He singing and learning language.

    c. They are sang and learned language.

    d. I am singing and learning language.

B. **Culture:** Based on the Cultural Note, decide which sentence is true (T) and which one is false (F)?

8- The COVID-19 pandemic is an ongoing disease (COVID-19), resulting in acute respiratory syndrome.[1] The outbreak was first identified in Hong Kong, China, in December 2020.

9- Teachers get up each day and report to hospitals that are struggling to provide care to the victims of the covid-19 virus.

10- The virus has had a very large impact upon communities of color.

Section 10: Endnotes

Museum Transcripts

Biography of Florence Nightingale

Florence Nightingale (1820 – 1913) was a British [117]social reformer, statistician, and the founder of modern nursing. She [118]came to public attention as a manager and trainer of nurses during the Crimean War. Nightingale organized and cared for wounded soldiers. She was known as the "The Lady with the Lamp," making rounds of wounded soldiers at night. Nightingale was a great and productive writer concerned with spreading [119]medical information. She wrote in simple English so that she could easily be understood by everyone. She was also a leader in data visualization with the use of infographics, effectively using graphical presentations of statistical data ("Florence Nightingale.," n.d.). But, most of all, she is famous for her care and [120]compassion for wounded soldiers. (Reef, C. (2016); Wikipedia contributors, 2022)).

Quotations

I took my lamp and medicines to reach wounded soldiers at night. Because I had love and passion, and I had no fear. There is no way to be successful under the spirit of fear. On your path to peace, evil appears in different shapes in your life, but you must stay strong and silent when someone or something contradicts you because then you will learn.

Yes, there is no better definition of a nurse than as a person who cares about patients and is attached to them. To be blessed, you need to be kind to others. If you only make your own joy, your pleasure, and not think about others, then you will be destined for eternal damnation" Now,

---

[117] social reformer: a person who tries to change the social rules to help people
[118] came to public attention: became famous
[119] medical: related to the treatment of illness and injuries
[120] kindness

I am longing to return to the battlefield and be of help to others. I want to say that wise and humane management of the patient is the best safeguard against any disease.

Quotations taken from Florence Nightingale's quotes on Life, Communication, and Nursing by Juma, 2020.

1- Direct Quotations, 2- Paraphrased Quotations

1- To reach: I would take my lamp and medicines to reach wounded soldiers at night.

2- No way: "How very little can be done under the spirit of fear.", There is no way to be successful under the spirit of fear.

3- Care about and attached to: "No man, not even a doctor, ever gives any other definition of what a nurse should be than this – 'devoted and obedient." 2- There is no better definition of a nurse than a person who cares about patients and is attached to them.

4- Longing: I am longing to return to the battlefield and be of help to others.

5- Still and Shattered: "If you knew how unreasonably sick people suffer from reasonable causes of distress, you would take more pains about all these things." 2-When you see a still and shattered body. You would take great pains to make them whole.

6- Silent: "Never dispute with anybody who wishes to contradict you, says a most reasonable saint." 2- Stay silent when someone contradicts you because then you will learn.

7- Joy: That "of His own good pleasure" He has" predestined" any souls to eternal damnation."2- If you only make your own joy, your pleasure, and not think about others, then you will be destined for eternal damnation."

Conversations

Model 1.

Topic: bad news, Participants: Natalia and Garcia

Garcia: Hi Natalia, how are you?

Natalia: Hi, I am worried. I was watching the news today. There is a virus in China, and it is so dangerous. When is your return ticket?

Garcia: Natalia, I have to give you the bad news. Unfortunately, I have become [121]infected with the virus. I am [122]quarantined in Wuhan, China.

Natalia: Oh, no, Garcia, oh, my God, what should I do now?

Garcia: Well, there is nothing that you can do baby.

Natalia: Where are you? Who is looking after you? Have you seen a doctor?

Garcia: I am quarantined in the hotel; A nurse has been assigned to come by and to check on me and to figure out if I need medication.

Natalia: Is there anything that I can do to help?

Garcia: No, there is nothing you can do at this time.

Natalia: Please take care of yourself.

Garcia: I will, you too.

Model 2.

Topic 2: When are you coming home? (a What's App conversation), Participants: Natalia and Garcia

Natalia: Hi, darling. How are you feeling? When are you coming home? I am feeling so sad.

Garcia: Oh, I miss you too, darling. You know I am so attached to you, and I care about you too, but no way for me to get back now. I am not feeling all that well, and all the flights have been canceled.

---

[121] containing bacteria or other things that can cause disease
[122] a period of time during which an animal or person that might have a disease is kept away from other people or animals so that the disease cannot spread

Natalia: Oh, I am sad and shattered. My world is so silent without you.

Garcia: Oh, I am longing to hold your hands again. I cannot leave my hotel room. Each day they bring me food, and they leave it at the door. I am spending my day watching TV. It is so boring.

Natalia: Darling, I miss you so much, and I feel so lonely. Tonight, I will send you my Christmas gift. It will be my surprise for you.

Garcia: Thank you, darling. I miss you and will talk to you again soon.

Model 3.

Topic: Chat between Natali and one of her followers on Facebook

Facebook follower: Hi, Natalia, you played this song so beautifully.

Natalia: Oh, Thank you, so sweet of you.

Facebook follower: I love it.

Natalia: It wasn't easy for me. I had to hold back the tears.

Facebook follower: I know it was hard, and I feel you.

Natalia: Thanks for listening to it.

Facebook follower: No problem. Stay strong as a tree and take good care of yourself.

Natalia: I am hanging in there.

Vocabulary list as a resource

	Vocabulary		
No.	Pronunciation Part of speech in the song	Meaning (synonym)	Example in sentence
1.	**To Wait** /weɪt/ **Verb**	to allow time to go by, esp. without doing much, until something happens or can happen, await	I am waiting for you.
2.	**Story** /ˈstɔːri/ **Noun**	a description of events that happened or that are invented (a drama: is a kind of story)	It is a long story.

3.	**Being** /ˈbiːɪŋ/ **present participle of** **be(noun)**	a person or thing that exists, or the state of existing, existence	Being a language learner and a singer is fun.
4.	**Here** /hɪr/ **Adverb**	in, at, or to this place, on this spot	Come here, I need your help!
5.	**Is** /ɪz/ **To be verb**	be, used with he/she/it, exists	This story is sad and full of sorrow.
6.	**Sad** /sæd/ **Adjective**	unhappy, sorrow	I am so sad that you can't come back.
7.	**Full** /fʊl/ **Adjective**	having filled	You are always full of energy.
8.	**Sorrow** /ˈsɑːrəʊ/ **Noun**	a feeling of great sadness, pain	His death was a great sorrow to everyone.
9.	**Without** /wɪˈðaʊt/ **Preposition**	not having or doing, not having the help of someone	She did it without him.
10.	**(There is) no way** /nəʊ weɪ/ **Phrase**	used to say someone that something is impossible, not at all	There is no way I can forget you!
11.	**Joy** /dʒɔɪ/ **Noun**	great happiness, pleasure	There is no joy without you.
12.	**Tomorrow** /təˈmɑːrəʊ/ **Adverb**	on the day after today, a future day	I hope to see you tomorrow.
13.	**To Come back** /kʌm bæk/ **Phrasal Verb**	to return, come again	Please come back, darling.
14.	**To hold** /həʊld/ **Verb**	to take and keep something in your hand, grasp	Hold my hands. They are cold.
15.	**My** /maɪ/ **Pronoun**	belonging to or connected with me; the possessive form of I, used before a noun	I think about my boyfriend.
16.	**Cold** /kəʊld/ **Adjective**	having a low temperature, chilly, freezing	- "It's cold today. Isn't it?" - "It is."
17.	**Hand** /hændz/ **Noun**	the part of the body at the end of the arm that includes the fingers and is used for holding,	Come back and hold my hands.

		moving, touching, and feeling things	
18.	**Again** /əˈgeɪn/ Adverb	once more, or as before, repeatedly	"Why are you late again?" "Sorry!"
19.	**To say** /dəʊnt seɪ/ Verb	to speak or pronounce words, to tell	I want to say I love you.
20.	**Goodbye** /ˌgʊdˈbaɪ/ Exclamation	used when someone leaves, bye-bye, ciao, adios	Say goodbye.
21.	**Or** /ɔːr/ Conjunction	used to connect different possibilities, either…… or	Is the tea cold or warm?
22.	**To see** /siː/ Verb	to look at something, to notice	I want to see you.
23.	**Eye** /aɪ/ Noun	one of the pair of organs of seeing in the faces of humans and animals, eyeball	Dracula's eyes are red.
24.	**To rain** /reɪn/ Verb	drops of water that fall from clouds, drizzle	It will rain tomorrow.
25.	**And** /ən/, /ənd/ Conjunction	in addition to; also, plus	You are sweet and lovely.
26.	**Darling** /ˈdɑːrlɪŋ/ Noun	a person who is very much loved or liked, sweetheart, sweetie, baby, dear	My darling, you are so beautiful.
27.	**can't** /kænt/ Modal verb	contraction of cannot, to not be able to	I can't live without you.
28.	**To Live** /lɪv/ Verb	to be alive or have life, or to continue in this state, get along	I can't live without her.
29.	**To Look** /lʊk/ Verb	to direct your eyes in order to see, to see	He looked at his girlfriend.
30.	**love** /lʌv/ Noun	the feeling of liking, sweetheart	She is my love.
31.	**Road** /rəʊd/ Noun	a route for traveling between places, avenue, lane	This road is a dead end.
32.	**dead-end** /ˌded ˈend/ Noun	a road or path that has one way out, impasse	That road is a dead end.

33.	**Without** /wɪˈðaʊt/ **Preposition**	not having or doing, in the absence of	Love is a dead-end road without you.
34.	**You** /juː/ **Pronoun**	the person or people spoken to	love road is a dead end without you.
35.	**no way** /nəʊ weɪ/ **Expression**	no or not in any way; used to tell someone that something is impossible	There is no way to be happy when you are not here.
36.	**I** /aɪ/ **Pronoun**	the person speaking	I am crazy about you.
37.	**Am** /əm/, /æm/ **To be verb**	(used with I) be	I am crazy about him.
38.	**So** /səʊ/ **Adverb**	to such a great degree; truly, very	You are so in love.
39.	**attached to somebody** /əˈtætʃt/ **Adjective**	feeling emotional close to, or loving; to like someone or something very much	I am very attached to her.
40.	**To Care about** /ker əˈbaʊt/ **Phrasal verb**	to feel that something is important and to feel interested in it or upset about it, love	He is only doing this because he cares about (= love) you.
41.	**Shattered** /ˈʃætərd/ **Adjective**	broken into very small pieces, extremely upset	My dreams are shattered.
42.	**Broken** /ˈbrəʊkən/ **Adjective**	suffering emotional pain usually as a result of an unpleasant event	Your lies have broken my heart.
43.	**Tree** /triː/ **Noun**	A tall plant	An oak tree is so strong.
44.	**Still** /stɪl/ **Adjective**	not moving; staying in the same position, quiet, calm, silence	The sea is still.
45.	**Silent** /ˈsaɪlənt/ **Adjective**	completely quiet; without any sound, mute	The empty room was completely silent.
46.	**For** /fər/ **Preposition**	Because, for the sake of	I am waiting for you.

47.	**to reach** **/riːtʃ/** **Verb**	to arrive somewhere, to come to	I am waiting for you to reach me.
48.	**Now** **/naʊ/** **Adverb**	at the present time, at this moment	Now it is the time to sing.
49.	**It's (It is)** **/ɪtz/** **Pronoun**	used to talk about the time, date, weather, or distances	It's the 25th of March. It's 9 o'clock. It's cold. It's a mile to my house.
50.	**New** **/nuː/** **Adjective**	different from one that existed earlier, novel	It is the new year. Happy new year!
51.	**Year** **/jɪr/** **Noun**	any period of twelve months	Is it the start of the new year?!
52.	**Time** **/taɪm/** **Noun**	the seconds, minutes, hours, days, weeks, months, years, etc., in which existence is measured	It is the time to learn.
53.	**Me** **/mi/** **Pronoun**	the person speaking; the objective form of I	Sweetie, come back to me.
54.	**Your** **/jʊr/** **Pronoun**	the possessive form of you, owned by you	Your love is important to me.
55.	**As** **/az/** **Proposition**	used to describe the purpose	You are the best.
56.	**Gift** **/gɪft/** **Noun**	something that is given, esp. to show your affection, a present	Your love is the best gift.
57.	**To bring** **/brɪŋ/** **Verb**	to take or carry someone or something to a place or a person, to carry	Should I bring a dish to the party?
58.	**Longing** **/ˈlɔːŋɪŋ/** **noun**	a feeling of wanting something or someone very much; a strong desire, a wish, craving	Her eyes were full of longing.
59.	**Christmas** **/ˈkrɪsməs gɪft/** **noun**	December 25th, a day celebrated each year to honor the birth of Christ (Noel)	When is Christmas?

Chapter 6

Section 1: Yoga Posture: Warrior

Yoga Posture: Warrior (Asana: Virabhadrasana)
Vira: bravery, courage; Bhadra: blessed, auspicious; Asana: Posture

When the lies, fear and negative energies in life find their way into your head and discourage you, do not give up. Turn it around, fight back, defeat them and show them you are a warrior!

Mythology of Virabhadrasana

This glorious standing pose is taken from the great hero warrior Virabhadra from Hindu mythology. This is an active posture that requires strength, steadiness, and a fierce determination to hold with integrity. We practice this pose not to condone violence but to honor our fight against our own ignorance and ego and to cultivate strength and courage to do the right thing under difficult circumstances.

The warrior Virabhadra was created by Shiva, one of the major Hindu Gods, to avenge the death of his beloved wife, Sati. Daksha, Sati's father, did not approve of her marriage to Shiva, so when Daksha decided to hold a huge festival, he did not invite Shiva or Sati. Sati was hurt by this snub and her father's refusal to accept her marriage, and she decided to go to the festival and confront him. Daksha asked why she was there since she was not invited, and he rudely asked if she had finally come to her senses and left that "wild animal of a husband." Sati was saddened and humiliated and decided to end her own life, not wanting to be associated with her father anymore. She throws herself into the sacrificial fires of the festival, and her body bursts into flames. When Shiva heard the news of his wife's death, he was at first devastated, then enraged. In a fury, he tore out one of his dreadlocks and threw it to the ground. Virabhadra was created, springing up from the energy released by the ferociously thrown dreadlock. "*Vira*" means "Hero," and "*Bhadra*" means "Auspicious." Virabhadrasana (Warrior) represents Virabhadra as he emerges up from under the ground, arms reaching up and gazing upwards (Karen, H.C, 2015).

Connections to the lesson

In this Part, Natalia feels devastated when she finds out about Garcia's lies, but she never gives up, and she starts to do some critical thinking (asking Aristotle's WH questions) and fighting not to repeat past mistakes. In this chapter, the author likens Natalia's personality to Virabhadrasana (Warrior), which represents Virabhadra as he emerges up from under the ground, arms reaching up, holding the critical thinking ball, and gazing upwards. Natalia gets angry and talks to her father. Then she is ready to fight. She calls the police to take her rights back.

Cautionary notes

- If you have a persistent circulatory or heart issue or high/low blood pressure, please consult your physicians.

- Avoid holding the posture for a long period of time, and do not raise your hands above your shoulder.

Yogic Breathing: Dirgha Pranayama

Meaning: Prana: air; life force; Yama: to restrain or hold back

Potential effects

Enhancement of complete and full breathing, decreasing stress and tension while calming the mind and the body, helping the lungs remain healthy by increasing the oxygen flow to the blood, it massages the abdominal organs, facilitating digestion, preparing you for a better learning experience.

Three Breathing Steps: (Visit website to listen)

1- Sit up straight with your shoulders back and down with relaxed abdominals.

2- Relax the face, close your mouth, and place your hands on your belly.

3- Breathe into your belly and feel it expands like a balloon. Repeat several times.

4- Now, put your hands to the sides of your rib cage and breathe into them, feeling the rib cage expand, and repeat several times.

5- Put your fingertips on your upper chest. Breathe into it and feel your hands lifting. Repeat several times.

6- Now, make a complete inhalation. As you are inhaling, feel the expansions of your belly, rib cage, and chest, and as you are exhaling, you feel the contractions of all three. Repeat this series several times (Refer to Figure 1 in Chapter 1).

Next, move into the warmup, which is the next section.

Warm-up: Standing Lunge (Visit website to listen)

- Stand tall with your feet hip-width apart. Keep your torso long and straight. Soften your shoulders back and down.

- On an inhale, step forward with one leg, lowering your hips until both knees are bent at about a 90-degree angle. Your front knee should be above your ankle. Do not let your back knee touch the floor. Keep the weight on your heels as you push back up to the starting position. Rest and try it on the other side (Figure 1).

Figure 1: Standing Lung

Posture steps for Warrior (Virabhadrasana): (Visit website to listen)

1- Stand tall with your feet hip-width apart, inhale, and as you exhale, step back with your left foot, about 3 to 4 feet. Bend your right knee and lower your hips. Be sure that the knee is stacked directly over the ankle. Align your feet so that they are hip width apart.

2- Square your hips and, on an inhale, lengthen your waist and raise your arms up to the sky into a V position. Roll your shoulders back and down and arch your upper back slightly. Ensure that your neck is aligned with the rest of your back. Hold the pose for a few seconds.

3- To release, on an exhale, lower your arms and step forward. Feel the difference of Virabadrasana/the Warrior pose and repeat on the other side (Figure 2).

1   2   3

Figure 2: Warrior 1

Section 2: Music and Lyrics: Liar

Part 1: Listening (Stage 1,2 and 3), (Visit website to listen)

Stage 1- (Listening for fun) Listen to the song several times, pat your feet, move your body, and enjoy the music! Do not worry about the meaning of the words yet!!!

Stage 2- (Attentive listening) Listen carefully several times to understand the lyrics.

Stage 3- (Listening and guessing) listen and read the lyrics several times to understand the lyrics. Try to guess the meaning of the words you do not know and understand. Do not look at the vocabulary list just yet. Listen to the lyrics again and guess the meaning of the words you do not know. Write down the words you do not know.

Guess words:

....

....

....

....

Part 2: Listening & Reading Lyrics (Stage 4, 5, 6, and 7)

SOS help, help 911

He has cheated me lied to me

it's over I am done

I got a phobia from his lies

Do something for me guys

911 my heart is on fire

It's burning (2) he is a liar (2)

Wanted, wanted by police

These lies have surely got to cease

This liar looks cute and chic

But he's nothing except slick

This liar is now in prison

Because of his lies and treasons

Stage 4- (Confirmation of guessing) Look at the vocabulary table to make sure that you know the meaning and the Part of speech of all the words in the lyrics.

Stage 5- (Humming) Now that you know the meaning of the whole song, listen to the music and hum along with the song several times.

Stage 6- (**Karaoke**) See the lyrics on the monitor and sing.

Stage 7- (Mastery) Listen to the music without any lyrics and sing away. Sing, Dance, and Enjoy!

Section 3: Reading a Short Story: Liar

Pre-Reading activity

a. **Listening and taking notes: (Visit website to listen)**

Please listen to the story and write down what you have understood.

……………………………………………………………………………………………………

……………………………………………………………………………………………………

……………………………………………………………………………………………………

……………………………………………………………………………………………………

……………………………………………………………………………………………………

b. Reading and Guessing

Please read the short story below, guess at the missing words and fill in the blanks.

"Liar"

Four months have passed, and Garcia has not returned from China. Garcia and Natalia have been in (1) …………………… through WhatsApp and FaceTime. Slowly, Garcia has become less interested in talking to Natalia. One day Natalia is (2) …………… Facebook, and suddenly she sees pictures of Garcia taken from an English-language newspaper in China. It is a story of a young businessman from America who has fallen in love with his Chinese nurse. The story received a lot of likes on Facebook because of the (3) …………… and positive (4) …………… of Covid-19. Natalia is UMSSAD ((5) ………., mad, sad, (6) …………., angry, and (7) ……………). She does not know what to do. Three months have passed, and she has been trying to get in touch with Garcia, but no reply from him. At that time, she receives an (8) …………… Facebook message sent by Li, the Chinese nurse who befriended Garcia in China. The nurse explains that she listened to the "waiting and waiting" song that Natalia sang on Facebook, and she loved the lyrics and (9) …………… that it was a gift to Garcia. Then she explains how (10) ………… and (11) ……………… she was because Garcia betrayed her. He (12) …………… to marry her and took her money and (13) ……………. .

When Natalia hears the story from the Chinese nurse, she becomes angry, but she tries to stay strong and put the anger aside. She starts to find her way to becoming a warrior. She begins to think (14) ……………. and asks the following questions: "Who can help me? How can I get (15) ………….? Why did this happen to me? When and where did I make a mistake? Should I call 911?". She sits down, talks to her dad, and tells him the whole story. Her dad is so (16) …………… and tells her, "I am sorry daughter that this jerk hurt you. I will do everything to support you.". They (17) ……………. that Garcia is an (18) …………… who has betrayed Natalia and the nurse in China. They decide to call the police because Natalia wants justice. She calls 911 and tells the police that she has been (19) ……………. and she knows of at least one other woman who has been swindled by Garcia. When Garcia returns from Wuhan to Logan International Airport, he is immediately (20) ……………. by the police. Now he is in (21) …………. and waiting for his (22) …………...

c. 🎧 **Listening and Checking your Guessing (Visit website to listen)**

Please read and listen to the short story. While you are listening, please check to see if the guesses you have made are correct. If your guess was not correct, please make a change and fill in the blanks. Then check your [123]answers in the footnotes.

d. **Clearing up all confusions**

---

[123] 1- communication: connection, 2- browsing: looking through, 3- reversed: the opposite, 4- effects: result of an influence, 5- upset: angry, 6- shocked: surprised or upset, 7- disappointed: desperate/ unhappy, 8- private: only for one person, 9- discovered: found information, 10- hurt: to feel emotional pain, 11- devastated: completely destroyed, 12- promised: said that he will certainly, 13- disappeared: got absent, 14- critically: to show that you have thought seriously about it, considering what is good and what is bad about it, 15- justice: fairness, 16- supportive: giving help and encouragement, 17- recognize: know, 18- criminal: someone who commits a crime, 19- swindled: got money dishonestly from Natalia by deceiving or cheating her, 20- arrested: taken away by police to be questioned about the crime, 21- prison: jail, 22- trial: the examination in a court of law of the facts of a case to decide whether a person is guilty of a crime

Please read the short story by yourself without listening to it. Highlight or underline the parts that are unclear to you in the story above. Use your dictionary or a partner to clarify highlighted parts. Write your notes below for further review.

………..

………...

………..

………...

e. Reading Comprehension based on the "WH Questions."

Look below for the boxes and read the questions (Q) and answers(A). While you are reading the questions, answer by filling in the blank with the "WH questions" (who, when, where, what, why, and how). Choose the answers that are the best fit. You do not have to use all the "WH questions." Notice that the title of the reading is in the middle of a circle, and the questions pivot around the title of the story in the figure. Both questions and answers are provided, and you only need to put the correct "wh question" in the blank.

- After you have finished filling in the blanks below, practice asking and answering the questions

 - Check your answers with the [124]answers key in the footnote.

---

[124]Answer Key: 1. When 2. why, 3. where 4. who 5. what, 6. how

                                    www.ez-model.com

Who? | When? | Where? | What? | Why? | How?

1- Q: ……. did Garcia stop communicating with Natalia?

A: Over four months, slowly Garcia has become less interested in talking to Natalia.

2- Q: …………. is Natalia shocked, angry, and upset with Garcia?

A: Because Natalia discovers that she has been deceived and betrayed by Garcia.

6- Q: ………... did Natalia discover Garcia's betrayal?

A: She discovered it on Facebook.

Liar

3- Q: …………. is Garcia now?

A: He is in prison.

4- Q: ………… told Natalia that Garcia was a liar?

A: Li, the Chinese nurse told Natalia.

5- Q: ………. did Natalia do after she received the message from the Chinese nurse?

A: Natalia gets angry, she immediately calls 911 and tells the police that she has been swindled.

Section 4: Syntax Notes: WH questions, Embedded questions

Example from a line in the lyrics:

Example 1: "When did your betrayals begin?"

Example 2: "Where did you betray me?(Who, how,…)"

Warm-up questions: What do you think the syntax point is about? Please Explain. Please Explain.

……………………………………………………………………………………………………

....

How to form a question:

Normal English sentence structure: Subject + Verb + Object (SVO)

I = subject, have = verb, a headache = object

What is a wh question? A WH question begins with WH words (what, when, where, how, who, why). Each of the questions is a request for specific information.

How to form a Wh question:

What= Question word, do = auxiliary verb, I = subject, have = main verb

WH question + Auxiliary Verb (do, does, did,..) + Subject + Main Verb (+ Object) or VSVO.

More examples:

No.	WH questions	Definition	Example
1	**what?** /wʌt/ **determiner, pronoun, exclamation**	used to ask for information about people or things	"What is the problem?" "He/She tells lie."
2	**why?** /waɪ/ **adverb**	for what reason	"Why does he/she tell lie?" "To hurt you."
3	**where?** /wer/ **adverb**	to, at, or in what place	"Where is he?" "He is in prison."
4	**How?** /haʊ/	what methods	"How did Natalia solve the problem?" "She called 911."
5	**who?** /huː/ **Pronoun**	used especially in questions as the subject or object of a verb, when asking which person or people, or when asking what someone's name is	"Who is angry?" "Natalia is angry."
6	**when?** /wen/ **adverb**	at what time; at the time at which	"When did Natalia get angry?" "After he lied to her."

Write a real-life example of the use of syntax point above in a sentence below.

……

Syntax Note 3: Embedded questions

Example from a line in the lyrics: "I wonder why you told me lie."

Warm-up questions: What do you think the syntax point is about? Please Explain. Please Explain.

……………………………………………………………………………………………………

……………………………………………………………………………………………………

Embedded questions: a question that is inside another statement

As you can see, the embedded question in the example above is not following a normal WH question pattern that you learned in the syntax note above. In other words, you use the normal subject+verb+object pattern when you use introductory phrases such as (I wonder, I gotta know, I wanna know, tell me, I don't know…). Embedded questions are used to show more politeness or being more indirect when we ask a question.

Another example from a line in the lyrics: "I gotta know when your lies begin."

If you say I gotta know when did your lies begin is awkward.

Write a real-life example of the use of syntax point above in a sentence below.

I wonder …………………………………………………………………………………

I Gott know…………………………………………………………………………………

I don't know …………………………………………………………………………………..

Section 5: Museum of Reincarnation: Hatshepsut

Wikipedia contributors. *Hatshepsut*

Stage 1. Completing the vocabulary list

Before going to the museum, please complete the vocabulary list below.

No.	Vocabulary	Meaning
1.	Wonder	
2.	Gotta know	
3.	Lies	
4.	Betrayals	
5.	Guys	
6.	Treasons	
7.	Burning	
8.	Phobia	

9.	**I don't care**	
10.	**Dead**	
11.	**Except**	

Stage 2. 🎧 **The Biography part of the museum, listening and taking notes (Visit website to listen)**

Who is the famous person? Why is the person famous?

…………………………………………………………………………………………………

…………………………………………………………………………………………………

…………………………………………………………………………………………………

Stage 3. Reincarnation with the famous person (Vocabulary part). (Visit website to listen)

a. 🎧 **Watching and Listening. (Visit website to listen)**

b. Watching, listening carefully, and writing down the usage of the words by the famous person.

c. Identifying the parts of speech.

d. Writing your own sentences using the vocabulary words and the syntax notes.

		a. Watching and Listening
No.	**Vocabulary**	**b. Sentences with the vocabulary word used by the famous person**
		c. Part of speech
		d. Sentences with the vocabulary word used by you

1	Wonder	b. Sentences by the famous person: ……………………………… ……………………………………………………………………… c. Part of speech: …………… d. Your sentence: ………………………………………………….. ………………………………………………………………………
2	Gotta know	b. Sentences by the famous person: ……………………………… ……………………………………………………………………… c. Part of speech: …………… d. Your sentence: ………………………………………………….. ………………………………………………………………………
3	Lies	b. Sentences by the famous person: ……………………………… ……………………………………………………………………… c. Part of speech: …………… d. Your sentence: ………………………………………………….. ………………………………………………………………………
4	Betrayals	b. Sentences by the famous person: ……………………………… ……………………………………………………………………… c. Part of speech: …………… d. Your sentence: ………………………………………………….. ………………………………………………………………………
5	Guys	b. Sentences by the famous person: ……………………………… ……………………………………………………………………… c. Part of speech: ……………

		d. Your sentence: …………………………………………….. ………………………………………………………………………
6	Treasons	b. Sentences by the famous person: ………………………………… ………………………………………………………………………
		c. Part of speech: ……………
		d. Your sentence: …………………………………………….. ………………………………………………………………………
7	Burning	b. Sentences by the famous person: ………………………………… ………………………………………………………………………
		c. Part of speech: ……………
		d. Your sentence: …………………………………………….. ………………………………………………………………………
8	Phobia	b. Sentences by the famous person: ………………………………… ………………………………………………………………………
		c. Part of speech: ……………
		d. Your sentence: …………………………………………….. ………………………………………………………………………
9	I don't care	b. Sentences by the famous person: ………………………………… ………………………………………………………………………
		c. Part of speech: ……………
		d. Your sentence: …………………………………………….. ………………………………………………………………………
10		b. Sentences by the famous person: …………………………………

	Dead	…………………………………………………………………………… c. Part of speech: ……………. d. Your sentence: ………………………………………………….. ……………………………………………………………………………
11	Except	b. Sentences by the famous person: ……………………………………… …………………………………………………………………………… c. Part of speech: ……………. d. Your sentence: ……………………………………………………….. ……………………………………………………………………………

Section 6: Conversation Creation; Developing a Relationship

a. Choosing a Topic

Choose one of the following potential topics and participants related to the short story/lyrics of the lesson.

Topic 1: A critical thinking Conversation with Garcia, Participant: Natalia talking to herself

Topic 2: Garcia betrayed me, too, Participants: Natalia and the Chinese Nurse, Li. (A chat on Facebook)

Topic 3: A critical thinking conversation with Dad, participants: Natalia and Dad

Topic 4: Reporting a crime, Participantes: Natalia and 911

b. Conversation Creation

After choosing your topic, create your conversation in the space below.

Note: There are four models of conversations in the endnotes to this chapter. You can look at the models and use or modify the conversation you have created. When you are creating your conversation, you should use the new syntax notes and some of the listed vocabularies.

Topic of Your Conversation:

Participants:

....

....

....

....

....

....

....

....

....

c. Role-playing

Practice and role-play the conversation with your partner, friend, brother/sister, or even with yourself in front of the mirror. The purpose of role-playing is to become comfortable using the language in a casual and conversational way.

Note: Role-play the other conversations in the endnotes for additional practice. Feel free to change the language as you see fit.

Section 7: Cultural Notes: Critical Thinking and Feeling of Justice

Hints: Aristotle's "wh questions" and an agricultural justice seeker

a. Warm-Up (Brainstorming)

Please look at the topic above and guess what the cultural Notes are about.

....

....

....

....

b. Reading: Cesar Estrada Chavez

Read the following cultural points. If you do not know a word or phrase, please use the guessing strategy (guess the meaning of the words based on the context) and use a dictionary when necessary.

Definition of lying: It is a clear decision made by a person to not tell the truth. All cultures and religions value honesty. Every culture judges lying as being wrong and truth as right.

Garcia is a liar! He made a choice not to tell Natalia the truth. Garcia did two things wrong: he lied to Natalia, and he also took her money. Lying is wrong and immoral. Taking her money is also immoral and a crime punishable by a jail sentence.
How do we know that someone is lying and immoral? An immoral act is an act that a culture agrees is wrong.

The Greek philosopher, Aristotle, gave us a way of telling right from wrong. You can tell if something is right or wrong by the feeling. You should ask yourself, "Is this right or

wrong?"; Life is complicated, and Aristotle devised critical thinking questions to help us decide if an act is right or wrong. His critical thinking questions were: (what happened, who did it, when, where, how, and why?); Over the centuries, these questions were adopted by the courts to determine if the testimony was truthful. If you ask the question why, what happened, who, where, when, and how the action was performed, we have enough information to judge if the person is telling the truth.

https://www.loc.gov/item/2016646413/

Cesar Estrada Chavez (1927-1993)

The civil rights leader Cezar Chavez says that right and wrong are something that you can see and feel. When he saw agricultural workers doing backbreaking work in the sun for low wages and no health care, he knew this was wrong.

Cesar Chavez is a critical cultural thinker who was a labor organizer, a leader, and a civil rights activist who transformed the lives and opportunities of tens of thousands of Mexican and Mexican American agricultural workers who labored in the fields of the west, southwest, and throughout the United States. Agricultural labor is backbreaking, hot, dirty work performed by immigrants and poor people. Cesar was introduced to injustice at a young age when his father was swindled out of the family land, and the family was forced to move from Yuma, Arizona, to San Jose, California. When his dad was injured in an auto accident, Cesar quit school and went to work in the grape vineyards. He was UMSSAD at the conditions in the fields, and he set out to organize the workers to get better wages and working conditions. His work was groundbreaking because no one had dared to organize agricultural workers before. After much struggle, he was successful, and today farm workers have much improved wages and working conditions because of this courageous and determined leader.

Cesar Chavez gives us a different way of critical thinking. He looked at the world, and he trusted his feelings to tell him right from wrong. Like Cesar Chavez, you can trust your feelings and your ability to tell right from wrong.

c. SPARCing the Cultural Notes

Using the information above, please complete the SPARC (Setting, Participant, Activities, Reasons, and Conclusion).

- Setting (when and where): …………………………………………………………………..
- Participants (who): …………………………………………………………………….
- Activities (how did they get there):

    …………………………………………………………………………………………….
- Reasons (why are they successful):

    …………………………………………………………………………………………..
- Conclusion (what is your SPARC):

    ……………………………………………………………………………………………

    ……………………………………………………………………………………………

Section 8: Creative Story/Lyrics Writing

Based on all the points you have learned in this chapter (Yoga (Mountain), vocabularies, grammar, lyrics, Museum of Reincarnation, conversations), follow the steps below:

Stage 1: Brainstorming/ SPARCing

Insert the title of your story/lyrics in the middle of the figure below and then fill in the other boxes about the participants in your story(who), the setting (when and where), the activities of your story (how), the reasons for your story (why), and the conclusion to your story (what).

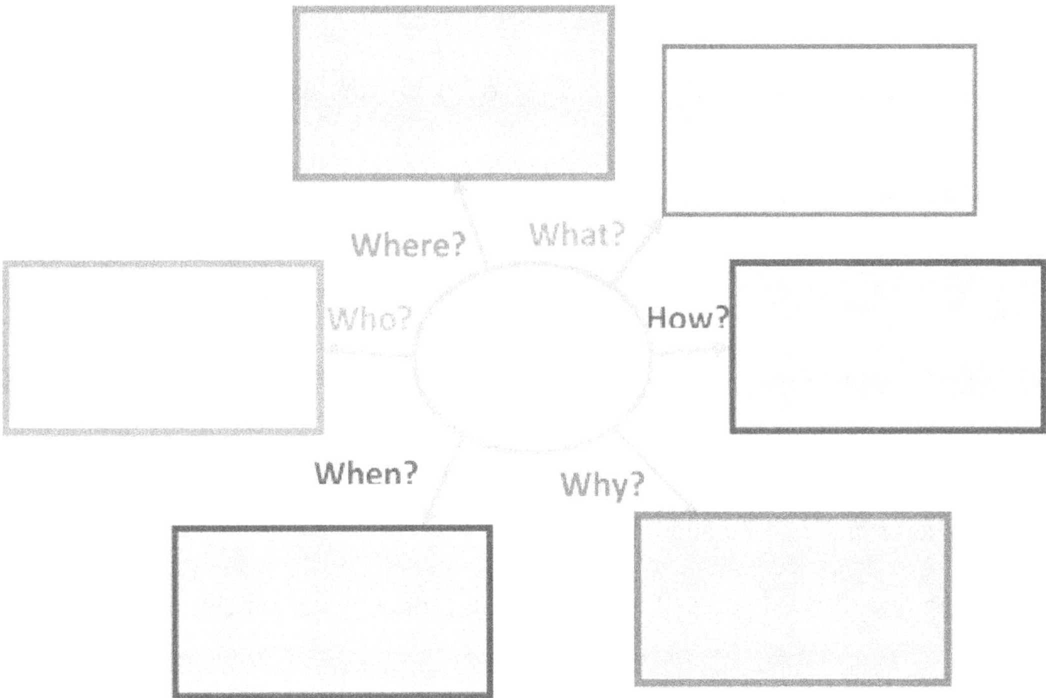

Stage 2- Writing Your Story/Lyrics

Now in the box below, write your story/ lyrics (Your story/lyrics can be rap, rhyming, etc., Be creative and let your imagination be your limit)

The Title of Your Story/Lyric: ……………………

………………………………………………………………………………………………

………………………………………………………………………………………………

………………………………………………………………………………………………

………………………………………………………………………………………………

………………………………………………………………………………………………

………………………………………………………………………………………………

Stage 3. Getting Feedback: Check your story/ lyrics with your teachers/parents/mentors to get feedback

Stage 4. Applying Music: Either apply your story/lyrics on the karaoke track of the song or click on the beat's website, such as https://www.8notes.com/metronome/. Choose the right beat for your story/lyrics. Even if you play a musical instrument, apply your writing to your playing. Don't limit yourself and be creative.

Stage 5. Singing: Practice, sing and enjoy!

Stage 6. Recording. Record yourself and share your product with someone else to get feedback, and revise if necessary.

Stage 7. Posting your creation.

Section 9: Quick Quiz

The quiz in this section is designed to help you review and remember the materials you have learned. The answer key is always provided in the footnotes. If you have any doubts about the correct answer, please check the footnotes.

Please answer the questions below and check your answers in the [125]answer key in the footnote.

a. Vocabulary: What is the Part of speech and synonym of the **Bolded** vocabulary?

1- Natalia has no real desire to travel by airplane and suffers from a **phobia** of flying.

   a. Noun: slick   b. Adjective: dangerous   c. Noun: fire   d. adjective: fear

2- I don't love him anymore because he is not honest with me. He **lied** to me.

   a. Verb: mislead   b. Adjective: loved   c. Verb: called   d. Verb: looked

3- She **dumped** her boyfriend.

   a. Verb: started the romantic relationship   b. Verb: began the romantic relationship

   c. Verb: ended the romantic relationship   d. Adjective: thought about the romantic relationship

4- They **wonder** when the police came.

   a. Verb: know   b. Adverb: guess   c. Verb: question   d. Verb: tell

5- You are a liar, and you **betrayed** me.

   b. Verb: You committed a treason   b. Verb: You committed a crime

   c. Adjective: You went to prison   d. Adjective: you reasoned

   d. Syntax: Which is the best way for an English speaker to express herself/himself?

6- When ………….?

   a. did his lies began?

   b. did his lies begin?

---

[125] Answer Key
1- D, 2- a, 3- c, 4- c, 5- a, 6- b, 7- b, 8- T, 9- F, 10- F

    c. did his lies beginning.

    d. his lies began.

7- I wonder……………..

    a. where did you see her.

    b. where you saw her.

    c. where did you saw her.

    d. did where you see her.

c. Culture: Based on the Cultural Note, decide which sentence is true (T) and which one is false (F)?

8- All cultures and religions value honesty.

9- The Greek philosopher, Einstein, gave us a way of telling right from wrong.

10- Cesar Chavez is a critical cultural thinker who was an art organizer, a singer, and a civil rights activist.

Section 10: Endnotes

Museum Transcripts

a. Biography of Hatshepsut

Hatshepsut (1507–1458 BC) was the fifth [126]pharaoh of the Eighteenth Dynasty of Egypt. she was the longest-reigning female pharaoh in Egypt, ruling for 20 years in the 15th century B.C. She is considered one of the most successful pharaohs.

According to American [127]archeologist and Egyptologist James Henry Breasted, she is also known as "the first great woman in the history of whom we are informed." Under her reign,

---

[126] (The title of) a king of ancient Egypt
[127] someone who studies the buildings, graves, tools, and other objects of people who lived in the past

Egypt [128]prospered. she was more interested in ensuring economic prosperity and building and restoring [129]monuments throughout Egypt rather than in [130]conquering new lands.

An attempt was made to remove all traces of Hatshepsut's rule. Her statues were torn down, her monuments were defaced, and her name was removed from the official king's list (Green, 2014). Why was the history of Hatshepsut's reign erased from Egyptian history? The reason for her removal was the fact that she was a woman. Her success was against the traditions of male supremacy.

b. Quotations

"I wonder why the men of my land could not accept the rule of a woman?" "You got to know I was a woman warrior" "When they destroyed my statues, they lied to the world about history. It was a betrayal to the world. No doubt that those guys committed treasons. I wanna show the truth to the world. Destroying and burning my statues does not burn my heart and my soul because "I have done things according to the design of my heart." Put aside your phobias and fears. Women are leaders, too. "I have commanded that my title abide like the mountains; when the sun shines, its rays shine brightly upon my majesty;" I don't care that "my name was removed from the official king list" because now my good work is shining in the history of the world. I am not dead; you destroyed my statue and everything except my majesty. I don't know what the future holds, and I wonder if people will one day understand women are the equals of men.

1- Quotes taken from Hatshepsut, wikiquotes, 2- Paraphrased Quotations

---

[128] Became successful
[129] a structure or building that is built to honor a special person or event
[130] Taking control

2. Wonder: "I wonder why the men of my land could not accept the rule of a woman?"

3. Gotta know: "You gotta know I was a woman warrior."

4. Lies and Betrayals: "When they destroyed my statues, you lied to the world about history. It was a betrayal to the world.

5. Guys and Treasons: No doubt that those guys committed treasons. I wanna show the truth to the world.

6. Burning: "I have done things according to the design of my heart." Destroying and burning my statues does not burn my heart and my soul.

7. Phobia: Put aside your phobias and fears. Women are leaders, too.

8. "I have commanded that my title abide like the mountains; when the sun shines its rays bright upon my majesty;."

9. I don't care I don't care that "my name was removed from the official king list" because now my good work is shining in the history of the world.

10. Dead and Except: I am not dead; you destroyed my statue and everything except my majesty.

11. Wonder: I don't know what the future holds, and I wonder if people will understand women are the equals of men.

Conversations

Model 1.

Topic: Garcia betrayed me, too. Participants: Natalia and the Chinese Nurse, Li. (A chat on Facebook)

Li: Hi Natalia, my name is Li. I came upon your Facebook page and heard your song. I love your song. I am the nurse who befriended Garcia. I discovered that this song was a Christmas gift to Garcia.

Natalia: Hi Li, thanks for liking my song. I am really UMSSAD with him.

Li: Natalia, he dumped me too. He got all my money and disappeared.

Natalia: Oh, my god, I cannot believe it.

Li: I am so hurt and disappointed.

Natalia: Ok, He is a liar, a fraud, a criminal.

Li: We should report this criminal. I know that he has a return ticket to the US for this weekend.

Natalia: Thanks for reaching out to me. I will do something.

Model 2.

Topic: An Imaginary Conversation (using Critical Thinking Questions) with Garcia, Participant: Natalia talking to herself

Natalia: I wonder *why* you lied to me.

Garcia: I did not mean to hurt you.

Natalia: I gotta know *who* cares about you more than me?

Garcia: Nobody

Natalia: I wanna know *when* you stopped loving me.

Garcia: Of course, I never stopped loving you.

Natalia: Let me know *where* you betrayed me.

Garcia: Nowhere, that story on Facebook is fake news.

Natalia: I wanna know *how* you could give me this heartache. No way, I wanna say goodbye.

W*hat* is the last thing you wanna say?

García: No, listen to me. I still care about you.

Natalia: Stop it. Oh my god, I cannot believe you are still lying.

Garcia: Oh, Come on. You are treating me like I have done a treason or crime.

Natalia: Of course, you did. You are nothing except a liar. You are dead to me

Model 3.

Topic 3: A critical thinking conversation with Dad, participants: Natalia and Dad

She begins to think critically and asks the following questions: "Who can help me? How can I get justice? Why did this happen to me? When and where did I make a mistake? She decides to talk to her dad.

Natalia: Dad, I want to have a heart-to-heart talk with you.

Dad: My daughter, how can I help?

Natalia: Dad, I am heartbroken. Garcia took my money and betrayed me.

Dad: I am sorry, baby, that this jerk hurt you. I will do everything to support you.

Natalia: Dad, I want justice. What can I do?

Dad: Let us think about it. We need to start by calling the police. When you call the police, they will ask you some questions: what happened? who did it? Where and when did it happen?

Natalia: Dad, I understand, and I am going to call the police.

Dad: My dear daughter, you are strong, and you can do this and find justice. I will always support you.

Natalia: Thank you, dad. I am going to do it now.

Model 4.

Topic: Reporting a crime. Participants: Natalia and 911

911: 911, how may I help you?

Natalia: Hi, I would like to report a crime.

911: Ok, tell me what happened. Who is this person, and when and where did the crime take place?

Natalia: This person who swindled another woman and me is coming back from China and arriving at Logan airport this weekend.

911: Yes, mam, you will have to file formal charges against this person and tell us the crimes that he has committed.

Natalia: Ok, thank you, I will come to the police department to file the charges.

Vocabulary list as a resource

Vocabulary No.	Vocabulary		
	Pronunciation Part of speech in the song	Meaning (synonym)	Example in sentence
1.	**Liar** /ˈlaɪər/ **Noun**	someone who tells lies, deceiver	You are a liar - I can't trust you.
2.	**Wonder** /ˈwʌndər/ **Verb**	- to ask yourself questions or express a wish to know about something, question - used in phrases at the beginning of a request to make it more formal and polite	- I wonder why you lied to me. - I wonder if you can help me.
3.	**what** /wʌt/ **determiner, pronoun, exclamation**	used to ask for information about people or things	What is your name?
4.	**Reason** /ˈriːzn/ **Noun**	the cause of an event or situation or something that provides an excuse or explanation	She has a reason for calling the police.
5.	**For** /fər/ **Preposition**	intended to be given to	This is a gift for you.
6.	**All** /ɔːl/ **determiner**	everyone (of), the complete amount or number (of)	All five women are hard workers.

	Word	Meaning	Example
7.	**Treason** /ˈtriːzn/ Noun	the crime of doing something that could cause danger to your country (in this song, it means causing a danger to a loved one: betrayal)	Those people see treason everywhere.
8.	**Why** /waɪ/ Adverb	for what reason, cause	Why did you lie to me?
9.	**To tell** /tel/ Verb	to say something to someone, to say	I want you to tell me the truth.
10.	**To Lie** /laɪ/ Verb	to say something that is not true in order to deceive, mislead	He is lying to me.
11.	**To tell a lie/lies** /tel ə laɪ/ Phrase	to say something/things that are not true	You are always telling lies.
12.	**How** /haʊ/ Adverb	in what way or by what methods	- "How do you know I am lying?" - "I saw you."
13.	**To dump** /dʌmp/ Verb	to suddenly end a romantic relationship	I am going to dump the liar.
14.	**Now** /naʊ/ Adverb	at the present time, this instant	Now, it is the time to dance.
15.	**Gotta** /ˈgɑːtə/ phrase	short form of "have got to" to need to or be forced to, must	I gotta go right now.
16.	**To know** /nəʊ/ Verb	to have information in your mind, to realize	"Do you know what her name is?" "I don't know."
17.	**Who** /huː/ Subject pronoun	which person, which people	Who knows?
18.	**To love** /lʌv/ Verb	to like someone or something very much, admire	I love my mother.
19.	**Way** /weɪ/ Noun	the manner in which someone behaves or thinks	I wonder who loves you the way I do (I love you).
20.	**To Do** /duː/ Verb	perform or have a part in an activity, go on	- "Are you going to sing it?" - "I am going to do it soon."
21.	**When** /wen/	at what time	When will we meet this weekend?

	Adverb		
22.	**Betrayals** /bɪˈtreɪəl/ Noun	the act of not being loyal when other people believe you are loyal	I felt a sense of betrayal when she refused to support me.
23.	**To begin** /bɪˈgɪn/ Verb	to start to happen, to start	I'd like to begin with a simple question.
24.	**Where** /wer/ Adverb	to, at, or in what place, location	- "Where is she?" - "She is at home."
25.	**Maybe** /ˈmeɪbi/ Adverb	used to show that something is possible or that something might be true, perhaps	- "Are you going to dance with me?" - "Maybe!"
26.	**Should** /ʃʊd/ Modal verb	used to say or ask what the best thing is to do, shall	If you're angry with his lies, you should tell him.
27.	**To care** /ker/ Verb	to think that something is important, and you want to protect it, to feel interested in it or upset about it, the process of protecting someone	I care about you.
28.	**Wanna** /ˈwɑːnə/ Short form of want to Verb	short form of "want to" or "want a" Want to: to wish for a particular thing or plan of action.	- "Do you wanna go now?!" - "Ye, it's late. I want to go."
29.	**To say (past tense: said)** /seɪ/ Verb	to tell something to someone, to speak	I want to say goodbye.
30.	**Goodbye** /ˌgʊdˈbaɪ/ Exclamation	used when someone leaves, bye-bye, ciao, adios	Don't say goodbye.
31.	**Cause** /kɔːz/ Conjunction	Because, as	This love is dead cause it is too late.
32.	**This** /ðɪs/ Pronoun	used for a person or thing to show which one is referred to	This guy is a bad guy.
33.	**love** /lʌv/ Noun	the feeling of liking	She is my love.
34.	**Dead** /ded/ Adjective	not now living	He had been dead for about five years now.
35.	**Late** /leɪt/	near the end of a period of time	It was late last night.

	Adjective		
36.	**To have** /həv/ Verb	to own or possess something, accept	I don't have his phone number.
37.	**Headache** /ˈhedeɪk/ Noun	a pain you feel inside your head, feelings of great sadness, suffering	You have caused me to have a headache.
38.	**To call** /kɔːl/ verb	to use a phone to talk to someone	I wanna call him.
39.	**Over** /ˈəʊvər/ Adverb	(especially of an event) finished	I will be sad when the party is over.
40.	**Done** /dʌn/ Adjective	If something is done, or you are done with it, it is finished	I am done with her/him. She/he is a liar.
41.	**SOS** /ˌes əʊ ˈes/ Noun	(Save Our Ship) an urgent request for help, alarm	911, SOS, help
42.	**Help** /help/ Noun	the act of making it possible or easier for someone to do something	I need your help.
43.	**To Cheat** /tʃiːt/ Verb	to behave in a dishonest way in order to get what you want, to deceive	They have cheated me.
44.	**Phobia** /ˈfəʊbiə/ Noun	a strong unreasonable fear of something, fear	I've got a phobia of stink bugs. I suffer from claustrophobia.
45.	**Something** /ˈsʌmθɪŋ/ Pronoun	a thing which is not known or stated, thing	Something is happening.
46.	**For** /fɔːr/ Proposition	to help	Do something for me, guys.
47.	**Guys** /gaɪz/ Plural Noun	used to address a group of people of either sex	Are you guys ready?
48.	**Fire** /ˈfaɪər/ Noun	strong emotion	My heart is on fire.
49.	**Burning** /ˈbɜːrnɪŋ/ Adjective	painful in a way that feels hot, a consuming desire	My heart is burning because of his lies.
50.	**Wanted** /ˈwɑːntɪd/	being searched for by the police because of a crime asked for	He is wanted by the police.

	verb (used with object)		
51.	**Police** /pəˈliːs/ Noun	an officer of the law	I think we should call the police.
52.	**Have got to** /ˈhæv ɡɑːt tə/ modal verb	used to show that you must do something, must	I have got to stop it.
53.	**Surely** /ˈʃʊrli/ Adverb	used to express that you are certain or almost certain about something	I will surely see you today.
54.	**To cease** /siːs/ Verb	to stop an action or condition, quit	They had to cease the process.
55.	**Look** /lʊk/ Verb	to seem or appear to be, sound	He looks very dapper.
56.	**Cute** /kjuːt/ Adjective	Adorable, charming, attractive	You look cute.
57.	**Chic** /ʃiːk/ Adjective	stylish and fashionable, elegant	He looks very chic.
58.	**But** /bʌt/ Preposition	not including, except	This liar has been nothing but trouble.
59.	**Nothing** /ˈnʌθɪŋ/ Pronoun	not anything, nothing	I have nothing to hide.
60.	**Except** /ɪkˈsept/ Preposition	not including, but not	Everyone was at the party except for Sara.
61.	**Slick** /slɪk/ Adjective	done or made in a way that is clever and efficient but often does not seem to be sincere, shrewd	He is slick.
62.	**Prison** /ˈprɪzn/ Noun	a building where criminals are forced to live as a punishment	The liars are in prison.
63.	**Because** /bɪˈkəz/ Conjunction	for the reason that, as, considering	"How are you?" "I am better now because I see you!"

Chapter 7

Section 1: Yoga Posture: Side Warrior

Yoga Posture: Side Warrior (Asana: Parshva Virabhadrasana)
Parshva: side; vira: bravery, courage; Bhadra: blessed, auspicious

Ride the waves of the difficulties and challenges on the sea of life because the higher the waves are, the greater the opportunities of a critical thinker and warrior to change the world!

Mythology of Parshva Virabhadrasana

In the previous warrior pose, when Shiva heard the news of his wife's death, he was devastated, then enraged. In a fury, he tore out one of his dreadlocks and threw it to the ground. Virabahdra was a huge and terrible being, with a thousand arms, three eyes, and wearing a garland of skulls. Virabhadra sprang from the energy of Shiva's dreadlock. Virabhadra was an angry force that killed all the gods at the festival and cut off Daksha's head. But when Shiva saw the bloody aftermath of this battle, his anger left him. The slain gods were miraculously healed, and Shiva replaced Daksha's head with a goat's head. Daksha and the other gods honored Shiva for this, calling him "Shankar,"," the "kind and benevolent one." Side Warrior portrays when Virabhadra drew his sword and sliced off Daksha's head.

In ancient Iranian mythology, a warrior whose name was Arash was a mighty archer. He lived in those days when the army of the Iranian king Manuchehr was defeated in Mazenderan by the king Turan Afrasiab. The Iranian king wanted to protect the country from the Turanians and made an agreement with Afrasiab. According to the agreement, one of the soldiers had to climb up the mountain of Damavand and shoot an arrow into the sky. The place where the arrow falls will be the border between Turan and Iran. King Afrasiab believed that the arrow would not fly far. Early in the morning, Arash the Archer climbed to the highest point of the mountain, pulled the bow, and shot. He put all his strength and love for his homeland into this arrow, and as soon as he shot the arrow, Arash died. His arrow flew for two days and finally fell next to the Amu Darya River on a land that was far from the Iranian border. Thus, the river became the border between Iran and Turan.

Connection to the lesson

In this chapter, Natalia's love is killed by Garcia. First, she became UMSSAD (upset, mad, sad, shocked, angry, and disappointed), then she overcame the emotional challenges and created a website to fight against the harassment of women. She began to teach other women to be strong like a warrior.

Cautionary notes

- If you have a persistent circulatory or heart issue or high/low blood pressure, please consult your physicians.

- Avoid holding the posture for a long period of time, and do not raise your hands above your shoulder.

Yogic Breathing: Dirgha Pranayama

Meaning: Prana: air; life force; Yama: to restrain or hold back

Potential effects

Enhancement of complete and full breathing, decreasing stress and tension while calming the mind and the body, helping the lungs remain healthy by increasing the oxygen flow to the blood, it massages the abdominal organs, facilitating digestion, preparing you for a better learning experience

Three Breathing Steps

1- Sit up straight with your shoulders back and down with relaxed abdominals.

2- Relax the face, close your mouth, and place your hands on your belly.

3- Breathe into your belly and feel it expands like a balloon. Repeat several times.

4- Now, put your hands to the sides of your rib cage and breathe into them, feeling the rib cage expand, and repeat several times.

5- Put your fingertips on your upper chest. Breathe into it and feel your hands lifting. Repeat several times.

6- Now, make a complete inhalation. As you are inhaling, feel the expansions of your belly, rib cage, and chest, and as you are exhaling, you feel the contractions of all three. Repeat this series several times (Refer to Figure 1 in Chapter 1).

Next, move into the warmup, which is the next section.

Warm-up: Standing Lunge (Visit website to listen)

- Stand tall with your feet hip-width apart. Keep your torso long and straight. Soften your shoulders back and down.

- On an inhale, step forward with one leg, lowering your hips until both knees are bent at about a 90-degree angle. Your front knee should be above your ankle. Do not let your back knee touch the floor. Keep the weight on your heels as you push back up to the starting position. Rest and try it on the other side (Figure 1).

-

Figure 1: Standing Lung

Posture steps for Side Warrior (Parshva Virabhadrasana): (Visit website to listen)

1- Stand tall in the mountain pose with your feet hip-width apart and your arms by your side.

2- As you are placing your hands on your hips, on an exhale, step back with your right foot, about one leg's length. Bend your left knee and lower your hips.

3- Rotate your back foot and align the arch of your back foot with the sole of your front foot. Level your hips and keep your left knee over your ankle.

4- Breathe deeply. Lengthen your waist and, on an inhale, lift your arms parallel to the floor, palms facing down. Shoulders back and down. Keep your neck straight and look out over your left shoulder. Hold the pose for a few seconds. Keep breathing.

5- To release on an exhale, lower your hands. Square your hips to the front. Exhale and step forward to Tadasana. Rest and feel the effects of Parshva Virabhadrasana. Repeat on the other side (Figure 2).

Figure 2: Side- Warrior (Parshva-Virabhadrasana)

Section 2: Music and Lyrics: Becoming a Fighter

Part 1: 🎧 **Listening (Stage 1,2 and 3), (Visit website to listen)**

Stage 1- (Listening for fun) Listen to the song several times, pat your feet, move your body, and enjoy the music! Do not worry about the meaning of the words yet!!!

Stage 2- (Attentive listening) Listen carefully several times to understand the lyrics.

Stage 3- (Listening and guessing) listen and read the lyrics several times to understand the lyrics. Try to guess the meaning of the words you do not know and understand. Do not look at the vocabulary list just yet. Listen to the lyrics again and guess at the meaning of the words you do not know. Write down the words you do not know.

Guess words: ………………………………………………………………………………………

………………………………………………………………………………………………………

………………………………………………………………………………………………………

………………………………………………………………………………………………………

………………………………………………………………………………………………………

………………………………………………………………………………………………………

………………………………………………………………………………………………………

………………………………………………………………………………………………………

………………………………………………………………………………………………………

Part 2: Listening & Reading Lyrics (Stage 4, 5, 6, and 7)

Just like a volcano
Ready to erupt you know
Can't put out this brutal fire
Can't forget my wild desire
Tonight
I can't help thinking
My damn mind is freaking
My beating heart is racing
My crazy thoughts are chasing
Tonight, I'm an insomniac
I am a maniac
Sound of clock ticking
The fast heart beating
I am a survivor
Who is still a fighter
I can break all the barriers
I am a warrior
I am a warrior

Stage 4- (Confirmation of guessing) Look at the vocabulary table to make sure that you know the meaning and part of speech of all the words in the lyrics.

Stage 5- (Humming) Now that you know the meaning of the whole song, listen to the music and hum along with the song several times.

Stage 6- (Karaoke) See the lyrics on the monitor and sing. (Visit website to listen)

Stage 7- (Mastery) Listen to the music without any lyrics and sing away. Sing, Dance, and Enjoy!

Section 3: Reading a Short Story: Becoming a Fighter

Pre-Reading activity

a. Listening and taking notes: (Visit website to listen)

Please listen to the story and write down what you have understood.

………………………………………………………………………………………………

………………………………………………………………………………………………

………………………………………………………………………………………………..

………………………………………………………………………………………………

………………………………………………………………………………………………

………………………………………………………………………………………………

b. Reading and Guessing

Please read the short story below, guess at the missing words and fill in the blanks.

"Becoming a Fighter"

While Garcia is in prison waiting for his trial Natalia is still UMSSAD (upset, mad, sad, shocked, angry, and disappointed). She was (1) …………….. ……… from what she does not know, and what she cannot (2) …………. . One night It is raining, it is (3) ……………….. . Suddenly she wakes up at 2:00 o'clock in the morning. She had a (4) ………….. dream, and her heart is racing. She thinks to herself, "my life is changing." She rushes to her desk to get her notebook and writes down what is on her mind. She writes: "I am an insomniac and a maniac listening to the rain drops on the rooftop." A picture comes into her mind. She is running from fear. Suddenly she stops and faces her fear. She is not afraid of (5) …………… anymore. Fear (6) …………… her (7) …………. . She continues writing: "no point in crying, and there is no

denying, this is a new beginning. I will face my fear. I am a warrior.

She decides (8) ………….. her (9) …………., she will tell the world that she was in love with a man who cheated on her and took her money. She (10) ………… a Facebook Page and shares her story with the world. The other women who were deceived by the Garcias in the world joined her page and posted their stories. Her Facebook page becomes famous because she started an (11) ………………. in which women can face their fears, tell their stories of being (12)……………., (13) ……………... , (14) …………..

…………. …. and fighting back.

A month later, Garcia's trial takes place. Natalia is the first (15) ………….. . She tells her story, and when she finishes, she turns to Garcia and says: "I told you my heart is tender, and my mind is tough." Next, Li, the Chinese woman, comes forward to tell her story. Garcia (16) ………… ………… and goes to jail for a long time, and the judge returns Li and Natalia's money plus (17) …………. for the suffering they have experienced.

Now Natalia is stronger. She is fighting hard to educate women about their rights, she has returned to college, and now she is majoring in women's studies. One day, while walking on campus, she happens to meet Sam, her high school crush. Now all the memories come flooding back about the moon.

c. Listening and Checking your Guessing (Visit website to listen)

Please read and listen to the short story. While you are listening, please check to see if the guesses you have made are correct. If your guess was not correct, please make a change and fill in the blanks. Then check your [131] answers in the footnotes.

d. Clearing up all confusions

Please read the short story by yourself without listening to it. Highlight or underline the parts that are unclear to you in the story above. Use your dictionary or a partner to clarify highlighted parts. Write your notes below for further review.

……..

……...

……..

---

[131] 1- Running away: leaving suddenly, 2- control: set a limit on, 3- pouring: raining quickly and in large amount, 4- scary: frightening, 5- failure: not succeeding, 6- caused: made it happen, 7- panic: a sudden strong feeling of fear, 8- to face: to confront, 9- demons: negative feelings, devil, 10- creates: makes, 11- movement: a group of people with a particular aims, 12- Deceived: cheated, 13- harassed: annoyed, 14- taken advantage of: treated badly in order to get something good from them, 15- witness: the person who knows about a legal case, 16- pleads guilty: gives an official answer to an accusation in a law court, 17- damages: harms

……...

e. Reading Comprehension based on the "WH Questions."

Look below for the boxes and read the questions (Q) and answers(A). While you are reading the questions, answer by filling in the blank with the "WH questions" (who, when, where, what, why, and how). Choose the answers that are the best fit. You do not have to use all the "WH questions." Notice that the title of the reading is in the middle of a circle, and the questions pivot around the title of the story in the figure. Both questions and answers are provided, and you only need to put the correct "WH question" in the blank.

- After you have finished filling in the blanks below, practice asking and answering the questions.

- Check your answers with the [132]answer key in the footnote.

____

[132] 1. how, 2. what, 3.who 4. why 5.why, 6. where

| Who? | When? | Where? | What? | Why? | How? |

1- Q: When Garcia is in prison waiting for his trial ……… is Natalia feeling?

A: Natalia is feeling UMSSAD.

2- Q: ………… does she decide to do in the morning?

A: She decides to face her demons, she will tell the world her story.

Becoming a Fighter

6- Q: ……….. does Natalia share her story?

A: She shares it on Facebook and in the court.

3- Q: ………… joins Natalia's Facebook page.

A: All the women who were victims joined her page and told their stories.

5- Q: ………. does she rush toward her desk?

A: She rushes toward her desk because she wants to write down what is coming to her mind.

4- Q: ………… does Natalia's Facebook page become famous?

A: Her Facebook page becomes famous because she has started a movement in which women can tell their stories of being deceived, harassed, and taken advantage of.

Section 4: Syntax Notes: Functions of "ing.", Usage of Who

Syntax Notes 1 & 2: Functions of "ing."

Examples from a line in lyrics: I am listening to the raindrops. Crying is useless. No point in crying.

Warm-up questions: What do you think the syntax point is about? Please Explain. Please Explain.

………………………………………………………………………………………

………………………………………………………………………………………

Functions of "ing"

There are different functions of "ing" forms in this song; We are reviewing some of them.

No.	The "ing" forms		Examples from lines in the lyrics
1	"ing" in GERUNDS (functions as a noun)	Gerund can be the subject of the sentence, and it functions as a noun.	Crying is useless.
		Noun (gerund) after propositions	No point in crying.
2	"ing" in the Present continuous tense	The "present continues tense" forms by the to-be verb (am-is-are) + base form of the verb + ing.)	I am listening to the raindrops.

*Find different functions of "ing" forms in the lyrics.

………………………………………………………………………………………

………………………………………………………………………………………

………………………………………………………………………………………

Write a real-life example of the use of syntax point above in a sentence below.

………………………………………………………………………………………

Syntax Note 3: Usage of Who

Example from a line in the lyrics: I am a survivor who is still a fighter.

 Warm-up questions: What do you think the syntax point is about? Please Explain. Please Explain.

....

....

Usage of who: a relative pronoun to introduce a relative clause about people

Natalia is the girl who is a fighter.

Write a real-life example of the use of syntax point above in a sentence below.

....

Section 5: Museum of Reincarnation: Albert Einstein

Turner O.J. (1947). Albert Einstein.

The EZ Model of Learning Language

Stage 1. Completing the vocabulary list.

Before going to the museum, please complete the vocabulary list below.

No.	Vocabulary	Meaning
1.	survivor	
2.	chasing	
3.	thoughts	
4.	mind	
5.	desires	
6.	brutal	
7.	I am done	
8.	debating	
9.	heartbeat	

Stage 2. **Listening to the Biography Part of the Museum, listening and taking notes**.

(Visit website to listen)

Who is the famous person? Why is the person famous?

....

....

....

Stage 3. Reincarnation with the famous person (Vocabulary part).

a. Watching and Listening. (Visit website to listen)

b. Watching, listening carefully, and writing down the usage of the words by the famous person.

c. Identifying the parts of speech

d. Writing your own sentences using the vocabulary words and the syntax notes.

a. Watching and Listening		
No.	**Vocabulary**	**b. Sentences with the vocabulary word used by the famous person**
		c. Part of speech
		d. Sentences with the vocabulary word used by you
1	**Survivor**	b. Sentences by the famous person: ………………………………… ………………………………………………………………………
		c. Part of speech: …………….
		d. Your sentence: ……………………………………………….. ………………………………………………………………………
2	**Chasing**	b. Sentences by the famous person: ………………………………… ………………………………………………………………………
		c. Part of speech: …………….
		d. Your sentence: ……………………………………………….. ………………………………………………………………………
3	**Thoughts**	b. Sentences by the famous person: ………………………………… ………………………………………………………………………
		c. Part of speech: …………….
		d. Your sentence: ………………………………………………..

		…………………………………………………………………
4	**Mind**	b. Sentences by the famous person: …………………………… …………………………………………………………………
		c. Part of speech: ……………
		d. Your sentence: …………………………………………….. …………………………………………………………………
5	**Desires**	b. Sentences by the famous person: ………………………………… …………………………………………………………………
		c. Part of speech: ……………
		d. Your sentence: …………………………………………….. …………………………………………………………………
6	**Brutal**	b. Sentences by the famous person: ………………………………… …………………………………………………………………
		c. Part of speech: ……………
		d. Your sentence: …………………………………………….. …………………………………………………………………
7	**I am done**	b. Sentences by the famous person: ………………………………… …………………………………………………………………
		c. Part of speech: ……………
		d. Your sentence: …………………………………………….. …………………………………………………………………
8		b. Sentences by the famous person: ………………………………… …………………………………………………………………

	Debating	c. Part of speech: …………….
		d. Your sentence: ………………………………………………….. …………………………………………………………………………
9	heartbeat	b. Sentences by the famous person: ………………………………. …………………………………………………………………………
		c. Part of speech: …………….
		d. Your sentence: ………………………………………………….. …………………………………………………………………………

Section 6: Conversation Creation

a. Choosing a Topic

Choose one of the following potential topics and participants related to the short story/lyrics of the lesson.

Topic 1: "Old friends getting reacquainted," Participants: Natalia and Sara

Topic 2: Natalia is telling Sara what happened and planning for the future. Participants: Natalia and Sara

b. Conversation Creation

After choosing your topic, create your conversation in the space below.

Note: There are two models of conversations in the endnotes to this chapter. You can look at the models and use or modify the conversation you have created. When you are creating your conversation, you should use the new syntax notes and some of the listed vocabulary.

Topic of the conversation:

Participants:

....

....

....

....

....

....

c. Role-Playing. Practice and role-play the conversation with your partner, friend, brother/sister, or even with yourself in front of the mirror. The purpose of role-playing is to become comfortable using the language in a casual and conversational way.

Note: Role-play the other conversations in the endnotes for additional practice. Feel free to change the language as you see fit.

Section 7: Cultural Notes: Women Are Fighters

a. Warm-Up (Brainstorming)

Please look at the topic above and guess what the cultural Notes are about?

....

....

....

....

b. Reading

Read the following cultural points. If you do not know a word or phrase, please use the guessing strategy (guess the meaning of the words based on the context) and use a dictionary when necessary.

"Beyond Wonder Woman: Mighty Female Warriors"

While the woman in the 2017 movie "Wonder Woman" is fictional, she has no [133]shortage of real-world [134]precedents. Throughout history and across cultures, women have been warriors, leading armies of both men and women, proving themselves to be great fighters and highly skilled leaders. (Weisberger, 2017)

"[135]"Fu Hao is the earliest known female general from the Shang Dynasty who lived about 3,000

years ago. More than 100 weapons were found buried in her tomb, confirming her status as a high-ranking military leader". Boudicca, a fierce military leader, led a tribe from eastern Britain in an uprising against interlopers during the Roman invasion and occupation of southern England in the first century. [136]"Ethiopia was once ruled by [137] Queen Gudit."[138]Tomoe Gozen, legendary female Japanese military leader, was

described as a skilled archer. Ana Nzinga ascended to rule as queen of Ndonga, an African state in what is now Angola, in 1624.[139] Nachiyar, who is the first Tamil woman to take up arms against British colonialism in India, grew up in South India, where she learned as a child to use weapons, practice martial arts, shoot a bow, and fight while on horseback. Bastidas was born in

---

[133] lack
[134] history
[135] according to the British Museum
[136] according to a study published in 2000 in the journal Bulletin of the School of Oriental and African Studies
[137] (circa 10th century A.D.)
[138] (circa 1157 – 1247)
[139] (1730 – 1796)

Peru; In 1780, when her husband Tupac led what would be a pivotal rebellion against the Spanish, she played an equal part in the uprising, according to historian Charles F. Walker in his [140]book." (Weisberger, 2017)

Atusa Shahbanu, the Empress of the Persian Achaemenid Empire [141]and daughter of Cyrus the Great, was the director of palace affairs. She had a say in deciding who would be sent on military missions. Artemis, another woman warrior, also joined the Persian Navy as a young woman. In her most renowned and recorded battle, the Battle of Salamis[142], she fought against the Greeks for King Xerxes. (Historical women, 2020)

Two Present Day fighters

Highsmith, C. M., (2021). George Floyd

George Floyd. (October 14, 1973 – May 25, 2020) died in police [143]custody in Minneapolis, Minn. Mr. Floyd died from [144]asphyxiation due to a [145]chokehold in which a policeman held a knee upon his throat for 8 minutes and forty-two seconds. This [146]horrific scene was videotaped; the video went viral and left people heartbroken. For the first time, people had a visual picture rather than a verbal description of [147]racial violence. His death created a global culture in which

---

[140] "The Tupac Amaru Rebellion" (Harvard University Press, 2016)
[141] (522–486 B.C.E.),
[142] (480 BC)
[143] the state of being kept in prison, especially while waiting to go to court for trial
[144] to cause someone to be unable to breathe, usually resulting in that person's death
[145] a way of holding someone with your arm tightly around their neck so that they cannot breathe easily
[146] very bad and shocking
[147] actions or words related to the race of people that are intended to hurt them

people stood together and fought for racial equality. He brought unity among people across race, skin color, religion, and nationality. This is the first time in history that people are united in their call for racial equality and an end to police brutality. He is the reason everyone can now breathe the word freedom in unity. The protests have resulted in local, state, and federal changes in policing policies and procedures. In death Mr. Floyd is a global and cultural warrior for racial equality and the "Black Lives Matter" movement.

Charlize Theon

The South African actress was only 15 years old when she [148]witnessed her mother shoot and kill her alcoholic and angry father out of self-defense. But instead of letting that bad experience define her future, she looked to her mother's protective example of strength and worked to build an amazing sense of confidence of her own. She continued to pursue her acting career, and she [149]ultimately became the first South African actress to win an Academy Award." (Hall, 2014).

c. SPARCing the Cultural Notes

Using the information above, please complete the SPARC (Setting, Participant, Activities, Reasons, and Conclusion).

- Setting (when and where?): …………………………………………………………………

- Participants (who?): …………………………………………………………………

- Activities (how did they get there?):

  …………………………………………………………………

---

[148] saw
[149] finally

- Reasons (why are they successful?):

……………………………………………………………………………………………..

- Conclusion (what is your SPARC?):

………………………………………………………………………………………………

………………………………………………………………………………………………

Section 8: Creative Story/Lyrics Writing

Based on all the points you have learned in this chapter (Yoga (Mountain), vocabularies, grammar, lyrics, video, conversations), follow the steps below:

Stage 1: Brainstorming

Insert the title of your story/lyrics in the middle of figure below and then fill in the other boxes about the participants in your story(who), the setting (when and where), the activities of your story (how), the reasons for your story (why), and the conclusion to your story (what).

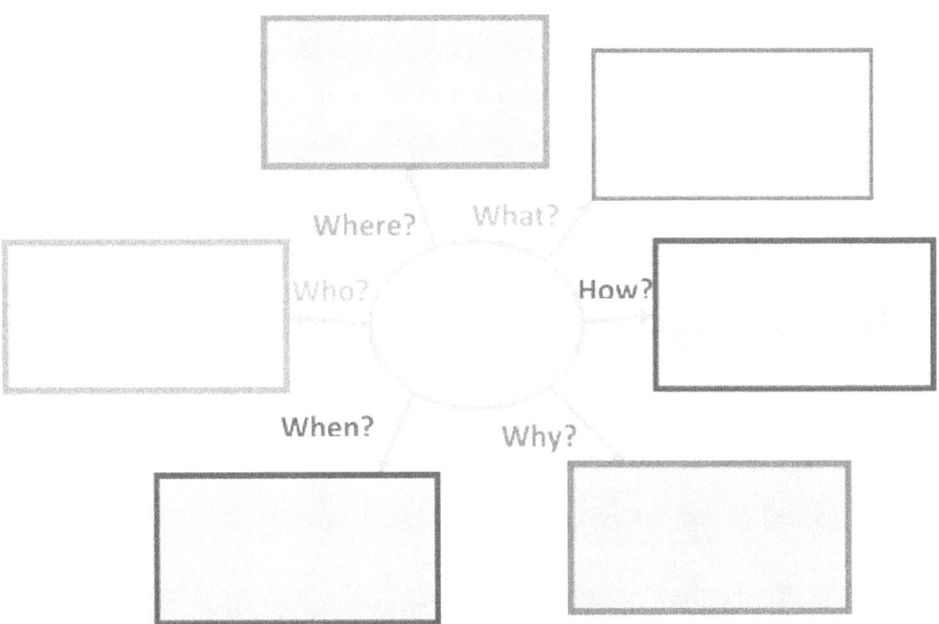

Stage 2- Writing your story/lyrics

Now in the box below, write your story/ lyrics (Your story/lyrics can be rap, rhyming, etc., Be

creative and let your imagination be your limit).

The Title of Your Story/Lyrics: ……………………

……………………………………………………………………………………………..

……………………………………………………………………………………………..

……………………………………………………………………………………………..

……………………………………………………………………………………………..

……………………………………………………………………………………………..

……………………………………………………………………………………………..

……………………………………………………………………………………………..

Stage 3. Getting Feedback: Check your story/ lyrics with your teachers/parents/mentors, to get

feedback

Stage 4. Applying Music: Either apply your story/lyrics on the karaoke track of the song or

click on the beat's website, such as https://www.8notes.com/metronome/. Choose the right beat

for your story/lyrics. Even if you play a musical instrument, apply your writing to your playing.

Don't limit yourself and be creative.

Stage 5. Singing: Practice, sing and enjoy!

Stage 6. Recording. Record yourself and share your product with someone else to get feedback,

and revise if necessary.

Stage 7. Posting your creation.

Section 9: Quick Quiz

The quiz in this section is designed to help you review and remember the materials you have learned. The answer key is always provided in the footnotes. If you have any doubts about the correct answer, please check the footnotes.

Please answer the questions below and check your answers in the [150]answer key in the footnote.

a. Vocabulary: What is the part of speech and synonym of the **Bolded** vocabulary?

1- It was raining. That was the night I became an **insomniac** and I was like a **maniac**.

    a. Adjective, adverb: crazy- fool   b. Adjective, Adjective: fool-crazy

    c. Adjective, Adjective: awake- crazy   d. Adverb, adverb: crazy- awake

2- We are strong women. We are survivors and **fighters**.

    a. Noun: Body-builders   b. Noun: teachers   c. Noun: warriors   d. Adverb: laughter

3- Life is full of difficulties. Life is sometimes **brutal**.

    a. Adjective: beautiful   b. Adjective: cruel   c. Noun: fire   d. Noun: desire

4- I have a big dream. I cannot **forget** my desire.

    a. Verb: forgive   b. Verb: fail to remember

    c. Verb: remember   d. Adverb: fail to forgive

5- When we are at the party, and we are dancing, **time flies**.

    a. Idiom: time passes surprisingly quickly   b. Idiom: time passes surprisingly slowly

    c. Proverb: time does not pass surprisingly quickly   d. Proverb: time does not normally pass slowly

---

[150] Answer Key

   1- c, 2- c, 3- b, 4- b, 5- a, 6- a, 7- a, 8- F, 9- F, 10- F

b. Syntax: Which is the best way for an English speaker to express herself/himself?

6-

   a.   It is raining, and I am listening to the raindrops now.

   b.   It was raining and I was listening to the raindrops now.

   c.   It raining and I am listening to the raindrops now.

   d.   It is raining and I listening to the raindrops now.

7-

   a.   Waiting for you is useless. You are the one who lied to me.

   b.   Wait for you is useless. You are the one which lied to me.

   c.   Waits for you is useless. You are the one that lied to me.

   d.   Waited for you is useless. You are the one whom lied to me.

c. Culture: Based on the Cultural Note, decide which sentence is true (T) and which one is false (F)?

8- Throughout history and across cultures, women have implemented military strategies and stormed battlefields, leading armies of women, proving themselves to be fierce fighters and highly skilled leaders.

9- The protests over Jorge Floyd's death have resulted in local changes in policing policies and procedures.

10- Instead of letting the trauma define her future, Charlize Theon looked to her father's protective example of strength and worked to build an amazing sense of confidence of her own.

Section 10: Endnotes

Museum Transcripts

a. Biography of Albert Einstein

Albert Einstein (1879-1965), born in Germany, was one of the great physicists of all time. His theory of relativity is one of the foundations of modern physics. The theory of Relativity is a picture and explains how the objects in the sky, earth, and the universe are related to each other using the laws of physics. The other foundation of physics is Quantum theory which is a picture of the sub-atomic world. Cause and effect are different in the quantum world. An element can be in two places at the same time. Now, how weird is that? The quantum world is a different place with different laws. A Munich schoolmaster wrote in Albert Einstein's school report, "He will never amount to anything," 1895., but he became everything in the world of physics ("Alber Einstein.," n.d.; Neffe, J. (2007); Isaacson, W. (2007); Wikipedia contributors (2022)).

b. Quotations

I finished my training as a physicist, and the only position I could find was as a clerk in the patent office. There were a lot of problems, but I learned we could not solve our problems with the same thoughts we used when we created them. This was one of the low points of my life and this was the time that I wrote the general theory of relativity, the publication that made me famous. Critical thinking can make you a survivor. When I was a young man hopes and striving were chasing me. Later, I realized we should not limit ourselves to our personal desires. We must free ourselves to embrace compassion for everybody and everything. We need to have great spirits to solve problems. Few are those who can see with their own eyes and feel with their heart beating. However, great spirits have always encountered wild and brutal opposition from mediocre minds, you need to be a fighter, and my last advice is when you are done with your share, leave elegantly. (Albert Einstein Quotes. (n.d.). BrainyQuote.com; Button, S. (2017); Goodread. (2020)).

1- Survivor: "A new type of thinking is essential if mankind is to survive and move toward higher levels."

2- Chasing: "When I was a fairly precocious young man, I became thoroughly impressed with the futility of the hopes and strivings that chase most men restlessly through life. Moreover, I soon discovered the cruelty of that chase, which in those years was much more carefully covered up by hypocrisy and glittering words than is the case today. By the mere existence of his stomach, everyone was condemned to participate in that chase. The stomach might well be satisfied by such participation, but not man insofar as he is a thinking and feeling being."

3- Thoughts: "Invention is not the product of logical thought, even though the final product is tied to a logical structure.", "We cannot solve our problems with the same thinking we used when we created them."

4- Mind: "Great spirits have always encountered violent opposition from mediocre minds.".

5- Desires: "Restricting us to our personal desires and to affection for a few persons nearest to us. Our task must be to free ourselves from this prison by widening our circle of compassion to embrace all living creatures and the whole of nature in its beauty."

6- Brutal: "We scientists, whose tragic destination has been to help in making the methods of annihilation more gruesome and more effective, must consider it our solemn and transcendent duty to do all in our power in preventing these weapons from being used for the brutal purpose for which they were invented, you know."

7- I am Done: "I want to go when I want. It is tasteless to prolong life artificially. I have done my share; it is time to go. I will do it elegantly."

8- Debating: "Currently, every coachman and every waiter is debating whether relativity theory is correct."; "Discussion and argument are essential parts of science; the greatest talent is the ability to strip a theory until the simple basic idea emerges with clarity."

9- Heartbeat: "Few are those who see with their own eyes and feel with their own hearts."

Conversations

Model 1.

Topic: "Old friends getting reacquainted", Participants: Natalia and Sara

Natalia: Hi, Sara, how are you?

Sara: Hi Natalia, it's good to hear your voice again. How are you doing?

Natalia: Honestly, I am not feeling so good, and I want to talk to you about it.

Sara: What's up, girl? Tell me.

Natalia: I have been thinking about the times that we were superstars. Do you remember the little red car?

Sara: Of course, I do. I remember the high heel shoes, dancing at the ball. I do remember your turning down the prince.

Natalia: Yes, I still regret not getting his number that night.

Sara: Yes, he was so handsome and polite.

Natalia: I am wondering if getting his number could have made my life different because I made bad choices.

Model 2.

Natalia is telling what happened and planning for the future. Participants: Natalia and Sara

Natalia: Let me tell you what happened. Last night I woke up. The raindrops were pouring on the rooftop. I was an insomniac and felt like a maniac.

Sara: Oh, Natalia, you have always been an insomniac. Ha, ha. I know some nights you feel like a volcano, ready to erupt.

Natalia: Yes, exactly, the clock was ticking, and my heart was beating so fast.

Sara: It sounds like your mind was freaking, and you were debating with your thoughts.

Natalia: Let me tell you what happened. I have been so UMSSAD. I fell in love with a "bad guy," and he took all my money, and he left me. To make the long story short, I called the police, and now he is in jail.

Sara: Oh my god, that's terrible. I am so sorry to hear that.

Natalia: At first, I was so depressed, but finally, I got myself together, and now I am done with waiting.

Sara: What's your plan now?

Natalia: I am planning to create a website for the survivors of harassment and injustice where all women can share their stories and learn from each other.

Sara: That is amazing girl. It seems you have a burning desire to help others.

Natalia: Yes, my heart is racing for this plan.

Sara: So, actually, you are chasing the dream of being a warrior for women's rights.

Natalia: Yes, and I need your help, girl.

Sara: I got your back. I am coming to Boston to help you this month.

Natalia: Thank you, my friend. We are still superstars.

Vocabulary list as a resource

No.	Vocabulary Pronunciation Part of speech in the song	Meaning (synonym)	Example in sentence
1.	**to become** /bɪˈkʌm/ Verb	to start to be	After going through hardships, she is becoming a fighter.
2.	**fighter** /ˈfaɪtər/ Noun	someone who fights, warrior	I'm a fighter.
3.	**tonight** /təˈnaɪt/ Adverb	the night of the present day, this evening	I have a date tonight.
4.	**to pour** /pɔːr/ Verb	it is raining heavily; rain is falling heavily	Tonight, it's pouring out there, take an umbrella with you.
5.	**to rain** /reɪn/ Verb	drops of water that fall from clouds, drizzle	It is raining.
6.	**to Feel /Feel like** /fiːl laɪk/ Verb	to want to do something, at a particular moment, to have a wish for something	I feel like flying.
7.	**life** /laɪf/ Noun	the state of being alive, existence	Life is tough.
8.	**to change** /tʃeɪndʒ/ Verb	to make or become different, difference, alteration	She was changing her dress.
9.	**to listen** /ˈlɪsn/ Verb	to pay attention to something you can hear, hear	I am listening to the raindrops.
10.	**raindrop** /ˈreɪndrɑːp/ Noun	a single drop of rain, rainfall	I am listening to the raindrops.
11.	**to slide** /slaɪd/ Verb	to cause something to move easily over a surface, move smoothly.	I love sliding down the hill.
12.	**rooftop** /ˈruːftɑːp/ Noun	the top surface of the roof of a building, ceiling	I am listening to the sound of rain on the rooftop.
13.	**insomniac** /ɪnˈsɑːmniæk/ Noun	someone who often finds it difficult to sleep, awake	Last night I became an insomniac.
14.	**maniac** /ˈmeɪniæk/ Noun	a person who has an unusually strong interest in an activity or subject, crazy, overenthusiastic	I am a maniac.

15.	**sound** **/saʊnd/** **Noun**	something heard, voice	The sound of your heartbeat is loud.
16.	**clock** **/klɑːk/** **Noun**	a device for measuring and showing time, alarm	The clock is ticking.
17.	**to tick** **/tɪk/** **Verb**	to make a quiet, short, regularly repeated sound like that made by a clock, to click	The clock is ticking.
18.	**fast** **/fæst/** **adjective**	moving or happening quickly, rapidly	Can you hear my fast heart beating?
19.	**heartbeat** **/ˈhɑːrtbiːt/** **noun**	the regular movement or sound that the heart makes, pulse, in this song it is the sound of the heart caused by passion	Can you hear my fast heart beating?
20.	**time** **/taɪm/** **Noun**	measure of existence, age	Time is flying, time is passing quickly. Time flies. (That time passes quickly)
21.	**to fly** **/flaɪ/** **Verb**	to move through the air	The bird is flying.
22.	**No point in doing something** **/nəʊ pɔɪnt ɪn ˈduːɪŋ ˈsʌmθɪŋ/** **Idiom**	no reason to do an activity	There is no point in doing that.
23.	**denying** **/dɪˈnaɪŋ/** **Noun**	saying that something is not true, declining	There is no point in denying.
24.	**crying** **/ˈkraɪŋ/** **Noun**	Producing tears because of strong emotion, sobbing	There is no point in crying.
25.	**this** **/ðɪs/** **Pronoun**	used for a person, object, idea, etc. to show which one is referred to, that	It is beautiful.
26.	**is** **/ɪz/** **To be verb**	form of be used with he/she/it	It is late. Go home.
27.	**new** **/nuː/** **Adjective**	recently created, modern	It's a new life.
28.	**beginning** **/bɪˈgɪnɪŋ/** **Noun**	the first part of something that continues, birth, the starting point	It's a new beginning.
29.	**Feeling**	affection, emotion	She has a feeling of loneliness.

	/ˈfiːlɪŋ/ Noun		
30.	**winning** /ˈwɪnɪŋ/ Noun	that has won something, being victorious	Winning is everything.
31.	**heart** /hɑːrt/ Noun	the organ inside the chest that sends the blood around the body; used to refer to a person's character, soul	She has a kind heart.
32.	**to debate** /dɪˈbeɪt/ Verb	to discuss, to argue	Again, I'm not here to convince or debate.
33.	**done** /dʌn/ Adjective	it is finished, complete If something is done, or you are done with it, it is finished	I am done with waiting.
34.	**to Wait** /weɪt/ Verb	to allow time to go by, delay, await	I am waiting for you.
35.	**just** /dʒʌst/ Adjective	Exactly, precisely	This veggie burger is just like hamburger.
36.	**like** /laɪk/ Preposition	in the same way, similar to	I have a car like that.
37.	**volcano** /vɑːlˈkeɪnəʊ/ Noun	a mountain with a large, circular hole at the top through which lava (= hot liquid rock) has been forced out, mountain	The volcano is ready to erupt.
38.	**ready** /ˈredi/ Adjective	prepared and suitable for action or use, eager	The volcano is ready to erupt.
39.	**to erupt** /ɪˈrʌpt/ Verb	to burst out suddenly or explode, blow up	I am a volcano waiting to erupt.
40.	**You know** /jə nəʊ/ Phrase	Some people say you know or (also y'know) at the end of a statement to make sure the person they are talking to understands; also used as a pause while speaking	I cannot wait any more, you know I am tired.
41.	**can't** kænt/ Modal verb	not able to, not capable of	I cannot wait any more.
42.	**to put out** /pʊt aʊt/ Phrasal verb	to extinguish fire, douse	I can't put out this fire.
43.	**brutal** /ˈbruːtl/ Adjective	cruel and violent, harsh, ferocious	This cold is brutal.
44.	**fire** /ˈfaɪər/	the state of burning, blaze	The house is on fire.

	Noun		
45.	**to forget** **/fərˈget/** **Verb**	fail to remember, obliterate	I cannot forget it.
46.	**wild** **/waɪld/** **Adjective**	Extreme, unusual, stormy	This is a wild wind.
47.	**desire** **/dɪˈzaɪər/** **Noun**	a strong feeling of wanting something, a passion	I have a burning desire to learn sign language.
48.	**stopping** **/stɑːpɪŋ/** **Present participle**	Finishing doing something, ending	There was no stopping me.
49.	**I can't help something** **Phrase**	to not be able to control or stop something	I can't help thinking.
50.	**damn** **/dæm/** **Adjective**	used for emphasis, especially to express anger or frustration	I am damn tired.
51.	**mind** **/maɪnd/** **Noun**	the part of a person that makes it possible for him or her to think, feel emotions, and understand things, head, brain	My mind is full of what happened last night.
52.	**to freak out** **/friːk aʊt/** **Phrasal verb**	to become extremely emotional (going mad) (In the lyrics the freaking is the short form of freaking out)	Stop making me angry. I am freaking out.
53.	**My beating heart is racing** **/maɪ hɑːrt ɪz ˈreɪsɪŋ/** **Idiom**	My heart is pounding, fluttering	My heart is racing because I am thinking about my desire.
54.	**thoughts** **/θɔːt/** **Noun**	considering something, opinion, (You may talk to yourself)	My thoughts are all about my desire.
55.	**to chase** **/tʃeɪs/** **Verb**	to hurry after someone or something in order to catch him, her, or it, to run after	The police car is chasing the speeding car.
56.	**survivor** **/sərˈvaɪvər/** **Noun**	a person or organization that continues to exist, especially after suffering difficulties	I'm a survivor who is always a fighter.
57.	**who** **/huː/** **Pronoun**	used as the subject or object of a verb to show which person you are referring to, or to add information about a person just mentioned. It is used for people, not things, that	I am the one who fought so hard.
58.	**still** **/stɪl/**	continuing to happen or continuing to be done, even now	I am still a fighter.

	Adverb		
59.	**to break** **/breɪk/** **Verb**	to separate something suddenly or violently into two or more pieces, to split	You are always breaking things.
60.	**barrier** **/ˈbærɪə(r)/** **Noun**	anything used or acting to block someone from going somewhere or from doing something, or to block something from happening, an obstacle, a wall	The mountains acted as a natural barrier to the spread of the disease.
61.	**warrior** **/ˈwɔːriər/** **Noun**	a soldier, usually one who has both experience and skill in fighting, especially in the past, hero	You are always a warrior.

Appendices

What do the A1, B2, C1, etc. labels mean in the following table?

These symbols show the English Profile level of a word, phrase, or meaning. For example, a word that has a B1 symbol is a word that intermediate learners of English usually know.
- o   A1 Beginner: 122
- o   A2 Elementary: 62
- o   B1 Intermediate: 68
- o   B2 Upper-Intermediate: 33
- o   C1 Advanced: 16
- o   C2 Proficiency: 16
- o   Unknown: Not mentioned in the dictionary

a. Vocabulary List

No	Level	Vocabulary Phonetics Part of Speech	Definition/ synonym
1	C2	411 /fɔːr wʌn wʌn/ Slang	Information (It is also the phone number of the service that you use in the US to find out a person's phone number)
2	A2	After /ˈæftər/ Preposition	following in time (afterward)
3	A2	After a while /ˈæftər ə waɪl/ Adverb	Following (coming)
4	A1	Again /əˈgeɪn/ Adverb	once more, or as before (repeatedly)
5	A1	All /ɔːl/ Adjective	every one of (entire)
6	A1	All /ɔːl/ determiner	everyone (of), the complete amount or number (of)
7	A1	Also /ˈɔːlsəʊ/ Adverb	in addition (too)
8	A1	Am /əm/ To be verb	I form of be
9	A1	And /ən/, /ənd/ Conjunction	in addition to; also; as well (plus)

10	A1	Are /ər/ To be verb	be, used with you/we/they
11	info	Aren't we /ɑːrn wi/ Contraction of are not	Contraction of are not
12	A1	At /ət/ Preposition	used to show a particular place or a particular time (near to)
13	B1	At all /ət ɔːl/ Adverb	in any way (of any type)
14	B2	attached to sb /əˈtætʃt/ Adjective	feeling close to emotionally, or loving; (to like someone or something very much)
15	C2	Awesome /ˈɔːsəm/ Adjective	causing feelings of great admiration (breathtaking, beautiful)
16	C2 Slang	Babe /ˈbeɪb/ Noun	Informal: an affectionate way of addressing a person you love (dear)
17	A1	Be /biː/ Verb	linking verb used when you are naming people or things, describing them, or giving more information about them In the lyrics: Be+ Adj
18	A2	Be born /bi bɔːrn/ Verb	to come out of a mother's body, and start to exist
19	A1	Beach /biːtʃ/ Noun	a flat, sloping area of sand or small stones beside the sea or a lake (coast, shore)
20	A2	Beautiful /ˈbjuːtɪfl/ Adjective	very attractive (gorgeous, fascinating)
21	A1	Because /bɪˈkəz/ Conjunction	for the reason that (as, considering)
22	A2	Beginning /bɪˈɡɪnɪŋ/ Noun	the first part of something that continues (birth)
23	C2	Being /ˈbiːɪŋ/ present participle of be(noun)	a person or thing that exists, or the state of existing (existence)
24	B1	Believe me /bɪˈliːv mi/ Believe = verb Me= object	said when emphasizing that something is true (trust me)

25	A1	Better /ˈbetər/ Adjective	comparative of good: of a higher standard, or more suitable, pleasing, or effective than other things or people (finer)
26	B1	Beyond /bɪˈjɑːnd/ Preposition	outside of a limit (above)
27	A1	Body /ˈbɑːdi/ Noun	the whole physical structure (physique)
28	A1	Boring /ˈbɔːrɪŋ/ Adjective	not interesting or exciting
29	A1	Both /bəʊθ/ Pronoun	used to refer to two people (the pair)
30	C1	Breezy /ˈbriːzi/ Adjective	Happy (cheerful) Also means windy but not in this song
31	C1	Brutal /ˈbruːtl/ Adjective	cruel and violent (harsh, ferocious)
32	A1	But /bʌt/ Preposition	Not including (except)
33	A2	By the way /baɪ ði weɪ/ Idiom	used to introduce a new subject to be considered or to give further information (apart from)
34	A1	Bye /baɪ/ Exclamation	Goodbye (adios, so long)
35	A1	Cali girls	Californian girls (Girls from California/kali)
36	A1	Can /kən/ Modal verb	to be able to (be capable of)
37	A1	can't /kænt/ Modal verb	contraction of cannot; not capable of (to not be able to)
38	A1	Car /kɑːr/ Noun	a road vehicle with an engine, four wheels, and seats for a small number of people
39	Infor B2	Cause /kɔːz/ Conjunction	Because (as)
40		Chai /tʃaɪ/	a drink, from India consisting of tea milk, spices and sugar (beverage)

		Noun	
41	B1	Cheers /tʃɪrz/ Exclamation	a friendly expression spoken before tasting a drink (a toast)
42	C1	Chic /ʃiːk/ Adjective	stylish and fashionable; elegant (modern)
43	A1	Christmas /ˈkrɪsməs ɡɪft/ noun	December 25th, a day celebrated each year to honor the birth of Christ (Noel)
44	A1	Clock /klɑːk/ Noun	a device for measuring and showing time (alarm)
45	A1	Cold /koʊld/ Adjective	having a low temperature (chilly, freezing)
46	A2	Cool /kuːl/ Adjective	fashionable in a way that people admire (excellent, neat)
47	A2	Crying /ˈkraɪɪŋ/ Noun	a period of strong emotion that results in producing tears (sobbing)
48	B1	Culture /ˈkʌltʃər/ Noun	the way of life of a particular people (A way of life)
49	B2	Cute /kjuːt/ Adjective	charming and attractive; beautiful; adorable (pretty)
50	infor	Damn /dæm/ Adjective	used for emphasis, especially to express anger or frustration
51	A1	Dancing /ˈdænsɪŋ/ Verb	Short form of We were dancing (Moving our body)
52	B2	Darling /ˈdɑːrlɪŋ/ Noun	a person who is very much loved or liked (sweetheart, sweetie, baby, dear)
53	C2	dead-end /ˌded ˈend/ Noun	a road or path that has one way out (impasse)
54	B2	Denying /dɪˈnaɪŋ/ Noun	saying that something is not true (declining)
55	C1	Desire /dɪˈzaɪər/ Noun	a strong feeling of wanting something (passion)
56	B1	Diet /ˈdaɪət/ Adjective	Diet food or drink contains less sugar or fat than the usual type, and often contains an artificial sweetener

57	B2	Distinguished /dɪˈstɪŋgwɪʃt/ Adjective	respected and admired for excellence (great)
58	B1	Do you have any idea? /ˈduː juː ˈhæv ˈeni aɪˈdiːə/ Expression	said for emphasis when you are describing how good or bad an experience is
59	B1	Done /dʌn/ Adjective	If something is done, or you are done with it, it is finished (complete)
60	B1	Dull /dʌl/ Adjective	not interesting or exciting; (boring)
61	A1	easy /ˈiːzi/ Adjective	effortless, smooth (simple)
62	A1	English /ˈɪŋglɪʃ/ Noun	the language of the United Kingdom and the United States, used also in many other parts of the world (speech)
63	A2	Ever /ˈevər/ Adverb	At any time (always)
64	A2	Except /ɪkˈsept/ Preposition	not including (but not)
65	C2	Extinguish /ɪkˈstɪŋgwɪʃ/ Verb	to stop (to kill)
66	A1	Eye /aɪ/ Noun	one of the pair of organs of seeing in the faces of humans and animals (eyeball)
67	B1	fall in love /fɔːl ɪn lʌv/ noun	If you fall in love you begin to love someone (to love)
68	A1	Fast /fæst/ adjective	moving or happening quickly (rapidly)
69	B1	Feeling /ˈfiːlɪŋ/ Noun	affection (emotion)
70	B1	Fighter /ˈfaɪtər/ Noun	someone who fights (warrior)
71	B1	Fine /faɪn/ Adjective	very good or very well; satisfactory or satisfactorily excellent or much better than average (great)
72	A1	Fire	the state of burning

	B2	/'faɪər/ Noun	(blaze)
73		Fireball /'faɪərbɔːl/ Noun	a large ball of fire (active person)
74	A2	For /fər/ Preposition	because (for the sake of)
75	B1	For /fər/ Preposition	intended to be given to
76	B1	For /fɔːr/ Proposition	instead of (to help)
77	B1	For a while /fɔːr ə waɪl/ Phrase	for a long time
78	B1	Forever /fər'evər/ Adverb	for all time, without end (always)
79	A2	Full /fʊl/ Adjective	Complete (whole)
80	A1	Fun /fʌn/ Noun	pleasure, enjoyment, amusement (joy)
81	B1	Further /'fɜːrðər/ Adverb	to a greater distance (farther)
82	A2	Gift /gɪft/ Noun	something that is given, esp. to show your affection (a present)
83	A1	Girl /gɜːrl/ Noun	a female child or young woman, especially one still at school (antique)
84	A1	Goodbye /ˌgʊd'baɪ/ Exclamation	used when someone leaves (bye-bye, ciao, adios)
85	B1	Gotta /'gɑːtə/ phrase	short form of "have got to" to need to or be forced to (must)
86	A2	Guy /gaɪ/ Noun	a man (boy)
87	B1	Guys /gaɪz/ Plural Noun	used to address a group of people of either sex
88	A1	Hand /hændz/ Noun	the part of the body at the end of the arm that includes the fingers and is used for holding, moving, touching, and feeling things

			(palm)	
89	B1	Handsome /ˈhænsəm/ Adjective	physically attractive (good-looking)	
90	A1	Have got to /ˈhæv gɑːt tə/ modal verb	used to show that you must do something (must)	
91	A2	Health /helθ/ Noun	the state of being well	
92	A2	Healthy /ˈhelθi/ Adjective	good for your health (healthful)	
93	A2	Heart /hɑːrt/ Noun	the organ inside the chest that sends the blood around the body; used to refer to a person's character, or the place within a person where feelings or emotions are considered to come from (soul)	
94	B1	Heartache /ˈhɑːrteɪk/ Noun	feelings of great sadness (suffering)	
95	B1	Heartbeat /ˈhɑːrtbiːt/ noun	the regular movement or sound that the heart makes (pulse)	
96	A1	Help /help/ Noun	the act of making it possible or easier for someone to do something	
97	A1	Her /hər/ Pronoun	to refer to a woman, girl, or female	
98	A1	Here /hɪr/ Adverb	in, at, or to this place (on this spot)	
99	A2	Hey /heɪ/ Noun	used to get someone's attention (hi; hello)	
100	A1	Home /hoʊm/ Noun	a house (apartment)	
101	A2	How /haʊ/ Adverb	in what way, or by what methods	
102	A1	How about you? /haʊ əˈbaʊt jə/ Expression Infor	How about you? (how are you?)	
103	A1	I /i/ Subject pronoun	used as the subject of a verb to refer to the person speaking or writing; the person speaking	
104	A1	I am seeing you /aɪ əm siː ɪŋ jɑː/ Informal	to meet or visit someone	

		expression	
105	A1	I don't know /aɪ dəʊnt nəʊ/ Idiom	used to express that you do not understand (I don't understand)
106	B1	I have no idea /aɪ həv nəʊ aɪˈdɪːə/ Informal expression	I don't have a belief about something I don't have an understating about it
107	B	I'll tell you / aɪlˈtel jə/ Idiom	Used to emphasize what you are saying (I believe what I am saying to you is true)
108	B2	Inner /ˈɪnər/ Adjective	inside (interior)
109	C2	Insomniac /ɪnˈsɑːmniæk/ Noun	someone who often finds it difficult to sleep (unsleeping, awake)
110	A1	Is /ɪz/ To be verb	he/she/it form of be
111	A1	It's /ɪtz/ Pronoun	used to talk about the time, date, weather, or distances (It is)
112	A2	It's so kind of you / ɪts kaɪnd əv jə/ Expression	generous, helpful, and thinking about other people's feelings
113	B2	Joy /dʒɔɪ/ Noun	great happiness (pleasure)
114	B1	Just /dʒʌst/ Adjective	Exactly (precisely)
115	B1	Just a moment /dʒʌs ə ˈməʊmənt/ Idiom	wait a short period of time (wait briefly)
116	B1	Lady /ˈdɑːnə/ Noun	Lady is often used as a polite way of addressing or referring to any woman (missy)
117	A1	Language /ˈlæŋgwɪdʒ/ Noun	a system of communication (speech)
118	A1	Last night /læst naɪt/ Adverb	the night immediately before the present (evening)
119	A1	Late /leɪt/ Adjective	near the end of a period of time
120	A2	Later /ˈleɪtər/ Adverb	at a time in the future or after the time you have mentioned (again)

121	B2	Learner /ˈlɜːrnər/ Noun	person who receives education (student)
122	B2	Learning /ˈlɜːrnɪŋ/ Noun	the activity of getting knowledge (education)
123	A1	Let's go (let us go) /letzɡəʊ/ Idiom	Let's move.
124	B2	Liar /ˈlaɪər/ Noun	someone who tells lies (cheater)
125	C2	[151]Liar liar pants on fire Proverb/ saying	to say something that's not true
126	A1	Life /laɪf/ Noun	the state of being alive (existence)
127	A2	Like /laɪk/ Preposition	in the same way or manner as (similar to)
128	A2	Little /ˈlɪtl/ Adjective	small in size or amount
129	A1	Long /lɔːŋ/ adjective	continuing for a large amount of time
130	C2	Longing /ˈlɔːŋɪŋ/ noun	a feeling of wanting something or someone very much; a strong desire (wish, craving)
131	A1	Look /lʊk/ Verb	to seem or appear to be (sound)
132	A1	love /lʌv/ Noun	the feeling of liking (sweetheart)
133	C1	Luxury /ˈlʌkʃəri/ Noun	something expensive that is pleasant to have but is not necessary
134	B2	Maniac /ˈmeɪniæk/ Noun	a person who has an unusually strong interest in an activity or subject (crazy, overenthusiastic)

---

[151] Children all over the United States know this simple rhyme. They say it when someone gets caught in a lie. In other words, when someone gets busted for lying. The word "lie" comes from Old English through even older German. https://learningenglish.voanews.com/a/liar s-liars-pants-on-fire/3084832.html

135	A2	Maybe /ˈmeɪbi/ Averb	used to show that something is possible or that something might be true (perhaps)
136	A1	Me /mi/ Pronoun	the person speaking; the objective form of I used, usually as the object of a verb or preposition, to refer to the person speaking or writing
137	A1	Men /men/ Noun	plural of man (fellows)
138	A2	Method /ˈmeθəd/ Noun	a way of doing something (design)
139	B1	Mind /maɪnd/ Noun	the part of a person that makes it possible for him or her to think, feel emotions, and understand things (head, brain)
140	A2	Mine /maɪn/ Pronoun	belongs to me
141	C2	Missy /ˈmɪsi/ Noun	miss (girl)
142	A2	Moon /muːn/ Noun	the object, like a planet, that moves through the sky (crescent)
143	A1	Morning /ˈmɔːrnɪŋ/ Adverb	during the early part of the day (AM)
144	A1	Music /ˈmjuːzɪk/ Noun	a pattern of sounds made by instruments or by singing or by a combination of both (song)
145	A2	Must /məst/ Modal verb	used to show that it is important that something happen in the present or future (need)
146	A1	My /maɪ/ Pronoun	belonging to or connected with me; the possessive form of I, used before a noun
147	B1	My heart is racing /maɪ hɑːrt ɪz ˈreɪsɪŋ/ Idiom	My heart is pounding (fluttering)
148	A1	New /nuː/ Adjective	different from one that existed earlier , recently created (modern)
149	A1	Nice to meet you /naɪs tu miːt jə/ Expression	(I'm) pleased to meet you (glad to meet you)

150	B1	No point in doing something /nəʊ pɔɪnt ɪn ˈduːɪŋ ˈsʌmθɪŋ/ Idiom	no reason to do an activity
151	B1	no way /nəʊ weɪ/ Expression	no or not in any way; used to tell someone that something is impossible (impossible)
152	A2	Nothing /ˈnʌθɪŋ/ Pronoun	not anything (no thing)
153	A1	November /nəʊˈvembər/ Noun	the eleventh month of the year, after October and before December
154	A2	Now /naʊ/ Adverb	at the present time rather than in the past or future, or immediately; right now (at this moment, today, instantly)
155	A1	Number /ˈnʌmbər/ Noun	phone number(digits)
156	A1	Oh /əʊ/ Exclamation	used to express different emotions, such as surprise, disappointment, and pleasure, often as a reaction to something someone has said (ah)
157	A1	Ok /əʊˈkeɪ/ Exclamation	agreed or acceptable; all right (yes, okay)
158	A1	Or /ɔːr/ Conjunction	used to connect different possibilities (either)
159	B1	Over /ˈəʊvər/ Averb	(especially of an event) finished
160	A1	Party /bɑl/ Noun	a social event at which a group of people meet to talk, eat, drink, dance, etc.
161	B1	Phobia /ˈfəʊbiə/ Noun	a strong unreasonable fear of something (fear)
162	A1	Please /pliːz/ Exclamation	used to add force to a request or demand
163	A2	Police /pəˈliːs/ Noun	Lawman (detective)
164	B1	Prison /ˈprɪzn/ Noun	a building where criminals are forced to live as a punishment
165	A1	Raindrop	a single drop of rain

		/ˈreɪndrɑːp/ Noun	(rainfall)
166	A1	Ready /ˈredi/ Adjective	prepared and suitable for action or use (apt, eager)
167	A2	Reason /ˈriːzn/ Noun	the cause of an event
168	A1	Red /red/ Adjective	of the color of fresh blood
169	B2	Rhythmic /ˈrɪðmɪk/ Adjective	a beat that is repeated (musical)
170	A1	Road /rəʊd/ Noun	a route for traveling between places (avenue, lane)
171	B1	Romantic /rəʊˈmæntɪk/ Adjective	Feeling of love (loving)
172	B2	Rooftop /ˈruːftɑːp/ Noun	the top surface of the roof of a building (ceiling)
173	A1	Sad /sæd/ Adjective	unhappy (sorrow)
174	B2	Sadness /ˈsædnəs/ Noun	the feeling of being sad or unhappy (unhappiness)
175	C1	Scorpio /ˈskɔːrpiəʊ/ Noun	the eighth sign of the zodiac, relating to the period October 23 to November 21 and represented by a scorpion (= a small creature that has a curved tail with a poisonous sting), or a person born during this period (zodiac sign)
176	A1	Sea /siː/ Noun	a large body of salty water, smaller than an ocean
177	A2	Should /ʃʊd/ Modal verb	used to say or ask what the best thing is to do (shall)
178	B1	Sign /saɪn/ Noun	a written or printed mark that has a standard meaning (mark)
179	B1	Silent /ˈsaɪlənt/ Adjective	completely quiet; without any sound (mute)
180	B1	Sir /sɜːr/ Noun	a polite word used to address a man (Mr)

181	A2	Sky /skaɪ/ Noun	the area above the earth in which clouds, the sun, and the stars can be seen (ether)
182	C2	Skyfall /skaifɑːl/ Noun	a great disaster great sorrow
183	B2	Slick /slɪk/ Adjective	skillful and effective but not sincere or honest(smooth)
184	B2	Slumber /'slʌmbər/ Noun	sleep
185	B1	Smile /smaɪl/ Noun	To have a happy expression (beam)
186	B1	Smooth talker /'smuːð ˌtɔːkə/ Adjective	a person who gets another person to do their bidding by using a slick, gently persuasive, practiced, or competent manner.
187	A2	So /səʊ/ Conjunction	Therefore (thus)
188	A2	So /səʊ/ Adverb	Extremely, to such a great degree; truly (very)
189	A2	Someone /'sʌmwʌn/ Pronoun	a person (character)
190	A1	Something /'sʌmθɪŋ/ Pronoun	a thing which is not known or stated (thing)
191	C2	Sorrow /'sɑːrəʊ/ Noun	a feeling of great sadness (pain)
192	C2	SOS /ˌes əʊ ˈes/ Noun	(Save Our Ship) an urgent request for help (alarm)
193	A2	Sound /saʊnd/ Noun	something heard (voice)
194	A2	Square /skwer/ Noun	an area of approximately square-shaped land in a city or a town, often including the buildings that surround it
195	A2	Star /stɑːr/ Noun	a large ball of burning gas in space; also, a famous and successful person (hero)
196	B1	Still /stɪl/ Adverb	despite that (nevertheless)

197	B2	**Still** /stɪl/ Adjective	not moving; staying in the same position (quiet, calm, silence)
198	A2	**Still** /stɪl/ Adverb	continuing to happen or continuing to be done (even now)
199	B1	**Stopping** /stɑːpɪŋ/ Present participle	Finishing doing something (ending)
200	A2	**Story** /ˈstɔːri/ Noun	a description, either true or imagined, of a series of events (an adventure)
201	B1	**Stress** /stres/ Noun	great worry (pressure)
202	B2	**Strongly** /ˈstrɔːŋli/ Adverb	very much or in a very serious way (highly, fully)
203	B1	**Suddenly** /ˈsʌdənli/ Adverb	Unexpectedly(abruptly)
204	B	**Superstar** /ˈsuːpərstɑːr/ Noun	an extremely famous actor, singer, musician, sports player, etc. (distinguished, well-known)
205	B2	**Surely** /ˈʃʊrli/ Adverb	used to express that you are certain or almost certain about something (absolutely, certainly)
206	B2	**Survivor** /sərˈvaɪvər/ Noun	a person or organization that continues to exist, especially after suffering difficulties
207	A2	**Sweet** /swiːt/ Adjective	If an emotion or event is sweet, it is very pleasant and satisfying (mellow and musical)
208	C2	**Sweetie** /ˈswiːti/ Noun	a very pleasant or kind person (sweetheart, honey, baby)
209	B1	**Technique** /tekˈniːk/ Noun	a way of performing a skillful activity (approach)
210	C1	**Testy** /ˈtesti/ Adjective	easily annoyed and not patient (grumpy)
211	A1	**That** /ðæt/ Conjunction	used to introduce a clause that reports something or gives further information, although it can often be left out
212	B1	**The best** /ðə best/ Noun	the most excellent in a group of things

213	C2	The sky's the limit /ðə skaɪ ɪz ðə ˈlɪmɪt/ Idiom	there is no limit (There is unlimited possibilities)
214	C1	There is no way /nəʊ weɪ/ Phrase	used to tell someone that something is impossible (not at all)
215	A2	Thinking /ˈθɪŋkɪŋ/ Noun	the activity of using your mind to consider something (reasoning)
216	A1	This /ðɪs/ Pronoun	used for a person or thing to show which one is referred (the one, that, this person)
217	B1	Thoughts /θɔːt/ Noun	considering something (opinion)
218	B1	Through /θru/ Preposition	By, using (via)
219	A2	Till /tɪl/ Preposition	Up to (until)
220	A2	Time /taɪm/ Noun	the seconds, minutes, hours, days, weeks, months, years, etc., in which existence is measured, or the past, present, and future considered as a whole measure of existence (age, life)
221	C2	Timid /ˈtɪmɪd/ Adjective	shy and nervous (bashful)
222	A1	Tired /ˈtaɪərd/ Adjective	in need of rest or sleep (drained)
223	A2	To become /bɪˈkʌm/ Verb	to start to be
224	A1	To begin /bɪˈgɪn/ Verb	to start to happen (to start)
225	A2	To bring /brɪŋ/ Verb	to take or carry someone or something to a place or a person (to carry)
226	C1	To burst into laughter /bɜːrst ˈɪntə ˈlæftər/ Idiom	To break open into laughter (to begin suddenly to laugh)
227	A2	To call /kɔːl/ verb	to use a phone to talk to someone

228	B1	To care /ker/ Verb	to think that something is important, and you want to protect it. and to feel interested in it or upset about it the process of protecting someone
229	B1	To Care about /ker ə'baʊt/ Phrasal verb	to feel that something is important and to feel interested in it or upset about it (love)
230	B2	To cease /siːs/ Verb	to stop an action or condition (quit)
231	A1	To change /tʃeɪndʒ/ Verb	to make or become different (difference, alteration)
232	B2	To chase /tʃeɪs/ Verb	to hurry after someone or something in order to catch him, her, or it (to run after)
233	A2	To Come back /kʌm bæk/ Phrasal Verb	to return (come again)
234	B1	To connect /kə'nekt/ Verb	to join two things (join)
235	A1	To dance (past tense: danced) /dæns/ Verb	to move the body and feet in rhythm to music (to rock, to move the body)
236	C2	To debate /dɪ'beɪt/ Verb	to discuss (to argue)
237	A1	To Do /duː/ Verb	perform or have a part in an activity (go on)
238	A1	To drink /drɪŋk/ Verb	to take in and swallow a liquid (consume)
239	C2	To dump /dʌmp/ Verb	to suddenly end a romantic relationship
240	C2	To erupt /ɪ'rʌpt/ Verb	to burst out suddenly or explode (blow up)
241	B1	To Feel /Feel like /fiːl laɪk/ Verb	to want to do something, at a particular moment (to have a wish for something)
242	A2	To fly /flaɪ/ Verb	to move through the air (hover)

243	B1	To forget /fərˈget/ Verb	fail to remember (obliterate)
244	B1	To forget about /fərˈget əˈbaʊt / Verb	to stop thinking about someone or something
245	C2	To freak out /friːk aʊt/ Phrasal verb	to become extremely emotional (going mad) (In the lyrics the freaking is the short form of freaking out)
246	A1	To get /get/ Verb	to receive or be given something (to receive)
247	A1	To Give /gɪv/ Verb	to offer something to someone, or to provide someone with something
248	A1	To go (past tense: went) /ˈpɑːrti/ Verb	to move or travel to another place (pass)
249	A2	To have /həv/ Verb	to own or possess something (accept)
250	C2	To Have a crush on someone /həv krʌʃ ɑːn ˈsʌmwʌn/ Idiom	To Like someone (To be attracted to someone) I have crush on you= I am attracted to you
251	B1	To hear /hɪr/ Verb	to be told or informed about (learned)
252	A2	To hold /həʊld/ Verb	to take and keep something in your hand (grasp)
253	C2	To integrate /ˈɪntɪgreɪt/ Verb	to combine two or more things to make something more effective (combine)
254	A1	To know /nəʊ/ Verb	to have information in your mind (to realize)
255	A1	To learn /lɜːrn/ Verb	to get knowledge (study)
256	A1	To leave /liːv/ Verb	to go away from someone that stays in the same place (get out)
257	B1	To let /let/ Verb	to allow something to happen (permit)
258	B1	To Lie	to say something that is not true in order to deceive

		/laɪ/ Verb	(mislead)
259	A1	To listen /ˈlɪsn/ Verb	to give attention to something you can hear (hear)
260	B1	To Live /lɪv/ Verb	to be alive or have life, or to continue in this state (get along)
261	A1	To Look /lʊk/ Verb	to direct your eyes in order to see (to see)
262	A1	To love /lʌv/ Verb	to like someone or something very much (admire)
263	B1	To make /meɪk/ Verb	to cause something (made is the past tense of make)
264	C1	To meet up /miːt ʌp/ Phrasal verb	to meet another person in order to do something together (meet)
265	B2	To notice (past tense: noticed) /ˈnəʊtɪs/ Verb	to become aware of, esp. by looking (to see)
266	B2	To panic /ˈpænɪk/ Verb	to suddenly feel so worried or frightened (To be scared)
267	B	To pour /pɔːr/ Verb	it is raining heavily (rain is falling heavily)
268	A1	To Put /pʊt/ Verb	to move something (place)
269	C2	To put out /pʊt aʊt/ Phrasal verb	to extinguish fire (douse)
270	A1	To rain /reɪn/ Verb	drops of water that fall from clouds (drizzle)
271	B1	To reach /riːtʃ/ Verb	to arrive somewhere (come to)
272	B1	To Recommend /ˌrekəˈmend/ Verb	to suggest that a particular action should be done (to suggest, to confirm)
273	B1	To regret /rɪˈɡret/ Verb	to feel sorry or unhappy about something you did

274	B1	To Rock /rɑːk/ Verb	to move something backward and forward or from side to side (to shake)
275	A1	To say (past tense: said) /seɪ/ Verb	to tell something to someone, to speak or pronounce words (to speak, to tell)
276	A1	To see /siː/ Verb	to meet, visit, or spend time with someone (to meet) look at something (notice)
277	B1	To shake /ʃeɪk/ Verb	to move something backward and forward or up and down in quick, short movements (Rock)
278	A1	to sing /sɪŋ/ Verb	to make musical sounds with the voice (chant)
279	B2	To slide /slaɪd/ Verb	to cause something to move easily over a surface (move smoothly)
280	B1	To smile /smaɪl/ Verb	a happy or friendly expression on the face (To beam)
281	A1	To stop /stɑːp/ Verb	to finish doing something or end (cease)
282	B1	To take care (of yourself) /teɪk ker/ Informal expression	used when saying goodbye to someone (goodbye, protect yourself)
283	A1	To tell /tel/ Verb	to say something to someone (to say)
284	A1	To tell a lie/lies /tel ə laɪ/ Phrase	to say something/things that are not true
285	B	To think (past tense: thought) /θɪŋk/ Verb	to have or to form an opinion or idea about something (realize, see)
286	C2	To tick /tɪk/ Verb	to make a quiet, short, regularly repeated sound like that made by a clock (to click)
287	B2	To turn into /tɜːrn/ Phrasal Verb	to develop from one thing to another (to change)
288	A1	To Wait /weɪt/	to allow time to go by, esp. without doing much, until something happens or can happen

		Verb	(await)
289	A1	To wake up (Past tense: Woke up) /weɪk ʌp/ Phrasal Verb	arise (get up)
290	B1	To Waste no time /weɪst nəʊ taɪm/ Idiom	to immediately begin an activity (to rush, to hurry up)
291	A1	To watch (had been watching) /wɑːtʃ/ Verb	to look at something for a period of time, especially something that is changing or moving
292	C1	Toast /təʊst/ Verb	to make a short speech and take a drink in honor of someone or in celebration of something (salute)
293	A1	Today /təˈdeɪ/ Adverb	on this day (current)
294	A1	Together /təˈgeðər/ Adverb	with each other (jointly)
295	A1 C2	Tomorrow /təˈmɑːrəʊ/ Adverb	- the day after today - a future period
296	A1	Tonight /təˈnaɪt/ Adverb	(during) the night of the present day (this evening)
297	A1	Too /tuː/ Adverb	(especially at the end of a sentence) in addition, also (likewise)
298	C2	Treason /ˈtriːzn/ Noun	the crime of doing something that could cause danger to your country (in this song it means betrayal)
299	B1	Unique /juˈniːk/ Adjective	special in some way (different)
300	B1	Valentine /ˈvæləntaɪn/ Adjective	someone you love or admire affectionately (honey)
301	B2	Volcano /vɑːlˈkeɪnəʊ/ Noun	a mountain with a large, circular hole at the top through which lava (= hot liquid rock) have been forced out (mountain)
302	B1	Wanna /ˈwɑːnə/ Short form of want to	short form of "want to" or "want a" Want to: to wish for a particular thing or plan of action.

303	C2	**Wanted** /ˈwɑːntɪd/ verb (used with object)	being searched for by the police because of a crime (asked for)
304	C1	**Way** /weɪ/ Noun	the manner in which someone behaves or thinks
305	A1	**We** /wi/ Pronoun	used as the subject of a verb to refer to a group including the speaker and at least one other person (you and I)
306	C2	**We are on Fire** /wi ɑːr ɑːn ˈfaɪər/ Idiom	We feel unstoppable. having a string of successes.
307	B2	**Wealth** /welθ/ Noun	a valuable possession (richness)
308	A1	**Weekend** /ˈwiːkend/ Noun	Saturday and Sunday, when many people do not work
309	A1	**what?** /wʌt/ determiner, pronoun, exclamation	used to ask for information about people or things
310	A1	**what's new?** /wʌtz nuː/ Expression Infor	What's new? What's up? informal (also whassup, what's up)
311	A1	**Where** /wer/ Adverb	to, at, or in what place (location)
312	A2	**Where are you from?** /wer ər juː frʌm/ expression	what city/state/country they consider "home," and that you assume it's someplace other than where you are right now. (What is your nationality?)
313	A1	**Which** /wɪtʃ/ Pronoun	used to add extra information (That)
314	A1 A2	**Who** /huː/ Pronoun	used as the subject or object of a verb to show which person you are referring to, or to add information about a person just mentioned. It is used for people, not things (that, which person)
315	A2	**Who cares?** /huː kerz/ Informal idiom	used to emphasize rudely that you do not think something is important (who pays attention)
316	A2	**Who knows?** /huː nəʊs/ phrase	A rhetorical question asked to show that the person asking it neither knows the answer nor knows who might. It could be one or the other, or both
317	A1	**Why**	for what reason

		/waɪ/ Adverb	(cause)
318	B2	Wild /waɪld/ Adjective	Extreme, unusual (stormy)
319	B1	Winning /ˈwɪnɪŋ/ Noun	that has won something (leading)
320	A1	With /wɪθ/ Preposition	used of people or things that are together (along)
321	A2	With /wɪð/, /wɪθ/ Preposition	using something
322	A2	Without /wɪˈðaʊt/ Preposition	not having or doing (in the absence of)
323	B1	Wonder /ˈwʌndər/ Verb	- to ask yourself questions or express a wish to know about something (question) - used in phrases, at the beginning of a request, to make it more formal and polite
324	C1	Worthy /ˈwɜːrði/ Adjective	worthy (of somebody/something) (formal) having the qualities that deserve somebody/something (deserved)
325	A2	Wonderful /ˈwʌndərfl/ Adjective	extremely good (great, amazing)
326	B1	Would /wʊd/ Modal verb	used to refer to a possibility or likelihood
327	A1	Year /jɪr/ Noun	any period of twelve months
328	A1	You /juː/ Pronoun	the person or people spoken to
329	C1	You are the one /juː ɑr ði wʌn/ Expression	You are my true love. You are my sweetie.
330	B1	You know /jə nəʊ/ Phrase	Some people say you know or (also y'know) at the end of a statement to make sure the person they are talking to understands; also used as a pause while speaking
331	A1	Your /jər/ Pronoun	the possessive form of you (owned by you) belonging or relating to the person or group of people being spoken or written to (belonging to you)

The background information including level, phonetics, part of speech, synonym and definition in the vocabulary lists were taken from the 3 dictionaries listed in the references.

b.Extra Grammar Explanations

Why is pronunciation important?
Because the English language is now a lingua franca (a bridge language or a common language used for communication between groups of people who speak different languages), so, it does not matter if you have an accent. Pronunciation matters when it affects the meaning and purpose of the conversations. It also matters when it is difficult for people whose first language is English to understand what you are saying. Then it is necessary to work on the pronunciation. In order to do so, we need to listen and repeat the words until the pronunciation is understandable. (Most of the time, you will see an expression of puzzlement on the person if they do not understand your pronunciation.)
There are two ways to work on the pronunciation. The first way to improve pronunciation is by listening to the pronunciation of vocabulary words and repeating the words. The second way to improve pronunciation is by reading the phonetic transcription in the vocabulary list. A pronunciation guide table from the Oxford dictionary is provided that will help you to read the phonetics.
The first column indicates part of speech of the words. Why is part of speech/functions important?
Learning the part of speech will help you to better understand grammar and English. Keep in mind that each word can function or be used as a different part of speech; the part of speech depends on the context in which the word is being used. The part of speech of each word in this book is based on their function in the lyrics.
Part of speech (word classes): Cambridge dictionary definition is "any of the groups into which words are divided depending on their use, such as verbs, nouns, and adjectives"
There are nine parts of speech in English words: verb, noun, adjective, adverb, pronoun, preposition, determiner, conjunction, and interjection.
Parts of speech
1-   Nouns: A person, a thing, a place, an idea (Natalia, Pepsi, party, restaurant, Boston, Natalia, Culture, Language…).
2-   Pronouns: Replace nouns (I, you, he, ….)
3-   Verbs: Shows an action or a state (To dance, (am, is, are…))
4-   Adjectives: Describe nouns or pronouns. (cute, handsome...)
5-   Adverbs: Describe verbs, adjectives, and other adverbs. They explain time, location, quantity, and quality of something. (Slowly, surely…)
6-   Prepositions: Indicate a relationship between the noun and pronoun in a sentence. There is always a noun or pronoun after preposition: (Example: at, to…)
7-   Conjunctions: connectors. They connect clauses and sentences together. (but, so, and...)
8-   Determiners: Determine nouns (an/a, numbers/ some…)
9-   Exclamations/ Interjections: a word that expresses sudden pain, surprise, anger, excitement, happiness, or other emotion (Ouch, ah…)
Useful Grammar Websites
https://www.englishclub.com/grammar/parts-of-speech.htm#table
The basic English Word order is Subject + Verb + Object (SVO).

Subject: Performer/doer of the action: Subject Pronouns (I, you, he, she, it, we, they), Proper nouns (Natalia, Garcia…) or noun phrases (A cute girl…)

Verb: a word or phrase that describes an action, state, condition, or experience (go, listening…)

Object: Receiver of the action, the thing, or person that the verb is applied. It can be a noun, a noun phrase, a pronoun, or a longer complex object, which is modified.

She went to the party. (She = subject, went = verb, to the party= object)

To be verbs: Present tense (am, is, are), Past tense (was, were)

You can analyze and understand a sentence better as you practice generating your own sentences using subject, verb, and object.

It is so helpful if you follow these steps in learning new words. Pay careful attention to the following:

1- (Meaning understanding): Learning the meaning/ definition and synonym

2- (Pronunciation learning): Listening or practicing the phonetics and repeating it several times to learn the pronunciation

3- (Analysis): Understanding the part of speech

4- (Stabilization): Reading the example in the sentence repeatedly

5- (Meaningful learning): Generating your own example. Try to use real-life examples (Examples about what happens in real-life situations rather than in a book, story, movie, etc.). for example, if you learn the word "wake up," your real-life example can be related to the time that you wake up in the morning like " I wake up at six every morning."

6- (Feedback): Getting feedback from someone can be helpful to you in the learning process. If what you have written is not completely true, generate more real-life examples and get more feedback until you are sure it is completely true. Be persistent!

7- (Mastery): Generate more real-life examples in a confident way. Find someone to teach it to (Your family, your friend, Online website, etc.)

The last section of the book is a list of all the vocabularies in all the songs based on English alphabetical order. After learning the whole album, you can refer to this part and make some real-life examples with each word.

The book ends with references. By clicking on each link, you can have more access to the information you need.

Pronunciation Guide (Oxford Dictionary)

https://www.oxfordlearnersdictionaries.com/us/about/english/pronunciation_english

<u>References</u>

Albert Einstein Quotes. (n.d.). BrainyQuote.com. Retrieved June 6, 2020, from

BrainyQuote.com Website: https://www.brainyquote.com/authors/albert-einstein-quotes

Arslan, G., Yıldırım, M., Zangeneh, M. & AK, I. (2022). Benefits of Positive Psychology-Based

Story Reading on Adolescent Mental Health and Well-Being. *Child Ind Res* 15, 781–793

(2022). https://doi.org/10.1007/s12187-021-09891-4

Bain News Services. P. *Mme. Curie*. Retrieved from the Library of Congress

https://www.loc.gov/pictures/item/2014687674/.

Bedrov, A., & Bulaj, G. (2018). Improving self-esteem with motivational quotes: opportunities

for digital health technologies for people with chronic disorders. *Frontiers in psychology*, *9*,

2126.

Button, S. (2017). *31 Amazing Einstein Quotes On Love, Life and Imagination*. Retrieved from

https://www.spiritbutton.com/albert-einstein-quotes/#ixzz6OpK28HvP

Carson, C. (2001). *The Autobiography of Martin Luther King, Jr.* (Reprint). Warner Books.

Charles River Editors. (2018). *Marie Curie: The Life and Legacy of the Legendary Scientist Who

Became the First Woman to Win a Nobel Prize*. CreateSpace Independent Publishing

Platform.

Coder, K. D. (2011). Cultural aspects of trees: Traditions & myths. Retrieved from

https://athenaeum.libs.uga.edu/bitstream/handle/10724/36443/Cultural%20Aspects%20of%20

Trees%2011-02.pdf?sequence=1

Corliss, J. 2021. Harvard Medical School. https://www.health.harvard.edu/heart-health/yoga-a-gateway-to-healthier-habits

Czuchry, M., & Dansereau, D. F. (2005). Using motivational activities to facilitate treatment involvement and reduce risk. *J. Psychoactive Drugs* 37, 7–13. doi: 10.1080/02791072.2005.10399744

Dadvar, A., & Rouzbahani, R. (2016). Role of nature in creation of Iranian Myths. *Asian Social Science*, *12*(6), 123-131. Retrieved from

https://pdfs.semanticscholar.org/3b3a/39c6d44db6392d088f5753de83c6ccf5b87a.pdf

Dictionary, C. (2008). Cambridge advanced learner's dictionary. PONS-Worterbucher, Klett Ernst Verlag GmbH. Retrieved from https://dictionary.cambridge.org/us/dictionary/english/

Dictionary, O. L. S. Breed. In oxford learners' dictionaries. com dictionary. Retrieved from https://www.oxfordlearnersdictionaries.com/us/definition/english/know_1#want_idmg_1

Ellasar, A.CNN. (2020). Rihanna's foundation donates $5 million to help fight coronavirus. Retrieved from https://www.cnn.com/2020/03/22/us/rihanna-coronavirus-relief-donation-trnd/index.html

Eradus, R., Harley, A., & Salcedo, I. (1999). Cambridge dictionaries online. Cambridge University Press. Retrieved from https://dictionary.cambridge.org/us/

Ferdowsi, A. (2021). *Shahnameh: The Persian Book of Kings*. Digireads.com.

France, L.R. CNN. (2019). Jennifer Lopez and Alex Rodriguez donate years' worth of food to Tennessee elementary students. Retrieved from

https://www.cnn.com/2019/10/24/entertainment/jennifer-lopez-alex-rodriguez-donate-food/index.html

France, L.R. CNN. (2014). Pitbull: 5 surprising facts about the superstar. Retrieved from https://www.cnn.com/2014/06/20/showbiz/celebrity-news-gossip/pitbull-cnn-spotlight/index.html

Gaab, N., Schlaug, G., & Wong, L. (2015). Music as Medicine: The impact of healing harmonies. In *Longwood Seminars* (pp. 1-46).

Gaia. (2018). *Vrksasana: Tree Pose*. Retrieved from https://www.gaia.com/article/vrksasana-tree-pose

Goodread. (2020). Albert Einstein Quotes. Retrieved from https://www.goodreads.com/quotes/555597-when-i-was-a-fairly-precocious-young-man-i-became

Green, K. (2014). *The pharaoh that wouldn't be forgotten.* (Hatshepsut) Retrieved from https://www.youtube.com/watch?v=8bYRy_wZEJI

Hall, A. (2014, August 24). *8 Celebrities Who Transformed Tragedy into Something Positive.* Retrieved from https://www.huffpost.com/entry/celebrities-overcoming-loss_n_5669363

Highsmith, C. M., photographer. (2021). Hennepin County United States Minnesota Minneapolis, 2021. -11-20. [Photograph] Retrieved from the Library of Congress, https://www.loc.gov/item/2021756279/.

Historical Women. (3/18/2020) Retrieved from http://www.persepolis.nu/queens.htm

Hutyra, H. (2019). *123 Of the Most Powerful Martin Luther King Jr. Quotes Ever.* Retrieved from https://www.keepinspiring.me/martin-luther-king-jr-quotes/#

Hutyra, H. (2019). 120 George Washington Quotes to Celebrate His Place In History Retrieved from https://www.keepinspiring.me/george-washington-quotes/

Ideal Immigration. (2019). Retrieved from https://www.idealimmigration.us/blog/immigrants-in-music

Isaacson, W. (2007). *Einstein: His Life and Universe*. Simon & Schuster.

Jang, M. (2017). Emma Watson, Beyoncé, 23 More Stars on Embracing Feminism and Empowering Women. Retrieved from https://www.hollywoodreporter.com/lists/international-womens-day-2017-feminist-quotes-25-celebrities-983702/item/uzo-aduba-international-womens-day-2017-984410

Gardner, H., & Hatch, T. (1989). Educational implications of the theory of multiple intelligences. *Educational researcher*, *18*(8), 4-10.

Juma, N. (2020). Florence Nightingale quotes on Life, Communication and Nursing. Retrieved from https://everydaypower.com/florence-nightingale-quotes/

Kaivalya, A. (2016). *Myths of the Asanas: The Stories at the Heart of the Yoga Tradition*. Simon and Schuster.

Karen, H.C. (2015). *The Story of the Yoga Warrior Poses*. Retrieved from http://www.whenlifeisgood.com/the-story-of-the-yoga-warrior-poses/

Kendall, J., Waddington, C., and Kendall, C. (2005). The daily moment: a stress reduction program for cancer center staff. *J. Oncol. Manage*. 14, 68–71.

Kokugo Dai Jiten, 1988. Revised Edition. Retrieved from: https://en.wikipedia.org/wiki/Tokyo

Kripalu/School of Yoga. (2019). 200-Hour Teacher Training Manual.

Leffler, W. K., photographer. (1965) *Martin Luther King Press conf*. , 1965. March 2. [Photograph] Retrieved from the Library of Congress, https://www.loc.gov/item/2016646651/

Ludwig van Beethoven Quotes. (n.d.). BrainyQuote.com. Retrieved June 6, 2020, from

BrainyQuote.com Web site: https://www.brainyquote.com/authors/ludwig-van-beethoven-

quotes

Mayor, L. (2000, July 1). "Oprah: The Soul and Spirit of a Superstar: An Unofficial Tribute."

Amazon, Triumph, 2000, www.amazon.com/Oprah-Winfrey-Soul-Spirit-

Superstar/dp/1572434082.

Marie Curie Quotes. (n.d.). BrainyQuote.com. Retrieved June 6, 2020, from BrainyQuote.com

Web site: https://www.brainyquote.com/authors/marie-curie-quotes

McGinley, K. (2017). *Uncover the Symbolism in 10 Common Yoga Poses.* Retrieved from

https://chopra.com/articles/uncover-the-symbolism-in-10-common-yoga-poses

Neffe, J. (2007). *Einstein: A biography*. Farrar, Straus and Giroux. Retrieved from

https://books.google.com/books?hl=en&lr=&id=B8K6n177ZwcC&oi=fnd&pg=PR7&dq=Ein

stein+Biography+jurgen&ots=_trvRoc0hO&sig=9mWHvsJ-

ypQYNtQL4w5IUmEdjxY#v=onepage&q=Einstein%20Biography%20jurgen&f=false

Newsday.com Staff. (02/01/2017) Celebrities who are immigrants: Justin Bieber, Mila Kunis,

Pamela Anderson, more. Retrieved from

https://www.newsday.com/entertainment/celebrities/celebrities-who-are-immigrants-justin-

bieber-mila-kunis-pamela-anderson-more-1.5579736

Pennebaker, J. W., & Seagal, J. D. (1999). Forming a story: The health benefits of

narrative. *Journal of clinical psychology*, *55*(10), 1243-1254.

Reef, C. (2016). *Florence Nightingale: The Courageous Life of the Legendary

Nurse* (Illustrated). Clarion Books.

Radha, S. S. (2006). *Hatha yoga: the hidden language*. timeless books.

Savage, M. (2020). Coronavirus: Stars take part in One World: Together At Home concert. BBC

Music Composer. Retrieved from https://www.bbc.com/news/entertainment-arts-52333890

Selinker, L. (1972). Interlanguage. *IRAL-International Review of Applied Linguistics in

Language Teaching, 10*(1-4), 209-232. Retrieved from

https://www.degruyter.com/view/journals/iral/10/1-4/article-p209.xml

Sjoman, N. E. (1999). *The Yoga Tradition of the Mysore Palace* (2nd ed.). Abhinav Publications.

Thayer, A. W., & Krehbiel, H. E. (2020). *The Life of Ludwig van Beethoven (Vol. 1-3):

Complete Edition*. e-artnow.

Tillich, P. (2008). *The courage to be*. Yale University Press.

Trejo, N. (2019, June 10). *Angelina Jolie Has Made the World A Better Place, One Deed at A

Time*. Retrieved from https://us.hola.com/celebrities/gallery/2019061024598/angelina-jolie-

humanitGarcian-work-gallery/1/

Trikosko, M. S., photographer. (1979) *Interview with Cesar Chavez. 4/20/. Chavez gesturing.* ,

1979. [Photograph] Retrieved from the Library of Congress,

https://www.loc.gov/item/2016646413/

Turner, O. J., photographer. (ca. 1947) *Albert Einstein, -1955.*, ca. 1947. [Photograph] Retrieved

from the Library of Congress, https://www.loc.gov/item/2004671908/.

Weidenbach, A. & Stuart, G. (ca. 1876) *"George Washington" / A. Weidenbach.* , ca. 1876.

[1876] [Photograph] Retrieved from the Library of Congress,

https://www.loc.gov/item/2009633671/

Weisberger, M. (2017, June 2). *Beyond Wonder Woman: 12 Mighty Female Warriors*. Retrieved

from https://www.livescience.com/59330-beyond-wonder-women-real-female-warriors.html

Whittaker, Elizabeth; Robin M. Kowalski (2015). "Cyberbullying Via Social Media". *Journal of School Violence*. 14 (1): 19. doi:10.1080/15388220.2014.949377. S2CID 144140856.

Wikipedia contributors. (2022, May 31). Albert Einstein. In *Wikipedia, The Free Encyclopedia*. Retrieved 11:31, June 6, 2022,

from https://en.wikipedia.org/w/index.php?title=Albert_Einstein&oldid=960064108

Wikipedia contributors. (2022, June 6). Florence Nightingale. In *Wikipedia, The Free Encyclopedia*. Retrieved 11:52, June 6, 2022,

from https://en.wikipedia.org/wiki/Florence_Nightingale

Wikipedia contributors. (2022, February 24). On the Floor. In *Wikipedia, The Free Encyclopedia*. Retrieved 22:02, March 11, 2022,

from https://en.wikipedia.org/w/index.php?title=On_the_Floor&oldid=942426674

Wikipedia contributors. (2020, March 4). Pitbull (rapper). In *Wikipedia, The Free Encyclopedia*. Retrieved 22:00, March 11, 2020,

from https://en.wikipedia.org/w/index.php?title=Pitbull_(rapper)&oldid=943882623

Wikipedia contributors. (2022, June 6). Martin Luther King Jr. In *Wikipedia, The Free Encyclopedia*. Retrieved 11:05, June 6, 2022,

from https://en.wikipedia.org/w/index.php?title=Martin_Luther_King_Jr.&oldid=961007646

Wikipedia contributors. (2022, June 6). Ludwig van Beethoven. In *Wikipedia, The Free Encyclopedia*. Retrieved 11:17, June 6, 2022,

from https://en.wikipedia.org/w/index.php?title=Ludwig_van_Beethoven&oldid=961002658

Wikipedia contributors. (2022, June 3). Marie Curie. In *Wikipedia, The Free Encyclopedia*. Retrieved 11:40, June 6, 2022,

from https://en.wikipedia.org/w/index.php?title=Marie_Curie&oldid=960619663

Wikipedia contributors. (2020, June 20). COVID-19 pandemic. In *Wikipedia, The Free Encyclopedia*. Retrieved 19:56, June 20, 2020.

Wikipedia contributors. (2022, November). Hatshepsut. http://en.wikipedia.org/wiki/Hatshepsut

Zandvakili, E., Washington, E., Gordon, E. W., Wells, C., & Mangaliso, M. (2019). Teaching Patterns of Critical Thinking: The 3CA Model—Concept Maps, Critical Thinking, Collaboration, and Assessment. SAGE Open. https://doi.org/10.1177/2158244019885142